Applied Equity Valuation

Edited by

T. Daniel Coggin, Ph.D.
Director of Research
TeamVest, LLC

and

Frank J. Fabozzi, Ph.D., CFA
Adjunct Professor of Finance
School of Management
Yale University

Published by Frank J. Fabozzi Associates

T. Daniel Coggin
To Jack Hunter,
Mentor and Friend

Frank J. Fabozzi
To my daughter Patricia Marie

© 1999 By Frank J. Fabozzi Associates
New Hope, Pennsylvania

ISBN: 1-883249-51-1

Printed in the United States of America

Table of Contents

Contributing Authors

James A. Abate	BEA Associates
Gary L. Bergstrom	Acadian Asset Management
Stephen J. Bruno	Dalton, Greiner, Hartman, Maher & Co.
Frank J. Fabozzi	Yale University
Ralph P. Goldsticker III	Vestek Systems
Mark R. Gordon	Sanford C. Bernstein & Co., Inc.
James L. Grant	Simmons College
Kenneth J. Greiner	Dalton, Greiner, Hartman, Maher & Co.
Robert A. Haugen	Haugen Custom Financial Systems
Bruce I. Jacobs	Jacobs Levy Equity Management
Kenneth N. Levy	Jacobs Levy Equity Management
Gerald J. Madigan	Smith Breeden Associates, Inc.
Michael P. McElroy	Independence Investment Associates, Inc.
Richard O. Michaud	Acadian Asset Management
Steven Pisarkiewicz	Sanford C. Bernstein & Co., Inc.
Gary G. Schlarbaum	Miller, Anderson & Sherrerd, LLP
Michael L. Steinberg	Smith Breeden Associates, Inc.
Lawrence S. Viehl	Columbia Management Company
Bruce D. Westervelt	First Madison Advisors
Brian K. Wolahan	Acadian Asset Management

About the Editors

T. Daniel Coggin is the Director of Research for TeamVest, LLC an investment management consulting firm in Charlotte, NC. Dan has 20 years of experience in investment management and consulting, and has a Ph.D. in political economy from Michigan State University. Before joining TeamVest, he was Director of Research for the Virginia Retirement System (a $35 billion state retirement fund) and a Visiting Professor of Applied Finance at the University of North Carolina at Charlotte. Dan has authored and co-authored over 25 articles in leading finance and investment management journals. He has also contributed a number of chapters to edited investment management books and co-edited three books on quantitative investment management. In addition to his duties at TeamVest, Dan serves on the editorial boards of the *Journal of Portfolio Management*, the *Journal of Investing*, and the *Review of Quantitative Finance and Accounting*.

Frank J. Fabozzi is editor of the *Journal of Portfolio Management* and an Adjunct Professor of Finance at Yale University's School of Management. Frank is a Chartered Financial Analyst and Certified Public Accountant. He is on the board of directors of the Guardian Life family of funds and the BlackRock complex of funds. He earned a doctorate in economics from the City University of New York in 1972 and in 1994 received an honorary doctorate of Humane Letters from Nova Southeastern University. Frank is a Fellow of the International Center for Finance at Yale University.

Preface

As the title indicates, this is a book about applied equity valuation. We feel that such a book is needed since we know of few places where one can find a comprehensive overview of applied equity valuation. Put another way, we know of few places where one can find detailed discussions by recognized experts who focus on the applied techniques practitioners actually use to manage equity portfolios.

Chapter 1 by Jacobs and Levy sets the stage by detailing the complex web of factors that influence equity returns and showing how systematic efforts to disentangle this web can result in enhanced returns. Chapters 2 and 3 discuss the two major approaches to equity valuation used by practitioners: bottom up and top down. Chapter 2 by Greiner and Bruno presents the bottom up approach to equity management with specific reference to small cap stocks. This chapter also contains a detailed discussion of the process of interviewing company management. Chapter 3 by Viehl presents the top down/thematic approach with specific reference to large cap stocks.

Chapter 4 by Goldsticker gives an exhaustive discussion of the process of applying the quantitative approach to equity valuation. Chapter 5 by Fabozzi describes a popular quantitative valuation technique known as the factor-based approach. Chapter 6 by Haugen compares the two major factor-based approaches from academia (the CAPM and the APT) to an *ad hoc* factor approach similar to that used by a number of practitioners. He finds the *ad hoc* approach to be a superior valuation model.

Chapters 7 and 8 give examples of applying the quantitative approach to equity management. Chapter 7 by Pisarkiewicz and Gordon discusses how to apply the dividend discount model to large cap equity valuation. Chapter 8 by Schlarbaum shows how to apply a multi-indicator, value-based approach to large cap equity management. Chapter 9 by Abate, Fabozzi, and Grant discusses a relatively new and popular topic in applied equity valuation called "value-based metrics." In this chapter they show how traditional methods of microeconomic and macroeconomic profit analysis can be combined to improve the equity selection process.

Chapter 10 by McElroy presents an example of the market neutral equity valuation model. In this approach, long and short portfolios are combined to form a zero-beta portfolio with a positive expected alpha. Chapter 11 by Steinberg and Madigan discusses the process of constructing enhanced S&P 500 equity index portfolios using futures and enhanced cash management. Following the growing interest in the topic of equity style management, Chapter 12 by Westervelt describes a dynamic style allocation methodology for equity portfolios.

Chapter 13 by Bergstrom, Michaud, and Wolahan discusses the use of fundamental value-based factors (e.g., earnings-to-price and book-to-price) in the process of international equity valuation.

T. Daniel Coggin
Frank J. Fabozzi

Chapter 1

Security Valuation in a Complex Market

Bruce I. Jacobs, Ph.D.
Principal
Jacobs Levy Equity Management

Kenneth N. Levy, CFA
Principal
Jacobs Levy Equity Management

INTRODUCTION

If the aim of security valuation is to determine the fair market price of securities, the aim of active security selection is to detect mispricing. Mispriced securities have the potential to provide superior returns as their prices correct, over time, to fair values. But mispricing offers opportunity only if it is significant enough, and consistent enough, to be detected and modeled.

If stock prices were totally random, as the efficient market hypothesis and random walk theory would have it, such opportunities would not exist. Mispricing, if it existed, would be so fleeting or so random as to defy detection and prediction. But stock prices are not random.

We find, rather, that price movements can be predicted, and with some consistency. At the same time, both research and reality have shown that this is not an easy task. Simple rules or screens such as low price/earnings ratios, or even elegant, Ivory Tower theories such as the Capital Asset Pricing Model and Arbitrage Pricing Theory, are inadequate.

Stock price behavior defies any simple analyses.[1] With the right research tools and enough perseverance, however, one can detect a complex web of interrelated return effects that form predictable patterns of mispricing across stocks and over time. These patterns may be exploited for superior performance.

---

[1] See, for example, Bruce I. Jacobs and Kenneth N. Levy, "The Complexity of the Stock Market," *Journal of Portfolio Management* (Fall 1989).

The authors thank Judith Kimball for her editorial assistance.

1

The equity market is what scientists would call a complex system. Random systems, such as Brownian motion and white noise (static), are the product of a large number of variables, cannot be modeled, and are inherently unpredictable. Ordered systems, such as the structure of diamond crystals or the dynamics of pendulums, are definable by a relatively small number of variables and predictable by relatively simple rules. Complex systems, such as the weather and the workings of DNA, can be at least partly comprehended and modeled, but only with great difficulty. The number of variables that must be modeled, and their interactions, are beyond the capacity of the human mind alone. Only with the aid of advanced computational science can the mysteries of complex systems be unraveled.[2]

A complex market, that is, requires a complex model. This chapter describes one such model, and its application to the stock selection, portfolio construction, and performance evaluation problems. We begin with the very basic question of how one should approach the equity market. Should one attempt to cover the broadest possible range of stocks, or can greater analytical insights be garnered by focusing on a particular subset of the market or a limited number of stocks?

A VIEW WITH BREADTH

Investment managers have traditionally followed several distinct approaches to stock selection. Value managers, for example, have concentrated on buying stocks selling at prices perceived to be low relative to the company's assets or earnings. Growth managers have sought stocks with above-average earnings growth not fully reflected in price. Small-capitalization managers have looked for opportunity in stocks that have been overlooked by most investors.

The valuation approaches of investment managers have left their tracks on the behavior of the stocks comprising the selection pool. Most prominent is the tendency for stocks to subdivide into distinct style segments — into growth and value, large- and small-cap groupings. Client preferences have encouraged this Balkanization of the market, and the actions of investment consultants have formalized it.

Consultants have designed style indexes and have defined managers in terms of their proclivity for one style or another. Managers may thus find a particular style orientation effectively imposed on them. To the extent that a manager's performance is measured against a given style index, deviations from the index give rise to added investment and business risk. Consequently, a manager may find it advantageous to stick closely to a given style.

An investment approach that focuses on individual market segments can have its advantages. Such an approach recognizes, for example, that the U.S. equity market is neither entirely homogeneous nor entirely heterogeneous. All stocks do not react alike to a given impetus, but nor does each stock exhibit its

---

[2] See, for example, Heinz Pagels, *The Dreams of Reason: The Computer and the Rise of the Sciences of Complexity* (New York, NY: Simon and Schuster, 1988).

own, totally idiosyncratic price behavior. Rather, stocks within a given style, or sector, or industry tend to behave similarly to each other and somewhat differently from stocks outside their group.

While style preferences and other forces act to segment the equity market, however, other forces act to integrate it. After all, there exist some managers who select their portfolios from the broad universe of stocks, and others who, while they may focus on a particular type of stock given current economic conditions, are poised to change their focus should underlying conditions change. The capital of these investors flows across style segments, integrating the overall market.

Most importantly, all stocks can be defined by the same fundamental parameters — by market capitalization, price/earnings ratio, dividend discount model ranking, and so on. All stocks can be found at some level on the continuum of values for each parameter. Growth and value stocks inhabit the opposite ends of the continuums of P/E and dividend yield, and small and large stocks the opposite ends of the continuums of firm capitalization and analyst coverage. Moreover, these positions are not static. An out-of-favor growth stock may slip into value territory. A small-cap company may grow into the large-cap range.

Arbitrage works toward market integration. If too many investors want low P/E, for example, low-P/E stocks will be bid up to higher P/E levels. Some investors will step in to sell them and buy other stocks deserving of higher P/Es. An investment approach that focuses on the individual segments of the market ignores the powerful forces that work to integrate, rather than segment, the market.

The market's tenuous balance between integration and segmentation is one dimension of its complexity. This dimension calls for an investment approach that is 180 degrees removed from the narrow, segment-oriented focus of traditional management. It requires an approach that takes into account the behavior of stocks across the broadest possible selection universe, without losing sight of the significant differences in price behavior that distinguish particular market segments.

Almost by default, this twin task demands a quantitative approach. Quantitative tools have the capacity to handle the widest selection universe and, at the same time, the capability of going into great depth and detail of analysis. To the same, myriad fundamental and economic data used in traditional security valuation, quantitative analysis can apply modern computing power, finance theory and statistical techniques that extend the reaches (and discipline the vagaries) of the human mind.

Starting off with the broadest possible view of the equity selection universe allows the investor to approach the investment problem with an unbiased philosophy. The investor can then, if desired, choose a more narrowly defined focal point from which to frame the market. But by beginning with the wider-angle lens, the investor is assured of two important qualities — coherence and completeness.

The interrelationships between the individual components, the stocks and stock subsets, of the equity market become clear only when viewed from the perspective of the whole. If the investor then chooses to zoom in on a particular subset of stocks, he or she can take advantage of insights garnered from this wider view. A wide-angle approach is thus poised to take advantage of more profit opportunities than a more narrowly focused, segmented approach proffers.[3]

Coherence and Completeness

To the extent that the market is integrated, an investment approach that models each industry or style segment as if it were a universe unto itself is not the best approach. Consider, for example, a firm that offers both core and value strategies. Suppose the firm runs a model on its total universe of, say, 3000 stocks. It then runs the same model or a different, segment-specific model on a 500-stock subset of large-cap value stocks.

If different models are used for each strategy, the results will differ. Even if the same model is estimated separately for each strategy, its results will differ because the model coefficients are bound to differ between the broader universe and the narrower segment. What if the core model predicts GM will outperform Ford, while the value model shows the reverse? Should the investor start the day with multiple estimates of one stock's alpha? This would violate what we call the "Law of One Alpha."[4]

Of course, the firm could ensure coherence by using separate models for each market segment — growth, value, small-cap — and linking the results via a single, overarching model that relates all the subsets. But the firm then runs into a second problem with segmented investment approaches: To the extent that the market is integrated, the pricing of securities in one segment may contain information relevant to pricing in other segments.

For example, within a generally well integrated national economy, labor market conditions in the U.S. differ region by region. An economist attempting to model employment in the Northeast would probably consider economic expansion in the Southeast. Similarly, the investor who wants to model growth stocks should not ignore value stocks. The effects of inflation, say, on value stocks may have repercussions for growth stocks; after all, the two segments represent opposite ends of the same P/E continuum.

An investment approach that concentrates on a single market segment does not make use of all available information. A wide-angle approach considers all the stocks in the universe — value and growth, large- and small-cap. It thus benefits from all the information to be gleaned from a wide and diverse range of stock price behavior.

Not Forgetting Depth

Breadth of inquiry must not come at the sacrifice of depth of inquiry. A complex security valuation model does not ignore the significant differences across differ-

---

[3] See, for example, Bruce I. Jacobs and Kenneth N. Levy, "Engineering Portfolios: A Unified Approach," *Journal of Investing* (Winter 1995).

[4] See Bruce I. Jacobs and Kenneth N. Levy, "The Law of One Alpha," *Journal of Portfolio Management* (Summer 1995).

ent types of stock, differences exploitable by specialized investing. What's more, in examining similarities and differences across market segments, it considers numerous variables that may be defining.

For value, say, a complex approach does not confine itself to a dividend discount model measure of value, but examines also earnings, cash flow, sales, and yield value, among other attributes. Growth measurements to be considered include historical, expected, and sustainable growth, as well as the momentum and stability of earnings. Share price, volatility, and analyst coverage are among the elements to be considered along with market capitalization as measures of size.[5]

These variables are often closely correlated with each other. Small-cap stocks, for example, tend to have low P/Es; low P/E is correlated with high yield; both low P/E and high yield are correlated with DDM estimates of value. Furthermore, they may be correlated with a stock's industry affiliation. A simple low-P/E screen, for example, will tend to select a large number of bank and utility stocks. Such correlations can distort naive attempts to relate returns to potentially relevant variables. A true picture of the variable-return relationship emerges only after "disentangling" the variables.

DISENTANGLING RETURNS

The effects of different sources of stock return can overlap. In Exhibit 1, the lines represent connections documented by academic studies; they may appear like a ball of yarn after the cat got to it. To unravel the connections between variables and return, it is necessary to examine all the variables simultaneously.

For instance, the low-P/E effect is widely recognized, as is the small-size effect. But stocks with low P/Es also tend to be of small size. Are P/E and size merely two ways of looking at the same effect? Or does each variable matter? Perhaps the excess returns to small-cap stocks are merely a January effect, reflecting the tendency of taxable investors to sell depressed stocks at year-end. Answering these questions requires disentangling return effects via multivariate regression.[6]

Common methods of measuring return effects, such as quintiling or univariate (single-variable) regression, are "naive" because they assume, naively, that prices are responding only to the single variable under consideration — low P/E, say. But a number of related variables may be affecting returns. As we have noted, small-cap stocks and banking and utility industry stocks tend to have low P/Es. A univariate

---

[5] At a deeper level of complexity, one must also consider alternative ways of specifying such fundamental variables as earnings or cash flow. Over what period does one measure earnings, for example? If using analyst earnings expectations, which measure provides the best estimate of future real earnings? The consensus of all available estimates made over the past six months? Only the very latest earnings estimates? Are some analysts more accurate or more influential? What if a recent estimate is not available for a given company? See Bruce I. Jacobs, Kenneth N. Levy, and Mitchell C. Krask, "Earnings Estimates, Predictor Specification, and Measurement Error," *Journal of Investing* (Summer 1997), pp. 29-46.

[6] See Bruce I. Jacobs and Kenneth N. Levy, "Disentangling Equity Return Regularities: New Insights and Investment Opportunities," *Financial Analysts Journal* (May/June 1988).

regression of return on low P/E will capture, along with the effect of P/E, a great deal of "noise" related to firm size, industry affiliation and other variables.

Simultaneous analysis of all relevant variables via multivariate regression takes into account and adjusts for such interrelationships. The result is the return to each variable separately, controlling for all related variables. A multivariate analysis for low P/E, for example, will provide a measure of the excess return to a portfolio that is market-like in all respects except for a single distinguishing feature — a lower-than-average P/E ratio. Disentangled returns are "pure" returns.

Noise Reduction

Exhibit 2 plots naive and pure cumulative excess (relative to a 3000-stock universe) returns to high book-to-price ratio.[7] The naive returns show a great deal of volatility; the pure returns, by contrast, follow a much smoother path. There is a lot of noise in the naive returns. What causes it?

Note the divergence between the naive and pure return series for the 12 months starting in March 1979. This date coincides with the crisis at the nuclear power plant at Three Mile Island. Utilities such as GPU, operator of the Three Mile Island power plant, tend to have high-B/Ps, and naive B/P measures will reflect the performance of these utilities along with the performance of other high-B/P stocks. Electric utility prices plummeted 24% after the Three Mile Island crisis. The naive B/P measure reflects this decline.

Exhibit 1: Return Effects Form a Tangled Web

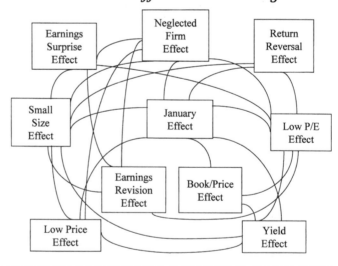

---

[7] In particular, naive and pure returns are provided by a portfolio having a book-to-price ratio that is one standard deviation above the universe mean book-to-price ratio. For pure returns, the portfolio is also constrained to have universe-average exposures to all the other variables in the model, including fundamental characteristics and industry affiliations.

Exhibit 2: Naive and Pure Returns to High Book-to-Price Ratio

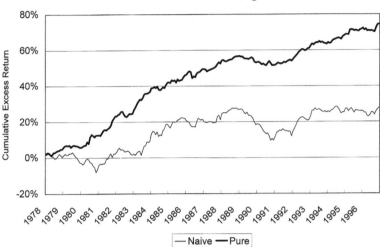

But industry-related events such as Three Mile Island have no necessary bearing on the book/price variable. An investor could, for example, hold a high-B/P portfolio that does not overweight utilities, and such a portfolio would not have experienced the decline reflected in the naive B/P measure in Exhibit 2. The naive returns to B/P reflect noise from the inclusion of a utility industry effect. A pure B/P measure is not contaminated by such irrelevant variables.

Disentangling distinguishes real effects from mere proxies and thereby distinguishes between real and spurious investment opportunities. As it separates high B/P and industry affiliation, for example, it can also separate the effects of firm size from the effects of related variables. Disentangling shows that returns to small firms in January are not abnormal; the apparent January seasonal merely proxies for year-end tax-loss selling and subsequent bounceback.[8] Not all small firms will benefit from a January rebound; indiscriminately buying small firms at the turn of the year is not an optimal investment strategy. Ascertaining true causation leads to more profitable strategies.

Return Revelation

Disentangling can reveal hidden opportunities. Exhibit 3 plots the naively measured cumulative excess returns (relative to the 3000-stock universe) to portfolios that rank lower than average in market capitalization and price per share and higher than average in terms of analyst neglect.[9] These results derive from

---

[8] See Bruce I. Jacobs and Kenneth N. Levy, "Calendar Anomalies: Abnormal Returns at Calendar Turning Points," *Financial Analysts Journal* (November/December 1988).

[9] Again, portfolios with values of these parameters that are, on average, one standard deviation away from the universe mean.

monthly univariate regressions. The "small-cap" line thus represents the cumulative excess returns to a portfolio of stocks naively chosen on the basis of their size, with no attempt made to control for other variables.

All three return series move together. The similarity between the small-cap and neglect series is particularly striking. This is confirmed by the correlation coefficients in the first column of Exhibit 4. Furthermore, all series show a great deal of volatility within a broader up, down, up pattern.

Exhibit 5 shows the pure cumulative excess returns to each size-related attribute over the period. These disentangled returns adjust for correlations not only between the three size variables, but also between each size variable and industry affiliations and each variable and growth and value characteristics. Two findings are immediately apparent from Exhibit 5.

First, pure returns to the size variables do not appear to be nearly as closely correlated as the naive returns displayed in Exhibit 3. In fact, over the second half of the period, the three return series diverge substantially. This is confirmed by the lower correlation coefficients in the second column of Exhibit 4.

Exhibit 3: Naive Returns Can Hide Opportunities: Three Size-Related Variables

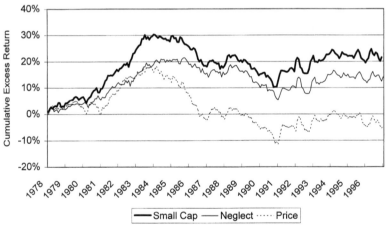

Exhibit 4: Correlations between Monthly Returns to Size-Related Variables*

Variable	Naive	Pure
Small Cap/Low Price	0.82	−0.12
Small Cap/Neglect	0.87	−0.22
Neglect/Low Price	0.66	−0.11

* A coefficient of 0.14 is significant at the 5% level.

Exhibit 5: Pure Returns Can Reveal Opportunities: Three Size-Related Variables

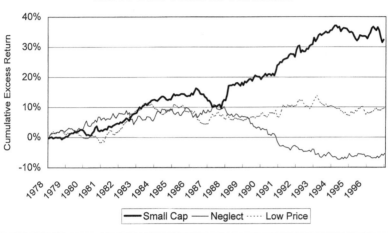

In particular, pure returns to small capitalization accumulate quite a gain over the period; they are up 30%, versus an only 20% gain for the naive returns to small cap. Purifying returns reveals a profit opportunity not apparent in the naive returns. Furthermore, pure returns to analyst neglect amount to a substantial loss over the period. Because disentangling controls for proxy effects, and thereby avoids redundancies, these pure return effects are additive. A portfolio could have achieved truly superior returns by selecting small-cap stocks with a higher-than-average analyst following (i.e., a negative exposure to analyst neglect).

Second, the pure returns appear to be much less volatile than the naive returns. The naive returns in Exhibit 3 display much month-to-month volatility within their more general trends. By contrast, the pure series in Exhibit 5 are much smoother and more consistent. This is confirmed by the standard deviations given in Exhibit 6.

The pure returns in Exhibit 5 are smoother and more consistent than the naive return responses in Exhibit 3 because the pure returns capture more "signal" and less noise. And because they are smoother and more consistent than naive returns, pure returns are also more predictable.

Predictability

Disentangling improves return predictability by providing a clearer picture of the relationship between stock price behavior, company fundamentals, and macroeconomic conditions. For example, investors often prefer value stocks in bearish market environments, because growth stocks are priced more on the basis of high expectations, which get dashed in more pessimistic eras. But the success of such a strategy will depend on the measures one has chosen to define value.

Exhibit 6: Pure Returns are Less Volatile, More Predictable: Standard Deviations of Monthly Returns to Size-Related Variables*

Variable	Naive	Pure
Small Cap	0.87	0.60
Neglect	0.87	0.67
Low Price	1.03	0.58

* All differences between naive and pure return standard deviations are significant at the 1% level.

Exhibit 7: Market Sensitivities of Monthly Returns to Value-Related Variables

Variable	Naive	(t-stat.)	Pure	(t-stat.)
DDM	0.06	(5.4)	0.04	(5.6)
B/P	−0.10	(−6.2)	−0.01	(−0.8)
Yield	−0.08	(−7.4)	−0.03	(−3.5)

Exhibit 7 displays the results of regressing both naive and pure returns to various value-related variables on market (S&P 500) returns over the 1978-1996 period. The results indicate that DDM value is a poor indicator of a stock's ability to withstand a tide of receding market prices. The regression coefficient in the first column indicates that a portfolio with a one-standard-deviation exposure to DDM value will tend to outperform by 0.06% when the market rises by 1.00% and to underperform by a similar margin when the market falls by 1.00%. The coefficient for pure returns to DDM is similar. Whether their returns are measured in pure or naive form, stocks with high DDM values tend to behave procyclically.

High book-to-price ratio appears to be a better indicator of a defensive stock. It has a regression coefficient of -0.10 in naive form. In pure form, however, B/P is virtually uncorrelated with market movements; pure B/P signals neither an aggressive nor a defensive stock. B/P as naively measured apparently picks up the effects of truly defensive variables — such as high yield.

The value investor in search of a defensive posture in uncertain market climates should consider moving toward high yield. The regression coefficients for both naive and pure returns to high yield indicate significant negative market sensitivities. Stocks with high yields may be expected to lag in up markets but to hold up relatively well during general market declines.

These results make broad intuitive sense. DDM is forward-looking, relying on estimates of future earnings. In bull markets, investors take a long-term outlook, so DDM explains security pricing behavior. In bear markets, however, investors become myopic; they prefer today's tangible income to tomorrow's promise, and so current yield is rewarded.[10]

---

[10] See also Bruce I. Jacobs and Kenneth N. Levy, "On the Value of 'Value'," *Financial Analysts Journal* (July/August 1988).

Exhibit 8: Forecast Response of Small Size to Macroeconomic Shocks

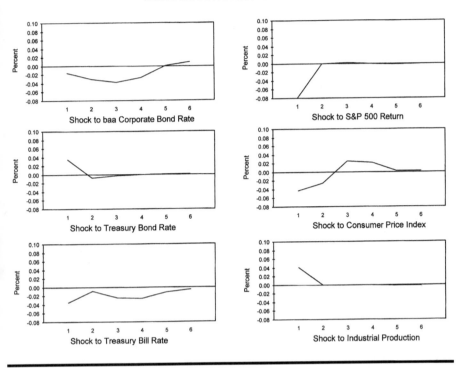

Pure returns respond in intuitively satisfying ways to macroeconomic events. Exhibit 8 illustrates, as an example, the estimated effects of changes in various macroeconomic variables on the pure returns to small size (as measured by market capitalization). Consistent with the capital constraints on small firms and their relatively greater sensitivity to the economy, pure returns to small size may be expected to be negative in the first four months following an unexpected increase in the BAA corporate rate rate and positive in the first month following an unexpected increase in industrial production.[11] Investors can exploit such predictable behavior by moving into and out of the small-cap market segment as economic conditions evolve.[12]

These examples serve to illustrate that the use of numerous, finely defined fundamental variables can provide a rich representation of the complexity of security pricing. The model can be even more finely tuned, however, by including variables that capture such subtleties as the effects of investor psychology, possible nonlinearities in variable-return relationships, and security transaction costs.

[11] See Bruce I. Jacobs and Kenneth N. Levy, "Forecasting the Size Effect," *Financial Analysts Journal* (May/June 1989).
[12] See, for example, Bruce I. Jacobs and Kenneth N. Levy, "High-Definition Style Rotation," *Journal of Investing* (Fall 1996), pp. 14-23.

Additional Complexities

In considering possible variables for inclusion in a model of stock price behavior, the investor should recognize that pure stock returns are driven by a combination of economic fundamentals and investor psychology. That is, economic fundamentals such as interest rates, industrial production, and inflation can explain much, but by no means all, of the systematic variation in returns. Psychology, including investors' tendency to overreact, their desire to seek safety in numbers, and their selective memories, also plays a role in security pricing.

What's more, the modeler should realize that the effects of different variables, fundamental and otherwise, can differ across different types of stocks. The value sector, for example, includes more financial stocks than the growth sector. Investors may thus expect value stocks in general to be more sensitive than growth stocks to changes in interest rate default spreads.

Psychologically based variables such as short-term overreaction and price correction also seem to have a stronger effect on value than on growth stocks. Earnings surprises and earnings estimate revisions, by contrast, appear to be more important for growth than for value stocks. Thus Intel shares can take a nose dive when earnings come in a penny under expectations, whereas Ford shares remain unmoved even by fairly substantial departures of actual earnings from expectations.

The relationship between stock returns and relevant variables may not be linear. The effects of positive earnings surprises, for instance, tend to be arbitraged away quickly; thus positive earnings surprises offer less opportunity for the investor. The effects of negative earnings surprises, however, appear to be more long-lasting. This nonlinearity may reflect the fact that sales of stock are limited to those investors who already own the stock (and to a relatively small number of short-sellers).[13]

Risk-variable relationships may also differ across different types of stock. In particular, small-cap stocks generally have more idiosyncratic risk than large-cap stocks. Diversification is thus more important for small-stock than for large-stock portfolios.

Return-variable relationships can also change over time. Recall the difference between DDM and yield value measures: High-DDM stocks tend to have high returns in bull markets and low returns in bear markets; high-yield stocks experience the reverse. For consistency of performance, return modeling must consider the effects of market dynamics — the changing nature of the overall market.

Finally, a complex model containing multiple variables is likely to turn up a number of promising return-variable relationships. But are these perceived profit opportunities translatable into real economic opportunities? Are some too ephemeral? Too small to survive frictions such as trading costs? Estimates of expected returns must be combined with estimates of the costs of trading to arrive at realistic returns net of trading costs.

---

[13] See Bruce I. Jacobs and Kenneth N. Levy, "Long/Short Equity Investing," *Journal of Portfolio Management* (Fall 1993).

ENGINEERING PORTFOLIOS

A broad-based approach to security valuation, one that also has the complexity to plumb the depths of security pricing behavior, provides the investment manager with the flexibility to tailor portfolios to a wide variety of client needs and the tools to fine-tune the portfolios' risks and enhance their returns relative to underlying benchmarks. Portfolios can in fact be "engineered" to multiple specifications, whether those are set by the client or by underlying performance benchmarks.

Consider, for example, a client that has no strong opinion about growth versus value, say, but believes that the equity market will continue to offer its average historical premium over alternative cash and bond investments. This client may choose to hold the market in the form of a broad-based core portfolio that can deliver the all-important equity market premium (at the market's risk level). Insightful security valuation can add to that the potential for some incremental return consistent with the additional risk incurred.[14]

For a client with a strong belief that value stocks will outperform, the investment manager can engineer a value portfolio that offers a given level of incremental return, based on the insights gleaned by the valuation model, consistent with the client's chosen level of incremental risk relative to a selected value index. In fact, with engineered portfolios, the client has the ability to fine-tune overall portfolio exposures. For example, the client can overweight growth stocks while retaining exposure to the overall market by placing some portion of the portfolio in core equity and the remainder in a growth portfolio, or by placing some percentage in a value portfolio and a larger percentage in a growth portfolio. Exposures to the market and to its various subsets can be precisely controlled.

This level of control helps to ensure portfolio integrity. Engineered style portfolios are non-overlapping; value portfolios contain no growth stocks, nor growth portfolios any value stocks. Furthermore, the style benchmarks are, in the aggregate, inclusive of all stocks in the selection universe. The underlying benchmarks for value and growth portfolios, say, or for large- and small-cap portfolios, will aggregate to the equity core.

Expanding Opportunities

Model insights are perhaps best exploited by portfolios that are not constrained to deliver a benchmark-like performance — by portfolios that are free to pursue the expected rewards from the model's insights, constrained only by the client's risk preferences.

For example, portfolios tied to a particular style benchmark will suffer relative to the overall market when that particular style is out of favor. The historical evidence suggests that any given style will tend to outperform the overall

---

[14] For a discussion of the appropriate level of risk for an investor of a given risk aversion level with a manager of given skill, see Bruce I. Jacobs and Kenneth N. Levy, "Residual Risk: How Much is Too Much?" *Journal of Portfolio Management* (Spring 1996).

market in some periods and to underperform it in others. A style rotation strategy seeks to deliver returns in excess of the market's by forecasting style subset performance and shifting investment weights aggressively among various style subsets as market and economic conditions evolve.

Style rotation takes advantage of the entire selection universe. A style-rotation portfolio can be engineered to offer a level of incremental return commensurate with the client's level of risk aversion. Rotation among passive style indexes may be able to offer incremental returns above the overall market return, at moderate levels of incremental risk. But a client that chooses to take advantage of the complex model's ability to disentangle style attributes and fine-tune style may expect even higher returns for not much more risk.

Allowing short sales, whether in conjunction with a core portfolio, a style portfolio, or style rotation, can further enhance return opportunities. While traditional management focuses on the selection of "winning" securities, the breadth of a complex quantitative approach allows the investor to profit from "losers" as well as "winners." With an engineered portfolio that allows shorting of losers, the manager can pursue potential mispricings without constraint, going long underpriced stocks and selling short overpriced stocks.

In markets in which short selling is not widespread, there are reasons to believe that shorting stocks can offer more opportunity than buying stocks. This is because restrictions on short selling do not permit investor pessimism to be as fully represented in prices as investor optimism. In such a market, the potential candidates for short sale may be less efficiently priced, hence offer greater return potential, than the potential candidates for purchase.[15]

Shorting can enhance performance by eliminating constraints on the implementation of investment insights. Consider, for example, that a security with a median market capitalization has a weighting of approximately 0.01% of the market's capitalization. A manager that cannot short can underweight such a security by, at most, 0.01% relative to the market; this is achieved by not holding the security at all. Those who do not consider this unduly restrictive should consider that placing a like constraint on the maximum portfolio overweight would be equivalent to saying the manager could hold, at most, a 0.02% position in the stock, no matter how appetizing its expected return. Shorting allows the manager free rein in translating the insights gained from the stock selection process into portfolio performance.

Long-Short Portfolios

If security returns are symmetrically distributed about the underlying market return, there will be fully as many unattractive securities for short sale as there are attractive securities for purchase. The manager can construct a portfolio that balances equal dollar amounts and equal systematic risks long and short. Such a

---

[15] See, for example, Bruce I. Jacobs and Kenneth N. Levy, "20 Myths About Long-Short," *Financial Analysts Journal* (September/October 1996).

long-short balance neutralizes the risk (and return) of the underlying market. The portfolio's return — which can be measured as the spread between the long and short returns — is solely reflective of the manager's skill at stock selection.[16]

Not only does such a long-short portfolio neutralize underlying market risk, it offers improved control of residual risk relative to a long-only portfolio. For example, the long-only portfolio can control risk relative to the underlying benchmark only by converging toward the weights of the benchmark's stocks; these weights constrain portfolio composition. Balancing securities' sensitivities long and short, however, eliminates risk relative to the underlying benchmark; benchmark weights are thus not constraining in long-short. Furthermore, the long-short portfolio can use offsetting long and short positions to fine-tune the portfolio's residual risk.

In addition to enhanced return and improved risk control, an engineered long-short approach also offers clients added flexibility in asset allocation. A simple long-short portfolio, for example, offers a return from security selection on top of a cash return (the interest received on the proceeds from the short sales). However, the long-short manager can also offer, or the client initiate, a long-short portfolio combined with a position in derivatives such as stock index futures. Such an "equitized" portfolio will offer the long-short portfolio's security selection return on top of the equity market return provided by the futures position; choice of other available derivatives can provide the return from security selection in combination with exposure to other asset classes. The transportability of the long-short portfolio's return offers clients the ability to take advantage of a manager's security selection skills while determining independently the plan's asset allocation mix.

Customizing Your Optimizer

To maximize implementation of the model's insights, the portfolio construction process should consider exactly the same dimensions found relevant by the stock selection model. Failure to do so can lead to mismatches between model insights and portfolio exposures.

Consider a commercially available portfolio optimizer that recognizes only a subset of the variables in the valuation model. Risk reduction using such an optimizer will reduce the portfolio's exposures only along the dimensions the optimizer recognizes. As a result, the portfolio is likely to wind up more exposed to those variables recognized by the model — but not the optimizer — and less exposed to those variables common to both the model and the optimizer.

Imagine an investor who seeks low-P/E stocks that analysts are recommending for purchase, but who uses a commercial optimizer that incorporates a P/E factor but not analyst recommendations. The investor is likely to wind up with a

---

[16] See Bruce I. Jacobs and Kenneth N. Levy, "The Long and Short on Long-Short," *Journal of Investing* (Spring 1997), pp. 73-86. See also Bruce I. Jacobs, Kenneth N. Levy, and David Starer, "On the Optimality of Long-Short Strategies," *Financial Analysts Journal* (March/April 1998), for an analysis of long-short balance.

portfolio that has a less than optimal level of exposure to low P/E and a greater than optimal level of exposure to analyst purchase recommendations. Optimization using all relevant variables ensures a portfolio whose risk and return opportunities are balanced in accordance with the model's insights. Furthermore, the use of more numerous variables allows portfolio risk to be more finely tuned.

Insofar as the investment process — both stock selection and portfolio construction — is model-driven, it is more adaptable to electronic trading venues. This should benefit the investor in several ways. First, electronic trading is generally less costly, with lower commissions, market impact, and opportunity costs. Second, it allows real-time monitoring, which can further reduce trading costs. Third, an automated trading system can take account of more factors, including the urgency of a particular trade and market conditions, than individual traders can be expected to bear in mind.

The performance attribution process should also be congruent with the dimensions of the selection model (and portfolio optimizer). Insofar as performance attribution identifies sources of return, a process that considers all the sources identified by the selection model will be more insightful than a commercial performance attribution system applied in a "one-size-fits-all" manner. Our investor who has sought exposure to low P/E and positive analyst recommendations, for example, will want to know how each of these factors has paid off and will be less interested in the returns to factors that are not a part of the stock selection process.

A performance evaluation process tailored to the model also functions as a monitor of the model's reliability. Has portfolio performance supported the model's insights? Equally important, does the model's reliability hold up over time? A model that performs well in today's economic and market environments may not necessarily perform well in the future. A feedback loop between the evaluation and the research/modeling processes can help ensure that the model retains robustness over time.

PROFITING FROM COMPLEXITY

It has been said that: "For every complex problem, there's a simple solution, and it's almost always wrong."[17]

A complex approach to stock selection, portfolio construction, and performance evaluation is needed to capture the complexities of the stock market. Such an approach combines the breadth of coverage and the depth of analysis needed to maximize investment opportunity and potential reward.

Grinold and Kahn present a formula that identifies the relationships between the depth and breadth of investment insights and investment performance:

$$IR = IC \times \sqrt{BR}$$

---

[17] Attributed to H.L. Mencken.

IR is the manager's information ratio, a measure of the success of the investment process. *IR* equals annualized excess return over annualized residual risk (e.g., 2% excess return with 4% tracking error provides 0.5 *IR*). *IC*, the information coefficient, or correlation between predicted and actual results, measures the goodness of the manager's insights, or the manager's skill. *BR* is the breadth of the strategy, measurable as the number of independent insights upon which investment decisions are made.[18]

One can increase *IR* by increasing *IC* or *BR*. Increasing *IC* means developing some means of improving predictive accuracy. Increasing *BR* means discovering more "investable" insights. A casino analogy may be apt (if anathema to prudent investors).

A gambler can seek to increase *IC* by card-counting in blackjack or by building a computer model to predict probable roulette outcomes. Similarly, some investors seek to outperform by concentrating their research efforts on a few stocks: By learning all there is to know about Microsoft, for example, one may be able to outperform all the other investors who follow this stock. But a strategy that makes a few concentrated stock bets is likely to produce consistent performance only if it is based on a very high level of skill, or if it benefits from extraordinary luck.

Alternatively, an investor can place a larger number of smaller stock bets and settle for more modest returns from a greater number of investment decisions. That is, rather than behaving like a gambler in a casino, the investor can behave like the casino. A casino has only a slight edge on any spin of the roulette wheel or roll of the dice, but many spins of many roulette wheels can result in a very consistent profit for the house. Over time, the odds will strongly favor the casino over the gambler.

A complex approach to the equity market, one that has both breadth of inquiry and depth of focus, can enhance the number and the goodness of investment insights. A complex approach to the equity market requires more time, effort and ability, but it will be better positioned to capture the complexities of security pricing. The rewards are worth the effort.

---

[18] Richard C. Grinold and Ronald N. Kahn, *Active Portfolio Management* (Chicago, IL: Probus, 1995).

Chapter 2

A Bottom-Up Approach to Small Capitalization Active Management

Kenneth J. Greiner, CFA
President
Dalton, Greiner, Hartman, Maher & Co.

Stephen J. Bruno, CFA
Senior Vice President
Dalton, Greiner, Hartman, Maher & Co.

INTRODUCTION

Within investing, two schools of thought regarding portfolio construction exist. The "top-down" approach attempts to utilize broad measures of economic activity, economic forecasts, and interest rate forecasts to determine which sectors of the economy are likely to outperform within the stock market. Thus, the economic sector a company represents (banks, energy, etc.) is more important than the individual company's characteristics. As shown in Chapter 3, top-down investors believe a company's industry classification determines much of a stock's relative performance in the market.

In contrast, "bottom-up" managers focus on the individual characteristics of each company and build a portfolio of attractive companies one at a time. The economic sector is a secondary consideration (i.e., no matter how attractive banks are, they would not represent 80% of a diversified portfolio). Bottom-up managers believe that it is the individual characteristics of a company that represent the underlying value and thus are the primary source of the stock's performance in the market.

We at Dalton, Greiner, Hartman, Maher (DGHM) are a bottom-up manager. In the small cap universe where we specialize, the individual company's characteristics are much more critical in determining how that company will perform. Small cap companies are often single product/single market companies, and

The authors would like to thank Bruce Geller, CFA (Dalton, Greiner, Hartman, Maher) and Steve Hardy (Zephyr Associates) for their assistance in writing this chapter.

19

the loss of a large customer, for example, is considerably more detrimental to a small company than a larger, more diversified one. The small cap universe is one where the bottom-up manager thrives by uncovering inefficiencies in the marketplace. In this chapter, we describe our bottom-up approach to small capitalization active management.

WHY INVEST IN SMALL CAP STOCKS?

We invest in small cap stocks because, to paraphrase Willie Sutton, "that's where the returns are." The first person to document the relationship between the size of a company, as measured by its market capitalization or market cap, and subsequent stock market returns was Rolf Banz in 1981.[1] Further research was done by Roger Ibbotson and Rex Sinquefield in 1982.[2] While this research covered a much broader spectrum of issues related to returns from various asset classes such as equities, bonds, and Treasury bills, and how they are related to inflation, the methodology used by Ibbotson and Sinquefield has become the standard method for researching how size (market cap) and returns are related. Ibbotson and Sinquefield utilized portfolios provided by the Center for Research in Security Prices (CRSP) at the University of Chicago. These portfolios ranked all operating companies on the NYSE by capitalization and then split them into 10 equally populated groups or deciles.

For example, if there were 1,000 companies on the NYSE, each decile would have 100 companies. These portfolios were held for one quarter and then rebalanced to reflect changing capitalizations. This process was repeated each quarter for the period 1926-1981. The resulting returns were analyzed and it was discovered that as you moved down the capitalization spectrum (Decile 1 → Decile 2 → Decile 3) the portfolio returns increased. This discovery led to the Wall Street axiom that small stocks outperform large stocks over the long term. Subsequent research added stocks listed on the American Stock Exchange and NASDAQ with no change in the conclusion. This research is updated on a yearly basis and is available from Ibbotson Associates.[3]

While comparing each decile to the other is interesting, it is more useful to look at broader categories of market capitalizations often referred to as large cap, mid cap, small cap, and micro cap. Although a concrete definition of these categories does not exist, many institutional investors would define the first two deciles of NYSE-listed stocks as large cap. Similarly, the next three deciles would be considered mid cap, the following three deciles small cap, and the final two deciles micro cap.

---

[1] Rolf W. Banz, "The Relationship Between Return and Market Value of Common Stocks," *Journal of Financial Economics* (1981), pp. 3-18.

[2] Roger G. Ibbotson and Rex A. Sinquefield, *Stocks, Bonds, Bills, and Inflation: The Past and the Future, 1982 ed.* (Charlottesville, VA: Institute of Chartered Financial Analysts, 1982).

[3] Ibbotson Associates, *Stocks, Bonds, Bills, and Inflation 1997 Yearbook*, Chicago, IL, 1983-1997.

Exhibit 1: Distribution of Returns

Name	CRSP Deciles	Geometric Return 1925-1996	Value in 1996 of $1.00 Invested in 1925
Large cap	1-2	10.4%	$1,183
Mid cap	3-5	11.7%	$2,567
Small cap	6-8	12.0%	$3,024
Micro cap	9-10	12.7%	$5,088

Source: Prudential Securities.

Exhibit 2: CRSP 9-10 versus CRSP 1-2 Relative Performance
3-Year Moving Average

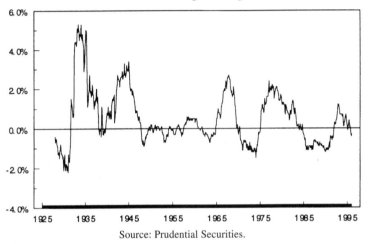

Source: Prudential Securities.

As shown in Exhibit 1, the ability to turn $1.00 into over $5,000 over a long period of time is the attraction of small cap investing in general and micro cap investing in specific. Investing in micro cap stocks has provided over 4 times the return as investing in large cap stocks over the long term. While 70 years would be considered a very long time for an individual, it must be remembered that large institutional portfolios such as pension funds and endowments are considered to exist in perpetuity. The power of compounding makes a huge difference over time.

It must also be remembered that micro cap stocks do not outperform in every single month. On the contrary, micro cap outperformance actually runs in cycles. As shown in Exhibit 2, if we compare a rolling 36-month moving average of micro cap performance relative to large cap performance, we can see a number of cycles have occurred over the last 70 years. These cycles are driven by a number of factors but relative earnings growth seems to be the predominant factor. In periods of economic strength, small cap companies are generally able to grow their earnings faster than large cap companies. Conversely, large cap companies, with their diversified markets and geographics, tend to suffer less in an economic downturn. Thus, economic forecasts should play a role in expectations for small cap relative performance.

Exhibit 3: Distribution of Market Capitalization

Sector	CRSP Deciles	Market Cap Range ($MM)	Median Market Cap ($MM)	Total Market Cap ($Bn)	No. of Names	Median Daily Shares Traded (000s)	Median No. of Analysts	% of Cos with Estimates
Large cap	1-2	≥4,212	9,055	7,543	422	540	14.0	99.0%
Mid cap	3-5	976-4,185	1,742	1,554	780	129	8.0	96.8%
Small cap	6-8	270-975	481	726	1,360	35	5.0	86.1%
Micro cap	9-10	≤270	71	312	3,438	8	2.0	64.6%

Source: FactSet Data Systems, First Call. Data as of 12/31/97.

What are Micro Caps?

The long-term results for micro cap investing are very compelling, but what are micro caps and why do they provide superior returns? Applying the CRSP 9-10 decile definition yields a market cap cut-off on 12/31/97 of approximately $270 million. Thus, the micro cap universe is defined as all listed companies (NYSE, AMEX, NASDAQ) with market caps below $270 million. Over 3,400 companies had market capitalizations below $270 million on 12/31/97. The *median* market cap of this universe is only $71 million, a sharp contrast to Microsoft, whose market cap on 12/31/97 was $156 billion!

Why Do Micro Caps Outperform?

While the stock market is thought to be generally efficient, it is likely that the degree of efficiency varies by market cap. Simply put, there is much greater Wall Street research being done on large cap stocks than on small cap stocks. This is driven by the economics of Wall Street. Wall Street analysts generally provide research on companies for two reasons: (1) large trading volumes earn their firms commissions and trading profits, and (2) security issuance and merger and acquisition activity reap investment banking fees. Small caps, in general, and micro caps, in specific, have neither of these traits. Research coverage is generally provided by small research boutiques and regional brokers who focus on specific sectors (e.g., technology) or regions of the country.

As shown in Exhibit 3, a dramatic difference exists between large caps and small caps/micro caps in terms of analyst coverage as well as trading volume. It is this lack of Wall Street coverage that drives the inefficiencies within the small cap/micro cap universe. As stated previously, there are over 3,400 companies within the micro cap universe. It is very difficult for investors to keep up with current trends within each of these companies, let alone perform the proper due diligence in order to invest in them. Nor can the entire micro cap universe be bought or sold efficiently and at low cost to capture the excess returns. Low liquidity, large bid-ask spreads, etc., make a passive or "complete indexing" approach not feasible within the micro cap universe. In order to capture the excess returns within the micro cap universe the ancient art of security analysis, also known as active management, must be applied.

Exhibit 4: Russell 2000 Value versus Growth (1979-1997)

	Annualized Return	Annualized Risk
R2000 Value	18.1%	16.7%
R2000 Growth	13.4%	21.7%

Source: Zephyr Associates/Frank Russell & Associates.

STYLES OF INVESTING WITHIN ACTIVE MANAGEMENT

Active management requires discipline. Simply researching each company within the universe starting with AAON Inc. and ending with ZYTEC Inc. is not only time consuming but counterproductive. Being able to rank stocks within the universe by traits deemed important is the most productive way of focusing research on the most attractive companies. It is these traits that distinguish what style of investing is adhered to. The two opposing camps in this investment style war are known as value and growth. Value investors focus on valuation driven traits such as price/EPS, price/book, price/cash flow, and yield. Growth investors focus on growth driven factors such as sales growth, earnings per share growth, and reinvestment rate. In reality, both sides pay attention to the other's factors yielding a spectrum of investment styles, but by and large investors consider themselves members of one group or the other. We at DGHM consider ourselves value investors. We focus on a value style because historically, value investing (buying cheap stocks) has outperformed growth investing (buying rapidly growing companies), particularly within the small cap universe.

Exhibit 4 illustrates this point by comparing the Russell 2000 (a recognized small cap index consisting of 2000 companies), after it has been divided between value and growth stocks. For the 19 years for which data are available, the value portion of the Russell 2000 index has outperformed the growth portion by 470 basis points. At the same time, the Russell 2000 Value index had less risk as measured by standard deviation of returns. Higher returns with lower risk seems to us like a very smart strategy to follow.

Small Cap Value Active Management

Now that the rationale for small cap value active management has been established, how can this strategy be successfully implemented? Our approach is a combination of quantitative and qualitative research. DGHM has developed a multi-factor model (MFM) comprised of nine factors which is designed to optimize the trade-off between valuation (low), profitability (high), and financial strength (strong). We have found through backtesting of historical data that our model's most attractive quintile (20% of names screened) will beat the CRSP 9-10 benchmark by 1,000 bps annualized over the last 15 years (*before* transaction costs).

Creating our multi-factor model was not simply a process of testing every variable we could think of and taking the nine best factors, a process known as data mining. The variables we chose to use were based upon more than 25 years of investment experience. That experience, combined with common sense (i.e., companies with higher profitability, sell at higher valuations), helped us create a model which outperformed many of the well-researched single-factor models such as low P/E or low P/Book investing. Optimizing the trade-off between valuation and profitability allows us to construct portfolios that outperform those that simply buy stocks with low P/E's or low P/Book measures.

A comparison between DGHM's MFM and low P/E and low P/Book investing is shown in Exhibit 5. By using our MFM, our eight analysts start their screening with a potential buy list or first quintile of 690 names rather than the original 3,400+. Our research has further shown that not only has the first or most attractive quintile outperformed the benchmark (CRSP 9-10), it contains an above average percentage of companies that outperform the benchmark. Quintile results are show in Exhibit 6.

While a 690 name list is more manageable than a 3,400 name list, the most attractive quintile is simply a starting point. As with any computer generated list, we must first delete from the potential buy list highly illiquid stocks as well as stocks with incorrect or out of date data. At this point the other portion of our process takes over. After deciding which of the names on our buy list warrant further research, our analysts apply rigorous securities analysis to those names in order to determine which companies offer a superior risk/reward trade-off.

Unlike large companies which are often involved in multiple industries and geographies, small companies tend to compete in much narrower industries with fewer products. This difference allows active management to add significant value to the process. It is much easier for the analyst to recognize and analyze the four or five critical issues that will enable a small company to be successful than it is when analyzing a global conglomerate such as General Motors. Thus, the focal point of the due diligence process is the management interview.

Exhibit 5: Model Comparison – Micro Cap Universe (1982-1997)

Model	Return
DGHM MFM (First Quintile)	23.0%
Low P/E	19.1%
Low P/Book	16.5%

Source: Dalton, Greiner, Hartman, Maher & Co.

Exhibit 6: Multi-Factor Model Backtest – Micro Cap Universe (1982-1997)

Quintile	Return
First Quintile	23.0%
Second Quintile	17.5%
Third Quintile	10.6%
Fourth Quintile	9.8%
Fifth Quintile	0.5%
CRSP 9-10	13.0%

Source: Dalton, Greiner, Hartman, Maher & Co., FactSet Data Systems, and Prudential Securities.

THE ART OF THE MANAGEMENT INTERVIEW

The management interview is a crucial aspect of the investment decision making process. It should be viewed as the analyst's opportunity to gain insights from senior management about the dynamics of their business and the industry or industries in which it operates, and to gauge the future prospects of the company. The analyst must take advantage of the interview opportunity in order to gain an edge over his competition. In a stock market that is fairly efficient, stock prices will generally reflect the market's view of a company's prospects. The interview will assist the analyst in determining whether this view is correct, or whether the market's pricing mechanism is missing something, albeit positive or negative. It is important to stay focused on information that may differ from Wall Street's perceived expectations. The interview is especially important for smaller companies who may not have a wide following among sell side analysts who publish research, because the critical decision making variables may not be as widely discussed or thoroughly understood by the investment community.

It is important to be thorough in the interview process, so that the analyst has as many decision inputs in his arsenal as possible. The goal is to achieve a high comfort level with each of the meaningful issues, and have considerable supporting information for those issues. The analyst should constantly be probing for things that excite or concern him.

The interview can be done via conference call, or perhaps more effectively, a face to face site visit to the company's headquarters. This can often be done in conjunction with a tour of some company facilities, which may afford an opportunity to speak with managers or employees at the operating level. This often provides further insights about how the company is run, and its overall management philosophy. One point to keep in mind is that questions should be geared to provide guidance and insights, but not specific budgeted numbers. It is highly inappropriate to attempt to gain access to any material nonpublic information.

The analyst must be sure to do substantial homework on the company ahead of time, and be prepared with a list of questions to pose — wasting management's time could hamper access in the future. A company executive will be much more patient and helpful if he believes that the analyst has some basic knowledge of the company, and a high degree of interest in learning more. Obtaining this fundamental knowledge entails reviewing the latest annual report, 10K, 10Q, proxy, recent press releases, product brochures, and Wall Street research reports if available.

The following sample interview outline is geared towards providing guidance on the topics that should be reviewed for companies across a wide array of industries. However, it is clearly not all encompassing, and there will always be company or industry-specific issues that need to be considered in addition to, or in place of, those given below.

Sample Interview Outline

Company Background Information

Review some basic company history in order to have an understanding of how the company has evolved into its current form:

- When was the company founded?
- When did it go public?
- How/why has it evolved into the businesses in which it currently operates?
- How long has the current management team been in place?
- What are the management team's primary long-term goals?

Market and Competitive Overview

Gain an understanding of the market profile and competitive landscape in which the company operates. The analyst should try to gauge the attractiveness of the market, as well as the company's relative competitive position, and its ability to improve on this position:

- Approximate size of the market(s).
- Competitive advantages/disadvantages of size.
- Market growth.
- Historical cyclicality.
- Position in the current economic cycle.
- Secular changes, if any, taking place that will affect the market profile going forward.
- Barriers to entry.
- Manufacturing capacity being added, and the impact on industry pricing structure.
- Fragmentation of the competitive landscape.
- Key industry competitors, ranked by strength.
- Market share breakdown among these industry participants.
- Market share shifts over the years, and the leading causes of these changes.
- Key differentiators (i.e., price, product quality, delivery times, technology, distribution).

Product Line Overview

The analyst wants to secure a solid understanding of the company's products, their competitive advantages, and their positioning in the marketplace. Special attention should be given to any product(s) that the company is particularly dependent upon, and the company's ability to maintain a competitive edge with respect to these products:

- Value added from a customer's perspective of the company's product line.
- Is any of the product line customized for customer specific applications?

- Product positioning in the market in terms of price point, and quality.
- Where is the product in terms of the its life cycle?
- How quickly do these cycles evolve?
- Proprietary aspects of the product line (i.e., patents, technology, trademarks, licenses, etc.).
- Products' drawbacks or competitive disadvantages.
- Risk of obsolescence.
- Company dependence on any single product or product line.
- Overall product mix profile in terms of revenue generation.
- How is this mix changing?
- How do operating margins differ within this mix?
- Level of resources put into research and development (R&D).
- Is R&D expensed or capitalized for accounting purposes?
- Company dependence on its ability to generate new and/or upgraded products.
- Ability to enter new markets.

Sales and Marketing

The analyst should try to understand how the sales and marketing functions are performed, and whether the company has gained any type of competitive advantage from these functions:

- Does the company have an internal sales force, or does it use independent representatives?
- Growth in sales force or number of independent representatives.
- How are the salespeople incentivized?
- Customer retention rates.
- Methodology for contacting new customers.
- Types of advertising used for marketing purposes.
- Ability to measure the impact of advertising on sales results.
- Significance of these costs in terms of the overall cost structure.
- Perceived competitive advantages/disadvantages of the company's sales and marketing efforts.

Distribution

The analyst should try to understand how the distribution functions are performed, and whether the company has gained any type of competitive advantage from these functions:

- Channels of distribution used.
- Percent of sales to Original Equipment Makers (OEMs), as opposed to the aftermarket.
- Percent of sales that are wholesale versus retail.
- How do margins differ by distribution channel?

- What changes are taking place industrywide in the way product is distributed?
- How is the company responding to these changes?
- Trends in distribution costs as a component of the overall cost structure.

Customer Overview

The analyst must gain an in-depth knowledge of the customer base, and an understanding of the company's strengths and weaknesses in regards to its customer base. This is determined by various factors such as the diversity of the customer base (diversification means less dependence on any one customer), the importance of the company's products to its customers (value added), and the financial health of the customer base:

- Composition of revenues by end market.
- By geography.
- By major customers.
- Diversity of the customer base.
- Does the company supply a dominant percentage of the customers' requirements?
- Price elasticity of customer purchasing decisions.
- Are sales done on a contractual basis?
- If so, how long do contracts typically last?
- Are they obtained through a competitive bidding process?
- Price escalators/deflators based upon changing factors such as volumes, raw materials, etc.
- Typical payment terms.
- What has the amount of bad debt writeoffs been?
- What is the current profitability/cash flow profile of the customer base?
- Customer capital spending plans relative to historical spending patterns.
- Does there appear to be pent up demand for the product(s)?
- How lean/full is the inventory pipeline?

Company Structure

The structure of the company's operations must be explored in order to gain an appreciation for the amount of operating leverage inherent in the business. This is important because the more operating leverage (fixed costs/total costs), the more profits will vary with changing volumes. It is also crucial to understand the relative cost advantages/disadvantages versus the competition. The analyst must determine whether the company is a low cost producer, and if not, then why not?

- Are the company's operations centralized or decentralized?
- To what degree is the company vertically integrated in its production processes?
- Level of capital intensity involved in running the business.

- Current capacity utilization.
- To what degree is the cost structure fixed versus variable?
- Components of costs of goods sold in percentage terms (i.e., raw materials, labor, overhead, etc.).
- Dependence on any one particular raw material supplier.
- Unionized labor force?
- Competitive advantage/disadvantage created by this.
- Geographic location of key production facilities, and reasons why.
- Is there a large need for capital to upgrade or expand facilities and equipment?
- How do the above factors affect the company's overall cost position relative to its competitors?

Earnings Model, Cash Flow, and Balance Sheet Discussion

The interview should provide the necessary guidance to build appropriate financial models. These models, which are helpful for valuation analysis, will also determine whether the profitability, cash flow, and balance sheet characteristics of the company can support its projected growth rate. These are all important variables which determine the ability to grow the value of an enterprise over the long-term, and they cannot be obtained from a static analysis of a company.

Earnings Model

It is critical to understand the relationship between sales growth and profitability. Ultimately the value the stock market places on the company will be derived from a company's secular profitability. The following issues should be reviewed:

- Assess the various components of revenue growth: volume, price, product mix changes, market share changes, acquisitions.
- Evaluate gross margins: trends in the components of COGS; incremental/decremental leverage on gross margins as volume changes; is COGS valued on a LIFO or FIFO basis?
- Any accounting methods considered too aggressive or too conservative?
- Evaluate selling, general, and administrative (SG&A) costs: Typically vary in line with changes in revenues? Ability to gain leverage on these costs as the company grows; How significantly can these costs be reduced as a percent of sales?
- Average interest rate on the company's outstanding debt.
- Recent or contemplated changes in capital structure that may change financing costs.
- Tax rate and any programs in place to try to reduce the tax burden?

Cash Flow

Even more important than the earnings model is the cash flow model. This model adjusts for the various accounting choices the company is able to make and exposes management's ability to efficiently run the enterprise. Whether a company is able to self-finance its growth or be forced to tap the capital markets, will be determined through analysis of the cash flow statement. The following issues should be reviewed:

- Trend in capital spending (CapEx) required over the next few years.
- Amount for replacement of the capital base versus growth.
- Compare to depreciation and amortization (D&A) levels.
- Any working capital required for growth? [4]
- If expected to generate free cash flow (FCF), what are the priorities for utilizing it (e.g., acquisitions, share repurchases, dividend payments, debt pay down)?
- If the company is in a negative FCF situation, how will it be financed (e.g., additional debt, stock offerings, etc.)?

Balance Sheet

Financial strength is critical to a company's ability to grow and compete. Financial flexibility as well as asset productivity (a sign of management ability) are important conclusions to draw from analysis of the balance sheet. The following issues should be reviewed:

- What is the company's optimal capital structure (debt/equity)?
- Does this differ significantly from the current capital structure?
- Strategy for bringing it in line.
- Discuss trends in asset productivity (e.g., receivables, inventory, and fixed asset turnover).
- Inventory levels versus expected revenue trends.
- Long-term liability funding issues (e.g., large debt maturity, post retirement obligations).

Review of Recent Trends

The analyst must assess current fundamentals. While the previous sections have helped the analyst gain insight into how the business is run and its long-term fundamentals, this part of the interview focuses on the short-term. While we are always looking to invest in businesses based on their longer term outlook, it would be foolish to overlook near term fluctuations. The following issues should be reviewed:

- Recent order rate trends.
- Backlog trends.
- Margins in this backlog versus typical margins in this type of operating environment.
- Customer indications that order levels may change significantly in the near future for any reason.

---

[4] The calculation to determine whether or not a company generates free cash flow (FCF) is as follows: Net income, plus D&A, minus working capital needs, minus CapEx.

- Impact of seasonality.
- Potential acquisitions (it's not appropriate to ask for specific targets, but markets served, size, and valuation are appropriate discussion points).

Reviewing Management Focus/Issues

An important issue that must be resolved in the analyst's mind during the interview is whether this management team has a coherent strategy, and the ability to execute it properly. By this point of the interview, the analyst should be able to determine whether management's long-term goals that were discussed early on are feasible. Any outstanding concerns should be addressed at this point. There should also be a review of management performance measurement, and it is always a plus when management's financial incentives are aligned with shareholder's best interests. In the case of small companies, the analyst must determine whether management has the capability and depth to grow the company to the next level.

- Review the stated long-term goals and the outlook for achieving them.
- Review the greatest challenges being faced by this company near term and long-term.
- How will the management team address these challenges?
- Review the largest opportunities for growth.
- How will they be exploited?
- Key financial benchmarks used in managing the businesses (i.e., ROA, ROE, EPS growth, etc.).
- Do these benchmarks vary at different levels in the company, such as by division, by plant, etc.?
- Where are these benchmarks currently versus long-term targets and versus their competitors?
- How is meeting benchmarks tied into management compensation.
- Compare total compensation (including stock, options, etc.) with similar companies.
- Discuss level of insider equity ownership, and how this has changed over the past few years.
- Is the proper management team in place to take this company into the future, or are there voids which must be filled?
- Discuss employee turnover trends, and ability to recruit talented managers.

Miscellaneous Topics

This is a catch-all section where various questions can be asked to help the analyst make a decision at the margin.

- Review currency or foreign exchange issues that could potentially impact earnings.
- Review outstanding legal or environmental issues which could have a material impact.

- Are there any shareholders that hold a significant share of the company (10% or greater)?
- If so, have they held the shares a long time?
- What is their investment strategy?
- Which sell side analysts have the best understanding of the company and its philosophy?
- Which customers and suppliers would be worthwhile to speak with regarding their experience in doing business with this company? (This is a good way to obtain more objective insights on the company.)
- What are some up and coming companies in this business to become more familiar with? (The answer to this question can often provide solid leads for other investment opportunities.)
- Any other outstanding issues that have not been covered.

Follow Ups

In addition to performing a thorough interview, the analyst will often want to follow up with shorter review sessions every so often. This will afford the ability to stay current on the issues discussed, and see whether events have played out as expected. Only through regular dialogue and review over a period of time will the analyst be able to determine a management team's ability to provide realistic guidance on their business. The perceptive analyst will be able to determine whether management is realistic about the prospects for their business, or whether they are overly optimistic or pessimistic. The analyst will also gain an appreciation for the importance of a dialogue with management as a key part of the active management of investment portfolios.

PORTFOLIO CONSTRUCTION

The focus of the analytical process and the management interview is to identify those companies with the characteristics that typically result in corporate success. But there is a difference between a good company and a good investment — and this centers on valuation. One of a portfolio manager's primary functions is to determine *when* a good company's stock is undervalued. In addition to the usual financial and valuation characteristics, there are also some subjective factors which often correlate with superior stock performance. We try to identify companies that have "the wind at their backs," or companies involved in an industry or sector that has strong cyclical or secular fundamentals. It is much easier to overcome temporary problems in a growing industry than in one that is contracting.

Another intangible is management's degree of focus on creating shareholder value. We prefer to invest in companies whose management has a significant equity stake and thus has their interests aligned with ours. These companies are less likely to make unattractive acquisitions and are more apt to use free cash flow to repurchase shares, which generally benefits all shareholders.

As a value manager, the valuation component is our primary focus and is accomplished through our multifactor screening model as previously discussed. The portfolio's manager marries this valuation underpinning with the analysts' estimates of improving corporate fundamentals. We typically look for a "double play" in our investments: a period of surprisingly good earnings which will result in an upward revaluation of the price/earnings multiple. For example, if a stock selling at a 10 P/E (due to unexciting historical growth) has two years of 15% growth and the P/E expands to 15, then the net result is a doubling of the stock price.

The portfolio manager's other responsibility is to assemble individual stocks into a portfolio. Two considerations are the number of stocks held in the portfolio and industry concentration. We run very diversified portfolios with 80-100 stocks. Typically, small cap portfolios tend to have more names and smaller positions (1%-2%) compared to large cap portfolios which are often concentrated in 20-50 positions. The primary difference is liquidity — it is much more difficult to trade small cap names. The other reason we like to own many stocks is that the timing of a fundamental improvement at a company and the market's recognition thereof is very uncertain in the inefficient world of small cap investing.

Industry concentration strategies differ significantly from manager to manager. Since we focus on "bottom-up" analysis, we restrict our industry sector bets to 50% over or under the sector weight in the corresponding index (e.g., the Russell 2000). This approach allows us flexibility in constructing the portfolio but retains our emphasis on stock selection.

While much of an analyst's or portfolio manager's effort is placed on the buy decision, the sell decision is equally important. As in buying, there are two primary reasons to sell: a change in fundamentals and/or a change in valuation. The analyst's job does not end with the decision to purchase a stock. Continued monitoring of the company's progress is required. Any deviations from expected results must be carefully scrutinized. Changes in the competitive or economic environment must be analyzed, and a dialog with management must be maintained. If the corporate outlook has significantly deteriorated, then the stock must be sold.

The more pleasant, but often more difficult, sale is one due to valuation. By definition, a sale for valuation reasons usually means the stock has done well and is no longer attractively valued. However, it is human nature to hold onto winners since they look so nice in the portfolio with that very low cost! Thus, a strict sell discipline is required. Target prices can be set, typically when a stock is purchased, based on a full-value P/E multiple. Another method, which we employ, continually ranks a stock in a relative valuation model. When the stock reaches an over-valued ranking, it becomes a sale candidate.

Once a purchase or sell decision has been made, trading becomes critical. The trading of small cap stocks is a specialty unto itself. Most of the stocks trade on NASDAQ and often have a very limited number of market makers. One result of limited liquidity is substantially higher volatility and a corresponding higher cost of execution as capitalization size declines. A very patient trader (and portfolio manager) is a necessity. In many cases, completing a buy or sell order may take a month or more. In recent years, trading in ECNs (electronic communications networks, i.e., Instinet) has become much more important as a means to access liquidity in illiquid markets. New electronic trading mechanisms will continue to emerge, as institutional investors seek natural liquidity while maintaining their anonymity.

SOUNDS GREAT, BUT DOES IT WORK?

We believe that all investors should have a long-term investment horizon, but this is especially true when investing in small cap. Our approach, combining quantitative screening, "bottom-up" security analysis, diversified portfolios, and patient trading has proved successful in adding value in small cap investing. To prove our point, we analyze the historical results for the DGHM Micro Cap MFM (multifactor model) in Exhibit 7.

Any quantitative model of value must backtest positively. DGHM's microcap multifactor model provides the desired results: the quintiles of relative attractiveness are arrayed sequentially, and the first two quintiles (buy and hold) are ahead of the index. The historical model has been tested over the 15-year period 1982-1997. The model portfolios are rebalanced annually.

Real life investment results from 1991-1997 are shown in Exhibit 8. The DGHM MFM Buys consist of the capitalization weighted buy list at the beginning of each year. This list is positively biased by the presumption that the portfolio's desired position can be purchased on day one, and *it does not incorporate transaction costs*. The final bar represents the actual annualized return for the DGHM Micro Cap portfolio for the 1991-1997 period (31.1%).

Exhibit 7: Historical Backtest Results for DGHM Micro Cap MFM 15-Year Annualized Return (1982-1997)

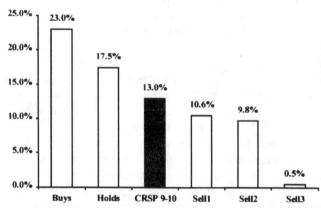

Source: Dalton, Greiner, Hartman, Maher & Co., FactSet Data Systems, and Prudential Securities.

Exhibit 8: Actual Results DGHM Micro Cap
7-Year Annualized Return (1991-1997)

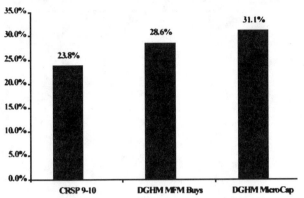

Source: Dalton, Greiner, Hartman, Maher & Co.

Exhibit 8 shows that our model has been productive and our security analysis and stock selection has further improved returns. The net result is a value added process that has delivered to our clients results that are 730 basis points ahead of the relevant benchmark for the 1991-1997 period (DGHM MFM outperformance of CRSP 9-10 by +480 basis points plus DGHM Micro Cap outperformance of DGHM MFM by + 250 basis points).

CONCLUSION

This chapter shows that disciplined, bottom-up stock selection can work very well in the inefficient world of small cap investing. We believe that analysts can gain more relevant insights in this sector of the market where the competition is less intense. Strong fundamental analysis combined with intelligent portfolio management can result in truly superior performance in small cap investing.

Chapter 3

Top Down/Thematic Equity Management

Lawrence S. Viehl, CFA
Vice President
Columbia Management Company

INTRODUCTION

It is generally recognized that there are many successful avenues to superior investment management. While we all may be familiar with investors or firms that have achieved extraordinary results following a particular philosophy or style, their specific approaches vary widely. No single approach has proven to be consistently better than another in spite of the superior returns associated with a particular individual or organization. One observes, however, a common element that is shared by all successful investors — whether their investment approach is oriented toward growth, value, contrarian, large or small cap. That is the consistent application of a disciplined, rational decision-making process for making portfolio asset allocation decisions with respect to industry and sector weightings, for selecting individual securities, as well as for shifting between equities, fixed income, and cash.

While the market does provide opportunities for superior returns, most often they are earned by those who can sift through the tremendous flow of information and anticipate its effect on the valuations of both individual securities and industry groups. Anticipating the impact a given piece of information could have on security prices can be difficult and is dependent on the intellectual, analytical, and intuitive skills of the investor. A well defined, rational decision-making process leverages these skills, giving structure and consistency to the analytical procedure.

TWO INVESTMENT APPROACHES

An investment decision process may take many forms. Two of the most generally recognized processes in investment management are known as "top down" and "bottom up."

Top Down Approach

Those who follow a top-down approach seek first to reach conclusions about the overall economic and market environment, looking for factors that will influence potential returns of the various asset classes as well as the earnings growth and/or profitability of particular industries or market sectors. Once these have been identified, the focus shifts to individual issues within industries to determine the extent to which they are subject to the critical variables in the environment, are positioned to capitalize on them, and are attractively priced.

The primary advantage of using a top-down approach in making investment decisions lies in its presumed efficiency. If one can properly identify those areas of the economy that are expected to experience accelerating revenue and profit growth, or broad investment themes likely to affect the valuation of certain industries, then the research effort to select attractive issues can be focused on those areas. The point is to identify macro forces that will affect the investment environment before they become obvious.

This chapter describes one approach of how a top-down analysis can be incorporated into the investment process.

Bottom Up Approach

A follower of the bottom-up process often uses a number of fundamental financial criteria to determine whether a specific security is under or over valued. These criteria may be measured in either absolute terms or relative to similar measures for the market. In its purest form, little time is spent in the bottom up process to analyze the industry or market sector of the security, or the economic backdrop, unless it directly affects the specific company.

The principle assumption underlying this approach is that each security has an intrinsic "value" that can be quantified by certain measurable criteria, and that the person using this approach is able to recognize the intrinsic value before the general market does. Then, when other market participants buy an issue priced below its perceived intrinsic value or sell a security priced higher, the true value of the stock will come to be reflected in the new price.

Portfolios structured using this approach can be viewed as being built security by security, without great attention to industry or sector weightings relative to a market average or benchmark index.

Supporting Research

Although this seems almost intuitive, there have been studies that tend to support the underlying principle of a top-down investment process. In his 1983 book, Richard Brealey noted that the price of any stock is subject to four different influences:[1]

---

[1] Richard A. Brealey, *An Introduction to Risk and Return from Common Stocks* (Cambridge, MA: The MIT Press, 1983).

- A market factor that affects all stocks.
- An industry factor that affects all stocks within the one industry.
- A variety of other factors that affect the performance of limited groups of stocks other than industry groups.
- An influence that affects only the one stock.

From an earlier study, Brealey found that 31% of the price variability of stocks during the period studied could be traced to the action of the market; 12% was due to the industry influence; 37% was due to the influence of other groupings; and the remaining 20% was on average unique to the individual security.[2] These percentages, of course, are not absolutes. Some industries are by nature more homogeneous than others, and the percentages almost certainly change over time and in response to changes in the broad market and economic environment. The importance of this study, from the point of view of those employing the top-down approach, is that the valuation and price action of a particular security is determined by much more than what can be found in an analysis of that security's financial statements. Furthermore, these other influences can be as or more critical to the price action going forward.

Empirical evidence supporting a top-down approach can be seen in a review of the increases and decreases in the relative weightings of industries in the Standard & Poor's 500 Stock Index over time. Exhibits 1 and 2 taken from work done by Thomas Galvin, chief investment officer of Donaldson, Lufkin & Jenrette, show how the S&P 500 weightings of certain market sectors have changed over time. The S&P 500 industry classifications were regrouped in 1996, and the historic weightings were reclassified here to match the new grouping, but the patterns of group rotation remain evident in Exhibit 2, even though the percentages have changed.

While there have been occasional changes in the individual companies represented in each of the industry sectors, the primary cause of the weightings changes has been the market price performance of the stocks within each industry. Those market areas outperforming the average have seen their relative weightings increase; those sectors underperforming the average have experienced a relative decline. Looking at Exhibits 1 and 2, it is easy to trace trends that were driven by macro changes in the environment and which, if understood and properly interpreted in a timely manner, would have significantly enhanced an investor's chances of generating superior returns. Particularly noticeable in Exhibit 1 is the increased weighting of the Consumer Noncyclical sector in the late 1960s that culminated in the "nifty fifty" phenomenon of the early 1970s; the rise of the Oil weighting from 13% of the Index in 1972 to 28% in 1980 followed by a drop to just 11% by 1986; the move back into Consumer Noncyclicals in the 1980s; and the jump in Finance, which began in 1990 and carried through 1995.

---

[2] Brealey, *An Introduction to Risk and Return from Common Stocks.*

Exhibit 1: Industry Group Shifts in the S&P 500*

Industry Group	1964	1966	1968	1970	1972	1974	1976	1977	1978	1980	1982	1984	1986	1987	1988	1989	1990	1991	1992	1993	1994	1995
Basic Goods	15%	13%	12%	12%	9%	13%	12%	10%	9%	10%	8%	7%	8%	9%	8%	8%	7%	6%	7%	7%	7%	6%
Consumer Cyclical	16%	14%	14%	15%	16%	11%	13%	12%	13%	10%	14%	15%	16%	16%	16%	14%	12%	13%	15%	16%	14%	13%
Consumer Noncyclical	11%	11%	13%	16%	18%	20%	15%	17%	17%	15%	18%	18%	20%	20%	21%	22%	26%	29%	26%	22%	24%	25%
Finance	1%	1%	1%	1%	1%	1%	6%	6%	6%	5%	6%	6%	7%	6%	8%	8%	7%	9%	10%	11%	11%	13%
Machinery	6%	8%	8%	7%	9%	9%	7%	8%	6%	5%	5%	5%	5%	6%	6%	6%	6%	6%	6%	6%	6%	6%
Miscellaneous	15%	16%	14%	13%	13%	13%	12%	11%	11%	8%	10%	4%	5%	6%	6%	3%	3%	3%	3%	3%	3%	2%
Oil	17%	16%	16%	15%	13%	16%	15%	16%	18%	28%	16%	15%	11%	11%	12%	12%	13%	10%	10%	10%	10%	9%
Technology	5%	8%	11%	11%	11%	9%	11%	11%	12%	11%	13%	17%	14%	13%	11%	8%	9%	8%	7%	8%	11%	12%
Telecommunications																3%	2%	2%	3%	3%	2%	3%
Transportation	3%	3%	3%	2%	2%	2%	2%	2%	2%	3%	3%	3%	3%	3%	2%	2%	2%	2%	2%	2%	2%	2%
Utilities	10%	10%	8%	8%	7%	7%	6%	7%	7%	6%	7%	11%	12%	11%	11%	13%	13%	12%	11%	12%	10%	10%
Industry Group Summary	100%	100%	100%	100%	100%	100%	100%	100%	100%	100%	100%	100%	100%	100%	100%	100%	100%	100%	100%	100%	100%	100%

* Numbers may not add due to rounding. Figures represent year-end data.
(a) New companies added

Source: Thomas M. Galvin, Chief Investment Officer, Donaldson, Lufkin & Jenrette. Reprinted with permission.

Exhibit 2: Sector Shifts in the S&P 500*

New Industry Group	1980	1982	1984	1986	1988	1990	1991	1992	1993	1994	1995	1996	1997
sic Materials	8%	8%	7%	7%	8%	7%	6%	7%	7%	7%	6%	6%	5%
pital Goods	11%	11%	11%	11%	11%	10%	9%	9%	9%	10%	10%	10%	9%
mmunications Services	6%	7%	8%	8%	8%	9%	8%	9%	9%	9%	9%	6%	7%
nsumer Cyclicals	10%	14%	14%	14%	14%	11%	12%	13%	14%	12%	10%	10%	9%
nsumer Staples	8%	10%	10%	12%	13%	17%	18%	17%	15%	16%	16%	16%	16%
ergy	27%	15%	14%	12%	12%	13%	10%	10%	10%	10%	9%	9%	8%
ance	6%	8%	8%	10%	9%	8%	10%	11%	12%	11%	13%	15%	17%
alth Care	6%	6%	6%	7%	7%	10%	12%	9%	8%	9%	10%	10%	11%
hnology	10%	12%	12%	9%	9%	7%	7%	7%	8%	10%	10%	13%	13%
nsportation	2%	2%	2%	2%	2%	1%	2%	2%	2%	1%	2%	1%	1%
lities	6%	7%	8%	8%	7%	7%	6%	6%	6%	5%	5%	4%	3%
ustry Group Summary	100%	100%	100%	100%	100%	100%	100%	100%	100%	100%	100%	100%	100%

Note: Numbers may not add due to rounding. Figures reflect year-end data.
* Historical data represent calculations for new S&P 500 groups.
Source: Thomas M. Galvin, Chief Investment Officer, Donaldson, Lufkin & Jenrette.
Reprinted with permission.

Some changes occurred over much shorter time periods, but were nevertheless quite dramatic. Note particularly the decline in the Basic Goods weighting in the period 1970-1972 and the seven-percentage point fall in Consumer Noncyclicals between 1991 and 1993. More recently, one can see the jump in the Technology weighting from 7% in 1992 to 12% in 1995. Similar patterns are shown in Exhibit 2 for economic sectors.

Each of the above examples illustrates a change in investor perceptions, which was a function of significant change or changes within the investment environment that in turn caused investors to assign a higher or lower valuation to a particular industry relative to the rest of the market. Often these changes are so significant or easily observed that they would be reflected in the analytical process of any investor regardless of approach. The advantage of using a top-down focus in the initial stages of the analytical process is that it leads the practitioner to look for those macro developments that will affect either the operating environment or the relative valuation of various market sectors before they become obvious. With a formal process for identifying such change, it is less likely that one will overlook the sometimes subtle changes that often have significant consequences over time. With that information, one can then concentrate the fundamental research effort much more efficiently to identify individual investment opportunities.

THE TOP-DOWN DECISION PROCESS

The top-down decision process involves four distinct steps and can be illustrated with the inverted triangle diagram in Exhibit 3.

Exhibit 3: Top Down Investment Decision Process

INVESTMENT TEAM

INVESTMENT ENVIRONMENT

ECONOMIC INDICATORS
GDP, Productivity, Employment, Inflation, Earnings

FINANCIAL FACTORS
Money Supply, Federal Reserve Policy, Interest Rates

GOVERNMENT POLICIES
Taxation, Budget, Regulation, Legislation

VALUATION
Current/Historical, Absolute/Relative

INVESTMENT THEMES
Developed from analysis of the
Investment environment

FAVORED SECTORS
Industries and representative companies
impacted by identified themes

FAVORED STOCKS
Subject to fundamental
technical analysis

Investment Environment

Often, the starting point of discussions for those using a top-down approach is the economy. As Exhibit 3 suggests, however, the analysis is much improved if the approach begins instead with an examination of the overall investment environment, including important influences such as financial factors, government policy, and broad valuation issues. While economic information holds many clues to the strength or weakness of conditions affecting industries or market sectors, other factors in the market environment are often as significant in influencing growth, profitability or valuation. For example, demographic growth patterns, regulatory decision making, or the prospect of new legislation often have a meaningful impact on corporate growth and/or earnings potential, as well as on market valuations assigned by investors, based on new operating conditions.

An example of a non-economic development that affected investment performance is the 1992 Presidential election and the resulting effect on the health care industry. During the campaign, the new administration placed a high priority on examining the delivery and cost of health care in the United States. Following the election, a special task force was appointed to study the question, with the goals of expanding heath care coverage to those who were not receiving care and controlling the cost of service. The prospect of a dramatic change in the way health care services are provided created considerable uncertainty about the ability of these companies to continue to grow earnings at their historic rates. Investors reacted to this uncertainty by revaluing these stocks relative to the market. Health care stocks fell from 12% of the S&P 500 Index in 1991 to 9% by the end of 1992 and 8% at the end of 1993.

This change in the relative valuation of health care stocks took place even though there was little, if any, change in the industry's growth rate during this period. The relative price action of the group was significantly influenced by the perceived risk to the industry's future profitability and growth rate. The top-down approach is oriented toward identifying just such a change in the environment for a sector of the market. By recognizing this change and acting on the uncertainty generated by the Presidential task force, the decision would be made to underweight health care versus the market, thus minimizing the impact of the group's underperformance on portfolio returns.

It is interesting to note how the health care industry began to regain investor favor once it became likely that there would be little change in the way the industry operated. From the 8% weighting at the end of 1993 in Exhibit 2, the industry began a steady climb back to 11% of the index by 1997. By continuously monitoring the environment, the top-down approach would focus on the prospects for change and whether the change was actually being realized. As it became less likely that any dramatic change would take place, this approach alerted the investor that reduced relative valuations had become unwarranted.

Because the investment environment is dynamic, the factors to be considered in this first step of the top-down process are not finite, but should include any influence that is likely to have a meaningful effect on the operating conditions or market valuation of an industry or group of companies. Exhibit 3 shows some of the most obvious topics one would usually consider. The issues, and the importance of each, will change with the progress of both economic and market cycles, as legislative and regulatory agendas are proposed and developed, and as other variables change.

Investment Themes

The second step in the process is one that is not always considered in many discussions of the top-down process. That is the attempt to identify broad investment themes at work in the environment. Ideally these themes would capture macro forces that extend beyond a single industry or market sector. These macro forces should become apparent as conclusions are drawn from the analysis of the investment environment. Examples of such themes are:

- "Corporate restructuring," which would include companies, regardless of industry, where management had indicated it was embarking on a plan to enhance shareholder value or where it was anticipated that outside forces would be brought to bear to effect such a change.

- "Agriculture," including farm equipment manufacturers, seed companies, and fertilizer suppliers, which would benefit from higher farm incomes resulting from higher crop prices.
- "Demographic aging," which seeks to capitalize on the probable changes in consumer spending and demand associated with demographic trends that indicate the average age of the population is increasing.

As with the initial review of the investment environment, the objective of this second step is to broaden the scope of the analyst or research organization from individual companies to potential opportunities or risks resulting from a macro change. Increased demand for the output of a particular industry is likely to translate into increased demand for that industry's suppliers. The analysis is not always linear or positive. Favorable consequences for one area of the economy are often mirrored negatively for others. A decline in crude oil prices, for example, may be interpreted positively for the airlines, truckers or other industries where energy is a large component of the cost structure. However, such a price decline could be perceived as a negative event for energy suppliers.

Sector Selection and Theme Monitors

Following identification of dominant investment themes, the next stage in the top-down process involves selecting the specific industries or market sectors that may be affected by the forces released as each theme develops and matures. The objective is to determine which industries or sectors are best positioned to capitalize on the macro changes that have been identified. It is a critical step in the process in that it provides the basis for monitoring the market impact of the investment themes.

Although following a top-down approach in selecting individual securities and determining sector weightings for a portfolio should result in the portfolio being in sync with the larger dynamics affecting the market and security valuations, there is always the risk that the trends and themes that appeared to be unfolding fail to develop as expected. From an investment perspective, there is little reward in having a well-reasoned theory if it fails to generate the desired market performance. It is important, therefore, to set up a procedure for monitoring the absolute and relative market performance of the stocks that are believed to be responsive to each theme. This can be accomplished by establishing paper portfolios for each theme and tracking the performance of this portfolio versus both the market and the expectations of the market impact of the theme. A frequent review of the monitor portfolio can yield clues as to how quickly the theme is developing.

Performance in line with expectations suggests both the trend and its market impact have been correctly identified and evaluated, and supports continuing or increasing the over or underweighting of the related securities in the portfolio. If the relative performance is at variance with expectations, it calls for a reexamination of the fundamental assumptions made in support of the theme.

Expectations for theme performance should be clearly defined, including the time frame over which the theme is expected to develop.

It is also important to review the performance of the individual securities in the monitor portfolio for consistency. The goal is to have a portfolio that reflects investor response to the theme. It is important to distinguish price changes that are a function of a group move that is independent from the theme from price changes driven by exposure to it. For example, a theme that attempts to capture the impact of demographic aging and the projected growth in this segment of the population might reasonably include increased exposure to drug stocks with products related to aging. If the selected securities outperform the market but do not act better than the drug group as a whole, their performance for the period may not be related to the theme, but may instead be a function of investment characteristics shared by drug stocks, generally.

The selection of the representative industries and stocks for each theme is perhaps the most difficult step in the top-down approach. Some companies fit nicely in a single industry. Others have product lines that cross several industries so that classification becomes somewhat subjective. In most cases, the guiding principle should be the degree to which the theme will influence the overall operating performance or market valuation of the company. A company might also be included if it were recognized as a major factor in the affected industry or market sector even though its exposure might not be as significant in terms of its current financial results.

In some situations, a company is believed to be subject to the influences of more than one theme. If both themes are perceived to have similar influences on the operation or market perception, the problem becomes one of determining the degree to which each is responsible for the outcome. If the themes are expected to exert opposing influences, special care is required to accurately assess the probable impact of each on the company. Such hybrid issues may be best analyzed as special situation stocks outside the themes rather than as bellwether indicators of any particular theme. Two current examples of this are Travelers Group and Warner Lambert. These two names are appropriate for the Aging of America theme but could also be strong candidates in a consolidation or takeover theme.

Selecting a Portfolio of Stocks

The final step in the top-down approach is the selection of the individual companies to be included in the active portfolio. At this stage there is essentially no difference between the top-down and bottom-up analytical approaches. All the qualitative and quantitative tools available to the analyst are applied to select the most attractive securities. By following a top-down approach to get to this point, however, the analyst should have a better contextual grasp of the operating environment of the companies being analyzed and can concentrate research and analytical effort on determining which securities are best positioned to benefit, or those that are at increased risk, from the macro trends at work.

AN EXAMPLE OF THEMATIC INVESTING

We can draw on the "Demographic Aging" example noted previously to illustrate how the top-down process moves from the analysis of the environment, through the identification of themes, to the selection of industries and stocks that are expected to be impacted by the theme. Population statistics reported by the U.S. Bureau of the Census show that, from 1995 to 2005, the greatest growth will occur in that portion of the population between the ages of 45-54 and 55-64. Those aged 45-54 are in their prime earning years. Equally as important, other studies show that the spending pattern for this age group is different versus the group 10 or more years younger. Outlays for household operation, food at home, and shelter decline, while those for travel, health care, entertainment, education, and financial services increase.

Of these two observations, the population projections and the historical spending patterns, the data on the growth of the population in the 45-54 and 55-64 age groups can be relied upon with reasonable confidence. Given the known numbers of those in the earlier ages we can estimate quite accurately the number that will survive to the subsequent category. It is not possible to be as confident that historic spending patterns will not change, but without solid evidence of any trends suggesting a change is underway, it seems valid to assume a continuation of past experience.

The task then, is to identify those industries and market sectors that will have exposure to and benefit from this demographic change. The most obvious candidates are health care — particularly those companies dealing with diseases and care associated with aging; providers of travel and entertainment services to more mature age groups; and those financial service companies with products targeted to those looking to accumulate assets for education expenses or retirement.

Exhibit 4 presents a portfolio of stocks selected by Columbia Management Company from each of these industries and which together would serve as a representative portfolio to monitor the market impact of the aging theme. Also included is the 1997 and first quarter 1998 price performance of each security and industry.

Exhibit 4 shows that the theme portfolio performed considerably better than the S&P 500 Index in 1997 and continued to lead the price change of the Index in the first quarter of 1998, suggesting that the theme has validity in the market. All but three of the sub-groups posted returns significantly better than average in 1997 and two of these, Hospital Supply and Deathcare, did nearly as well. In addition, price performance between the sub-sectors was relatively uniform. Only the HMO sector meaningfully underperformed, as the accounting problems of Oxford Health Plans and the growing realization that past premium rates had underestimated the cost of service throughout the industry led to a downward revaluation of the stocks by investors. This, and the sub-par performance of individual issues within otherwise strong sectors, serves to illustrate how the particular dynamics of an industry or company can override the favorable macro influences of an investment theme, and reinforce the importance of thorough fundamental analysis of the expected beneficiaries of a theme before such stocks are purchased for a portfolio.

Exhibit 4: Portfolio Theme: Aging of America

	% S&P 500	% Price Change (Market Weighted)	
		1997	First Quarter 1998
Asset Gatherers/Financial Services	2.1	61.0	17.6
Merrill Lynch	0.3	79.0	13.8
Morgan, J.P.	0.3	15.6	19.0
Price, T.R.	0.0	44.5	11.9
Jefferson-Pilot	0.1	37.5	14.2
Lincoln National	0.1	48.8	9.1
Morgan Stanley/Dean Witter	0.5	78.5	23.3
Travelers	0.8	78.1	11.4
Drug Manufacturers	7.5	55.9	15.0
American Home Products	0.7	30.5	24.7
Warner-Lambert	0.5	65.6	37.1
Lilly, Eli	0.9	90.8	−14.4
Pharmacia Upjohn	0.3	−7.6	19.5
Bristol Meyers	1.3	73.6	10.2
Pfizer	1.3	79.7	33.7
Glaxo Holding ADS	0.0	50.8	13.1
Schering-Plough	0.7	91.9	31.6
Merck	1.8	33.1	20.9
Drug Retail	0.5	55.2	13.6
Walgreen	0.2	55.9	12.4
Rite Aid	0.1	47.8	16.6
CVS	0.2	54.8	17.9
Hospital Supply	1.3	30.2	12.4
Abbot Laboratories	0.7	29.1	15.0
Bard C.R.	0.0	11.8	17.4
Baxter Int'l	0.2	23.0	9.3
Becton Dickenson	0.1	15.3	36.1
Medtronic	0.3	54.4	−1.2
U.S. Surgical	0.0	−25.6	12.6
Assisted Living	0.0	136.2	4.2
ARV Assisted Living	0.0	37.6	−12.5
Assisted Living Concept	0.0	159.0	7.6
Carematrix	0.0	119.0	7.0
Emeritus	0.0	−5.6	2.0
Regent Assisted Living	0.0	21.1	34.8
Alternative Living	0.0	105.7	12.1
Death Care Services	0.1	27.6	13.6
Service Corp Intl	0.1	31.3	15.5
Hillenbrand Ind	0.0	41.2	20.3
Loewen Group	0.0	−34.2	−1.9

Exhibit 4 (Continued)

	% S&P 500	% Price Change (Market Weighted)	
		1997	First Quarter 1998
HMOs	0.4	−13.9	22.9
Aetna	0.2	−11.8	18.2
Humana	0.1	9.2	19.6
United Healthcare	0.2	10.4	30.3
Oxford Health Plans	0.0	−73.5	−4.0
Pacificare Health A	0.0	−38.2	47.3
Nursing Homes	0.2	41.6	2.7
Beverly Enterprises	0.0	44.6	2.4
Manor Care	0.0	29.6	5.7
Health South	0.1	43.7	1.1
Leisure Time/Travel	1.8	41.5	8.5
American Express	0.5	58.0	2.9
Circus Circus	0.0	−40.4	3.0
Disney	0.9	41.9	7.8
AMR	0.2	45.8	11.4
Mirage Resorts	0.1	5.2	6.9
Hilton Hotels	0.1	13.3	7.1
Marriott Intl	0.1	25.3	−46.3
Carnival Cruise	0.0	67.8	26.0
Total S&P Weighting	13.9		
Theme Performance*		49.8%	15.4%
S&P Performance*		31.0%	13.5%

*Returns are based on price performance and do not include reinvested dividends.
Source: BaseLine

CONCLUSION

The top-down style of investment management described here provides a disciplined approach for examining the overall environment in order to identify opportunities that may offer superior returns. Recognizing macro forces and refining those ideas to form investment themes are critical to the process of selecting the industries and stocks best positioned to outperform the market. The consistent application of this type of approach provides a useful analytical framework to achieve investment success.

Chapter 4

Implementing an Integrated Quantitative Investment Process

Ralph P. Goldsticker III, CFA
Director of Research
Vestek Systems

INTRODUCTION

The amount of information provided by a quantitative stock selection model about any one stock's future performance is very small. The models work better at the portfolio level, but they still only explain a portion of a portfolio's relative return. Therefore, to successfully add value, all parts of a quantitative investment process must be structured to capture the models' predictive information and to try to minimize the intrusion of other variables that may otherwise overwhelm it.

In this chapter, I will illustrate the steps of developing, implementing, and monitoring an integrated quantitative investment strategy. I will also try to point out as many of the pitfalls and difficulties that I can. The steps that I will present are:

1. *Research* — Developing the strategy
   • Constructing the component models
   • Combining the models into a composite multiple factor model
   • Statistical evaluation of the models
   • Backtesting — Portfolio simulation
2. *Implementation* — Putting it into action
   • Portfolio construction — Optimization
   • Portfolio analysis
3. *Performance Attribution* — Evaluating the strategy
   • Portfolio performance
   • Model performance
4. *Process Enhancement* — Closing the loop

In the real world, you will have to do the best you can with the time, data, and other resources available to you. You may not be able to follow all of the steps and avoid all of the problems highlighted here, but it should be helpful to keep all of the issues in mind. You can decide which ones are likely to cause problems and which ones can safely be overlooked.

The investment approach that I will present will have a stock selection process based on a combination of two of the models from Vestek System's MultiFactor System. I will use the Earnings Estimate Revision Model (Erev) and the Dividend Discount Model (DDM). The portfolio that will be used to illustrate the sections on portfolio analysis and performance attribution will be constructed to be neutral versus economic sectors and have relatively low tracking error. The benchmark will be the Russell 2000 index.

THE RESEARCH PROCESS

Model Construction

The first step of the research process is building the stock ranking models. They should incorporate all of your knowledge about the market, the data, and your strategy. For example, if you think that the whisper forecast of earnings is a better consensus than the IBES mean, you should try to model it when creating an earnings surprise model. If you have the time and resources, you should build a different model for each investment strategy. For example, the models that perform well in a large cap value universe may not work as well in a small cap value universe. You may find it efficient to utilize models that have been refined and tested by vendors and integrate them into your process. But, when possible, you should adapt them to fit your specific requirements.

A partial list of the issues that you should consider when constructing models and fitting them to your strategy includes:

- If you plan to manage your portfolio without making economic sector bets, you should construct sector neutral models. To do that, rank each stock against the others in its sector rather than against all other stocks. If you can't do that, you should at least test the models in a sector neutral simulation.
- Make sure that all of your models fit the characteristics of the stocks that they are ranking. For example, if your cash flow to price model doesn't work for bank stocks, construct a different model for that sector.
- Try to eliminate all unintended biases from your models.
  - You cannot eliminate the bias against growth stocks in a P/E model and a low P/E portfolio will be concentrated in stocks with less than average growth rates. If you are uncomfortable with this bias, you may want to use a PEG model instead.
  - Without an adjustment, most earnings revision models tend to place small cap stocks in the tails. If you do not adjust the model, your portfolios will tend to be concentrated in small cap stocks.

- Examine the pattern of returns in the models' performance and relate them to how your models will affect your portfolios.
  - Is the payoff to the model ranks linear? That is, do expected returns always increase with model ranks? Or, does all of the performance come from the tails or does the model work in only one tail?
  - If only the top 25% of the stocks in the model tend to outperform the benchmark, you should assign the other 75% the same rank.
  - Does the model work only on the sell side or the buy side? If so, you should adjust the model ranks accordingly.

Combining the Models

Most quantitative managers use a stock selection model that is a composite of several other models. They rank each stock on each of the component models and then combine the component models to create the composite. There are several advantages of building a model that is a composite of several others. These advantages are:

- You have identified more than one model that selects stocks that will outperform.
- You can combine several disparate models into one that captures information from all of them.
- The research process is more manageable because you can test each model individually. However if the models are highly correlated, at some point you will still have to evaluate them simultaneously.
- Different models work better in different market environments. A properly constructed multiple factor model will provide diversification in that it should add value in all environments.
- All models are subject to estimation error in the model inputs. By using several models and incorporating different data from multiple sources, you are less exposed to data problems.
- Some models may only work on the sell side or on the buy side. By combining them, you will have a model that captures the information in both.

In building a composite model from several component models, you have another problem to resolve. You must decide the best way to combine the component models into the composite. You want the combination that maximizes the performance of the composite model. You should consider the magnitude, volatility, and consistency of its value added. Some of the issues that you should consider include:

- What weights will you use? Will you combine percentiles, standardized values or use some other process? Will you vary model weights across sectors? Will you vary the model weights through time? If so, what time period and weighting method will you use?

- If you have models whose ranks are highly correlated, how will you adjust the weights? For example P/E and P/B models give similar rankings. When combining these models with a different type of model such as an earnings surprise model, you must think about the independence of the rankings. A model that is uncorrelated with the others should get more weight in the composite than one with similar performance but that is correlated with the others.
- If you have models whose patterns of performance through time are highly correlated, how will you adjust the weights? In periods when one value model works well, all tend to work. If you have a model that performs on a different cycle than the others, you should give it additional weight.
- Is there an interaction or synergy between models? For example, if you have two models that perform equally well, does a stock that ranks in the 75th percentile on each of the two component models perform better than one that ranks in the 85th on one and the 65th on the other? If there appears to be an interaction you should use a nonlinear combination of the models that incorporates the interaction.
- If you use different model weights for different sectors, you should be able to justify the differences. You should not just "mine" the data, but you should have a reasonable theory to support each of your models. If you vary the models weights through time, you must have a rationale for that as well.
- Make sure that your model ranks are as uncorrelated with as many other security attributes as possible. You should try to adjust the model's construction if you can do so without losing too much information. You don't want your models to cause an inadvertent bet on risk factors such as size or growth. If your models are correlated with risk factors, you can control the size of the bet during the optimization process, but your optimized portfolios will no longer fully reflect the unadjusted performance of your models.

In later sections, I will refer to the ranks for the composite model as the stocks' alphas.

Eliminating Bias from the Models

In this section, bias means that the test results do not reflect the predictive information in the underling data. Rather the test results will be affected by some other factor that is unrelated to the theory that you are testing. If you base your judgments on the biased results, you are at greater risk of making a poor decision. In most cases, the bias will result in a model's performance appearing to be better than it really was.

You should be aware of all of the sources of bias in your research and modeling. You cannot eliminate all bias but you should make the attempt. One type of bias that cannot be avoided is the bias that comes from being aware of the types of models that have worked in the past. For example, we all "know" that earnings revision has been a successful strategy, and most backtests will confirm that. If you test an earnings revision model, you should recognize that you are only producing evidence that confirms prior research not testing a new model or theory. If the performance of earnings revisions during the last several years was spurious and will not repeat in the future, you will not be able to see it from your tests. They will incorporate similar models and the same data as the other tests, all of which produced positive results. Even though you cannot eliminate the bias that comes from following in the footsteps of others, you should do everything that you can to eliminate all other sources of bias.

Some examples of other types of bias include:

Look ahead — incorporating data that you could not have known at the time:
- Underestimating how long it will take data to make it into your portfolios. If you are working with a model like earnings surprise, it is easy to underestimate how long it will take you to capture the earnings report, rerun your models, optimize your portfolios, and make the necessary trades.
- Compustat includes only restated data in the quarterly database.
- Using corrected data. In many cases errors in the databases have been cleaned up after the fact. If you have a sanitized database your backtests will not show how errors in live data may affect your results.

Survivorship and ex-post selection bias — selecting from a biased list of stocks:
- Using a database that does not include bankrupt and other "dead" companies. If the model leads you to take over candidates, and these stocks are not in your data, your tests will not reflect the effect of owning these stocks.
- The history of the constituents for a number of indices was backbuilt. Evaluating a model based on the backbuilt constituents of an index creates a bias because the smaller stocks in the backbuilt portion of the history are included because they are be larger in the future.
- Compustat and Worldscope backbuild history. That is, when these two data vendors add stocks to their databases, they include a number of years of history. Since the stocks that they add are selected because they have been successful, the use of the backbuilt history will introduce a bias.

Data Problems and Model Construction

It is critical when constructing the models that the data used are as clean and robust as possible. It is also important that to the extent possible the data used to build the models reflect what would have been available at the time they would have been constructed. Common problems include:

Bad or not meaningful data: One example of this problem is IPOs. Often there are records in the Compustat database for fiscal years before the company went public. If you don't guard against it, you can calculate a price to book ratio using the pre IPO book value per share and the post IPO price.

Mismatched tickers across multiple data sources: For most publicly traded U.S. stocks, all of the data services use the same tickers. However for ADRs, foreign stocks, and stocks with multiple share types, the ticker conventions vary. If you get your data from more than one source you will need to make sure that the data are lined up correctly.

Missed or mis-timed splits or capital changes: This is most frequently an issue when you are calculating ratios using data from more than one source. For example, if your price is adjusted for a 2 for 1 split and your earnings are not, the P/E will be too low.

Multiple share types: Many companies have more than one share type of common stock trading. They may have the same call on dividends and earnings and trade at about the same price, or there may be fundamental differences between the share types and they will trade at substantially different prices. If the latter is the case, how will you calculate variables such as capitalization, P/E, and P/B? In global investing, there are multiple share types as well as ADRs and other depository receipts trading around the world. It is critical that all of these are matched up correctly.

Restructurings and M&A activity: While prices reflect the current makeup of a company, other data may not. It may take days or even weeks for the effects of an acquisition to be reflected in earnings estimates. Sources of fundamental data such as Compustat and Worldscope will not reflect the changes until after the next set of financial statements are filed. A major acquisition or restructuring will prevent you from calculating ratios such as price to book and return on equity. Even after new financial statements are available, any model that evaluates a time series history of fundamental data will need to be adjusted.

Late database updates and bad transmissions: In the real world, you will receive late transmissions of data, miss updates, and otherwise have less than perfect data. If in your backtests you assume that data always arrive on time and you get your models updated without a hitch, you are too optimistic.

Timeliness of the data — are "cheap" stocks cheap, or are your data stale? When a stock drops significantly, it is usually because its future prospects have suffered. However, most value models will take time to adjust. Even expectational models such as Forecast P/E may take a while to adjust as all of the analysts that follow the stock update their forecasts. One way to spot these events that are not captured in your models is to add a filter to spot any large price moves over the period of a day or two. These stocks should be investigated before being traded.

Once you have solved all of the above data cleansing problems, there are still other modeling and data questions to address. There are two you must consider. First, will you Winsorize the model values of outliers, or will you remove the company from consideration? Second, if you are developing a multiple factor model and you are missing data or some of the required data are not meaningful for one of the component models for a stock, how will you calculate the stock's composite rank?

STATISTICAL ANALYSIS OF MODEL PERFORMANCE

The statistical analysis of model performance is different from what is frequently referred to as backtesting. I will use the term "backtesting" to apply to the simulation of the performance of a portfolio management strategy. In a backtest, you will simulate all of the aspects of your investment process. In the statistical analysis of performance you will examine the performance of the component models and the composite in a statistical sense. You will try to learn if your models contain information about excess returns. Once you are satisfied with these analyses, you should then run a backtest to simulate how the model will work in a portfolio management process.

Like your backtests, the statistical analyses should reflect the investment process as closely as possible. If you are a large cap growth stock manager, make sure your model works in a large cap growth stock universe. Think about the real world delays in implementing your portfolio strategy and reasonable levels of turnover. Are there any institutional constraints that will affect your performance? Don't just focus on summary statistics, but rather focus on how well the models performed using real world criteria. Make sure that the tests of your models and your interpretation of the results differentiate between economically meaningful information and statistical differences that are too small or isolated to be of value in portfolio management.

A partial list of the statistics you should examine includes:

- *Cumulative performance* — How well did the model perform on average?
- *Time series of performance* — How did the model perform through time? This is more important than the model's average or cumulative performance. It allows you to answer questions such as: Did all of the performance come in a short period? Were there extended periods of significant underperformance? If so, how long and how bad were they? What percent of the months did the model add value? How has the model been working recently?
- *Incremental return* — Does all of the value added appear in the first month after the model ranks are formulated, or do the highly ranked stocks continue to perform over longer periods? This will give you an indication of the amount of turnover that will be required to capture the information in the model. It will also tell you how aggressively you will need to trade.
- *Turnover* — How long do your top ranked stocks stay at the top? Does this fit with the turnover allowed by your investment guidelines? For the composite model, is the turnover in ranks due to stocks ranks changing on the constituent models or the models' weights changing through time?

- *Performance by sector* — Does the model work equally well in all economic sectors? Does it work better for growth stocks than it does for value stocks?
- *Performance in up and down markets* — If the model consistently works better in bull markets and poorly in bear markets, its performance may be due to a beta or growth bet rather than the intrinsic value of the model.
- *Batting average* — What percentage of highly ranked stocks outperformed the benchmark? This question will help you decide how many stocks you need to hold in the portfolio.

Sample Reports Investigating Model Performance

The exhibits in this section show examples of how to evaluate model performance. Each one of them shows the performance of Vestek's Earnings Estimate Revisions Model (Erev) for the five years from 1993 through 1997. Two methods of calculating a model's performance are illustrated. The first runs an OLS cross sectional regression of month end model ranks versus the subsequent total returns for the stocks. The second method is to group the stocks into several portfolios based on their month end model ranks (quartiles, quintiles, ...) and then calculate the performance of each of the portfolios for the subsequent month.

The advantage of the regression method is that it produces one number per month and it is easy to evaluate the time series. By adjusting the regression methodology, it is possible to control for other factors in calculating the model's performance. The advantages of the portfolio method are that it is more intuitive, and it will show any nonlinear results.

A modification of the regression method is the use of multiple regression. It regresses monthly returns against the ranks of several models. It has the advantage of the simple regression in that it produces one number for the performance of each model for each month. It also allows a portfolio manager to disentangle the returns from several correlated models. For example, rankings based on P/E and P/B ratios are highly correlated. If you evaluate their performance separately, you will see that they both add value. By using a multiple regression, you will learn if they have independent effects. You will also learn if a strategy that uses both models will have better results than only using one.

Exhibits 1a, 1b, and 1c show results calculated using the simple regression method. "Naïve Returns" are regression coefficients produced by a cross sectional regression of the stocks' standardized model scores against the stocks' subsequent monthly returns. They are naïve in that there is no attempt to control for other factors such as industry or growth. To illustrate this, consider a simple P/E strategy. The portfolio will be heavily overweighted in utilities and other stocks in slow growing sectors. When these sectors do well, it will appear that the low P/E strategy was working when in fact it may have had nothing to do with the stocks' P/Es. "Pure Returns" are regression coefficient produced by cross sectional regression of the stocks' standardized model score against the stocks' specific returns for the subsequent month. The specific returns are calculated using Vestek's Fundamental Risk Model. The returns are "pure" in that by using the stock specific returns as the dependent variable in the regressions, we have controlled for the confounding effects of industries and common factors such as beta, yield, and capitalization.

Looking at the exhibits, the interpretation of the Naïve and Pure Returns are different. The Naïve Returns can be viewed as the return above a benchmark of a portfolio with a 1 standard deviation higher exposure to the Erev Model than the benchmark. The Pure Returns can be viewed as the return above the benchmark of a portfolio with a 1 standard deviation higher exposure to the Erev Model and optimized so that it has no active exposure to industries or the factors in Vestek's risk model.

Vestek calculates monthly Naïve and Pure Returns for each of the models in its MultiFactor System for each of several stock universes. The graphs in Exhibits 1a, 1b, and 1c illustrate how regression-based model analyses can be used. All of the graphs have the same format. The horizontal axis shows time from 1/93 through 12/97. The left vertical axis is used for the monthly returns in percentage points. The right vertical axis is used for the cumulative returns.

Exhibit 1a shows the monthly and cumulative performance of the Pure Returns for the Earnings Revision model in the Vestek 1000 (VT1000) and in the Second 1000 (VT2000) Universes. The VT1000 is a large cap universe. It is a capitalization weighted portfolio containing the 1000 largest U.S. stocks. The VT2000 is a small cap universe. It is a capitalization weighted portfolio containing the U.S. stocks ranked from 1001 to 2000 in market capitalization. You can see that the pattern of monthly returns is similar. In most cases when the Pure Return for the VT1000 was positive, so was the return for the VT2000, and visa versa. However, you can see that the Erev Model worked much better in the small cap universe. It had a cumulative Pure Return of 23.8% versus 12.6% for the VT1000.

Exhibit 1b shows the monthly and cumulative performance of the Naïve and Pure Returns for the Earnings Revision model in VT2000 Universe (the second 1000 by market capitalization). Pure Returns measure the performance of the model while controlling for industries and common factors such as beta, yield, and capitalization. You can see that the pattern of monthly returns is similar. In most months both the Naïve and Pure Returns were positive. When one of the models produced negative returns, most of the time they both did. The models' cumulative returns were different. The cumulative Naïve Return was 35.6% while the cumulative Pure Return was only 23.8%. The standard deviation of the monthly Naïve Returns was 0.82% while the standard deviation of the monthly Pure Returns was 0.52%. This suggests that a portfolio management strategy based on the Erev Model without imposing constraints on economic sector weights or similar types of risk control would have outperformed one with the risk controls. A strategy of keeping all of the industry and factor bets out of the portfolio would have reduced its tracking error, but it would have underperformed a strategy that simply purchased the most attractive stocks based on the Erev Model.

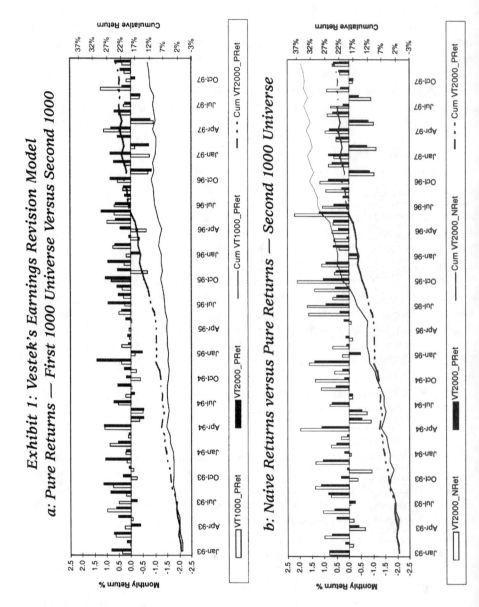

Exhibit 1: Vestek's Earnings Revision Model

a: Pure Returns — First 1000 Universe Versus Second 1000

b: Naive Returns versus Pure Returns — Second 1000 Universe

Exhibit 1 (Continued)

*c: Pure Returns — Second 1000 Universe versus Second 1000 Growth versus
Second 1000 Value*

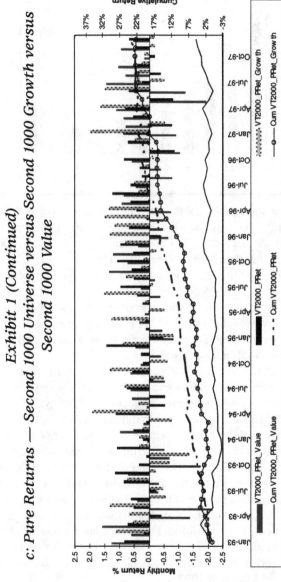

Exhibit 2: Cumulative Performance Ranked by Earnings Revision Model
Rebalanced Monthly 1993-1997

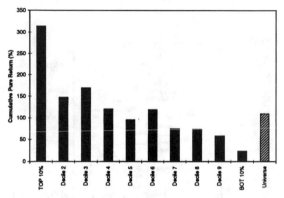

Exhibit 1c shows the monthly and cumulative performance of the Pure Returns for the Erev Model in the Vestek's Second 1000 Universe. It also shows its performance in the Second 1000 Growth and in the Second 1000 Value Universes. You can see that the model worked much better in the Growth than in the Value Universe. In the Growth Universe, it had a cumulative excess return of 22.3% (4.2% per year) versus only 4.9% (0.96% per year) in the Value Universe.

In managing a portfolio against a small-cap or a small-cap growth benchmark, using the Erev Model should add value. Using an earnings revision model in a small-cap value universe does not appear to be a successful strategy. Since the model worked as well in the full universe as it did in the Growth Universe and better than it did in the Value Universe, it tells us that as the list of attractive stocks shifted between growth stocks and value stocks, rotating the portfolio from growth to value stocks would have been a successful strategy.

Exhibits 1a, 1b, and 1c were used to illustrate how to interpret a model's performance using cross sectional regressions. We were able to draw several conclusions. Although it worked in both universes, the Earnings Revision Model worked better in small-cap than large-cap stocks. It also worked better in growth than value stocks. Lastly, using an investment strategy that limits sector rotation and tracking risk would have forced out a significant portion of the information in the Erev Model.

Exhibits 1, 2, and 3 are examples of examining the Earnings Revision Model's and Dividend Discount Model's performance using a fractile portfolio method. It allows examination of the cross sectional behavior of the models rather than just the time series. All three are calculated using the Second 1000 universe for the five years 1993 through 1997.

Exhibit 2 is a bar chart that shows the cumulative performance of 10 decile portfolios formed by ranking monthly on the Erev Model. It illustrates how a model's performance can be viewed to see if the payoff is linear or if another pattern emerges.

Exhibit 3: Performance of Earnings Revision versus Dividend Discount Models*

		Vestek's Earnings Revision Model					
		Most Attractive	Quintile 2	Quintile 3	Quintile 4	Least Attractive	All Earn Rev	Most-Least Attractive
	Most Attractive	29.3	24.9	22.0	13.6	12.9	19.8	16.4
	Quintile 2	28.8	26.6	21.7	15.8	13.8	21.3	15.0
	Quintile 3	23.8	22.8	16.7	12.5	4.0	16.2	19.8
DDM	Quintile 4	30.2	15.6	12.3	5.7	1.0	14.2	29.2
	Least Attractive	28.4	9.9	5.6	4.1	0.5	11.7	27.9
	All Earn Rev	27.4	19.5	16.0	11.9	7.9	16.7	19.5
	Most-Least Attractive	0.9	15.0	16.4	9.5	12.4	8.1	

* Average Annual Returns, Second 1000 Universe, 1/93-12/97

In this case, the returns were nearly monotonic. The higher the portfolios' ranks, the better they performed. However, the top decile performed significantly better than the second and third. For a strategy that is not concentrated in a few stocks and traded aggressively, the performance of the second through fourth deciles may be a better indicator of the performance that may be expected than is the first decile.

Exhibit 3 shows how the Earnings Revision Model (Erev) works in conjunction with the Dividend Discount Model (DDM). Examining tables such as this will help you to decide how best to combine models. To produce this table, each month each of the stocks in the Second 1000 Universe was assigned two quintiles. Each based on one of the model ranks. The stocks were then grouped into three sets of portfolios. One set of five portfolios was based on Erev quintiles, one set of five was based on DDM quintiles and one set of 25 portfolios (5 × 5) was based on the combination of the stocks' Erev quintiles and DDM quintiles. The cumulative returns of the 25 portfolios based on both ranks are in the middle of the table. The cumulative returns of the five portfolios based on the Erev Model are shown in the second column from the right, and the cumulative returns of the five portfolios based on the DDM are shown in the second column from the bottom. The columns on the right and on the bottom of the table show the difference in cumulative returns between the portfolio with the most attractive stocks and the portfolio with the least attractive stocks for each row or column.

Reading across a row, the columns show the performance of the Erev Model. The first five columns show the performance of each Erev Model quintile if you look only at stocks in the one DDM quintile. For example, if you examine the top row of the table (the 20% of the universe that were ranked most attractive on the DDM), the top quintile of stocks on the Erev returned 29.3% per annum while the bottom quintile (least attractive) only returned 12.9%. Reading down a column, the rows show the performance of the DDM. The first five columns show the performance of each quintile if you control for the ranking on the Erev Model.

For example, if you examine the first column (the 20% of the universe ranked most attractive on the Erev Model), the top quintile of stocks on the DDM returned 29.3% per annum while the bottom quintile returned 28.4%.

Performance of the DDM Model

From Exhibit 3, it is clear that in the top quintile of estimate revision stocks, a value based model such as the DDM did not provide much incremental return. The return for the most attractive minus least attractive quintiles was only 0.9% per year. However, the DDM did add significant value in all of the other Erev Model quintiles. The decision on whether on not to incorporate the DDM into your investment strategy would depend on whether it is possible to implement one that is very concentrated in the stocks in the top quintile of the Erev Model.

Performance of the EREV Model

Even though the Erev Model worked best in the most expensive stocks (DDM quintiles 4 and 5), it added value in all of the quintiles. If these data were being used to investigate whether adding an earnings revision component to a value driven strategy such as a DDM, it would look promising.

Exhibits 4a and 4b show the performance of the DDM and the Erev Model by economic sector. Each table shows the models' performance by quintile. The tables are sorted by the performance of the model's "buys" (quintiles 1 and 2) minus its "sells" (quintiles 4 and 5) for the economic sector.

Exhibit 4a: Performance of Vastek's Earnings Revision Model by Economic Sector*

Economic Sector	Most Attractive	Quintile 2	Quintile 3	Quintile 4	Least Attractive	Universe	Buys-Sells**
Retail	38.4	17.8	6.4	5.3	-17.5	7.7	34.2
Business Equip & Serv	39.4	27.4	11.3	2.3	-0.2	15.0	32.4
Multi-Industry	27.9	39.5	6.9	5.6	11.0	44.2	25.4
Health Care	13.8	17.9	12.7	2.7	-4.0	10.7	16.5
Technology	25.3	13.8	10.5	0.6	7.6	15.3	15.5
Consumer Non-Durable	17.3	17.9	4.9	3.4	5.6	8.7	13.1
Consumer Services	32.1	16.7	19.0	24.1	-0.4	18.2	12.6
Capital Goods	27.7	16.8	20.0	14.3	8.7	18.0	10.8
Consumer Durables	18.5	4.7	6.0	6.1	-1.9	8.0	9.5
Energy	34.1	29.2	14.1	19.2	29.1	26.9	7.5
Raw Materials	18.3	8.4	14.0	10.0	3.0	10.5	6.9
Financial Services	28.2	27.9	21.0	22.5	20.3	24.9	6.7
Utilities	17.1	17.9	15.5	16.4	9.3	15.7	4.7
Transportation	28.9	18.2	6.6	11.5	29.1	20.4	3.3
Shelter	15.9	7.8	19.7	0.7	16.7	13.5	3.2
Universe	26.1	18.4	16.2	11.5	6.9	15.9	13.1

* Average Annual Returns, Second 1000 Universe, 1/93-12/97
** Buys-Sells = Average of (Quintile 1 + Quintile 2) minus (Quintile 3 + Quintile 4)

Exhibit 4b: Performance of Vestek's Dividend Discount Model by Economic Sector*

Economic Sector	Most Attractive	Quintile 2	Quintile 3	Quintile 4	Least Attractive	Universe	Buys-Sells**
Shelter	23.1	15.4	9.9	-4.9	-4.0	14.0	23.7
Consumer Durables	28.5	5.4	9.0	4.2	-13.2	9.0	21.5
Energy	40.7	32.7	45.2	24.1	12.5	29.0	18.4
Technology	14.0	37.3	24.9	7.6	12.3	17.2	15.7
Financial Services	28.2	26.2	17.1	23.4	3.1	25.0	14.0
Raw Materials	13.5	20.7	9.7	4.2	3.7	11.7	13.2
Multi-Industry	33.7	23.8	18.7	9.8	23.5	47.2	12.1
Retail	9.2	13.5	4.4	1.3	4.2	7.8	8.6
Business Equip & Serv	16.2	21.7	17.3	11.6	11.3	15.3	7.5
Consumer Non-Durable	6.5	15.6	7.9	12.0	2.0	8.8	4.1
Health Care	4.3	16.2	21.9	11.4	3.5	11.6	2.8
Utilities	12.1	12.2	20.6	15.7	5.1	15.1	1.8
Capital Goods	16.7	18.4	8.6	24.8	12.5	17.7	-1.1
Consumer Services	30.3	11.9	19.0	23.3	24.3	19.0	-2.7
Transportation	19.7	-4.3	18.8	21.1	0.9	20.5	-3.3
Universe	19.9	21.4	16.2	14.2	11.7	16.7	7.7

* Average Annual Returns, Second 1000 Universe, 1/93-12/97
** Buys-Sells = Average of (Quintile 1 + Quintile 2) minus (Quintile 3 + Quintile 4)

Exhibit 4a shows the performance for the Erev Model by economic sector for the entire universe. The stocks in the top two quintiles (buys) outperformed the stocks in the bottom two quintiles (sells) by 13.1% per year. The Erev Model's performance varied significantly by economic sector. In Retail, the best performing sector, the buys outperformed the sells by 34.2%, while in Shelter the buys outperformed the sells by only 3.2%. Examining the exhibit, a pattern emerges. The Erev Model worked better in the sectors that contain the faster growing stocks. It worked well in Retail, Health Care and Technology. It did not work as well in Utilities, Transportation, and Shelter. There is a logical explanation for this difference. Faster growing stocks are more sensitive to changes in earnings expectations, and they react more to changes in estimates. If the market does not immediately fully incorporate changes in estimates, the Erev Model should work better for these stocks. If this argument makes sense to you, in constructing a multiple factor model you would vary the Erev Model's weights by economic sectors, giving it greater weight in the faster growing sectors.

Exhibit 4b shows the performance by economic sector for the DDM. From it we learn several things. On average the model worked reasonably well, although only half as well as the Erev Model. Looking at the bottom row of the exhibit (Universe), we see that the buys outperformed the sells by 7.7% per year (versus 15.9% for the Erev Model). Like the Erev Model, the DDM's performance varied by economic sector. In Shelter the buys outperformed the sells by 23.7%, while in Transportation the buys underperformed the sells by 3.3%. We do not see a logical reason that explains this pattern of performance. If you can explain it and believe the performance will persist, you would use the DDM aggressively in the Shelter sector and ignore it in Transportation. If you cannot explain the relative performance across sectors, in constructing your composite model, you would assume that it is spurious and use the average performance of the model for all sectors.

Comparing Exhibits 4a and 4b, we can draw several conclusions. On average the Erev Model worked better than the DDM. In constructing a composite multiple factor model we should give it more weight. If we vary the weights of the composite by economic sector, the variability should be driven by the relative performance of the Erev Model not the DDM. This is because we can explain the Erev Model's pattern of performance but not the DDM's.

To summarize the statistical testing of the models, we are looking for compelling evidence that will support or refute our theory of why stocks ranked using our models should outperform. Regressions provide a single number for each month which are easy to analyze in a time series framework. Multiple regressions can be used to separate the effects of several correlated models. Fractile portfolio analysis allows the examination of cross sectional behavior of returns and interactions between models.

Backtesting — Simulation of Investment Strategy

Once you have constructed your models, tested them, refined them, and tested them again, the next step is to use them to simulate your investment process. Ideally, you will have reserved your out-of-sample data for this analysis. The portfolio simulation process should track the investment process as closely as possible. (For the purpose of this discussion, I will assume that the simulated portfolios are constructed using the same optimization process that you will use to manage the "real" portfolio. You will use the same reports to evaluate the portfolios in your backtests as you use to evaluate your "real" portfolios. I will save the discussion of optimization, portfolio analysis, and performance attribution for the later sections.)

You should incorporate as many of the real world delays, constraints, and influences into the simulation as possible. Also think about trading. What is a reasonable level of turnover? If you have experience in managing similar strategies, think about how you will trade. What has been your experience in real world transactions costs? How often does an attractive stock "run away" from you? If you will be running the portfolio as a pure quantitative strategy, the simulation will be relatively straight forward. If you will be adding a fundamental overlay, you will have to decide how you will you simulate it.

It is in the simulation phase that you can investigate the tradeoffs between risk, turnover, and return. Run multiple simulations to look for patterns of behavior. Do not try to develop the ultimate strategy. Rather evaluate questions such as: If I increase turnover to 100%, how much does my alpha go up? How much does the performance improve if I reduce the number of stocks in the portfolio to 75?

Don't approach the problem by trying to answer questions such as: What combination of risk and turnover maximized the Sharpe ratio? You will tend to overfit the process and will be lead to very aggressive or very low risk approaches that don't fit your needs. Instead, work to refine the strategy so that it works reliably given your investment guidelines.

Don't run too many simulations and modifications to fine tune the strategy in an attempt to improve its performance. You will end up with a strategy that works well in the backtest and is unreliable in the real world. Remember that even if you have reserved your out-of-sample data for simulation, as soon as you run the first simulation and modify the parameters to run a second, your out-of-sample data are no longer out-of-sample.

Your portfolio construction and rebalancing rules should simulate as closely as possible how you plan to manage the fund. It will help if you keep the following list of considerations in mind:

- Use the appropriate level of turnover and apply reasonable estimates of transactions costs to the results.
- Be honest about how quickly information can be incorporated into the portfolio. You may want to add a week between the time you update the model and you trade the stocks. This is one of the most overlooked sources of look-ahead bias.
- Incorporate all of your normal investment guidelines. These should include: sector diversification, the maximum and minimum number of stocks, concentration limits, tracking error, and others.

You will also need to determine any sell rules. Will you automatically sell poorly ranked stocks, will you have a separate sell model or will you let the optimizer decide? Will you sell a mediocre stock to purchase an attractive one? Will you hold a mediocre stock for diversification?

After you have simulated the portfolio's performance, the critical step is to evaluate its performance. The goal here is to understand how well the strategy worked? Focus your attention on the out-of-sample results rather than the entire backtest. As in the statistical analysis of the models, concentrate on the time series of the portfolio's performance rather than just the summary statistics such as cumulative return. You should also evaluate the portfolio's structure and risk characteristics. Examine data such as:

- The average annual outperformance after transactions costs.
- The tracking error or risk relative to benchmark.
- The percentage of months the strategy worked
- The longest period of underperformance and how bad it was.
- The performance correlation with other factors such as bull and bear markets.
- How often the investment policy constraints were binding.

After you have convinced yourself that the strategy worked in the simulation, the next step is to understand why. This is the object of performance attribution. Use the same reports that you use to evaluate the performance of your "real" portfolios. (Exhibit 8 shown later in this chapter is a sample of this kind of report.) Use performance attribution to answer questions such as:

- Did the model put the portfolio in the right stocks or the right sectors? Even if the portfolio was run on an economic sector neutral basis, was it making a bet on size or some other factor? How did these bets contribute to the return?
- Did the model work in all sectors?
- Did the performance come from a handful of home runs?

You should use backtesting and portfolio simulation as a way to gather compelling evidence that the strategy would have performed well in the past and is likely to be successful in the future. Remember that the market's behavior during the time of analysis is only one of many possible outcomes and the future will be different. The next time, history may not repeat itself and it will not repeat itself exactly. Gather and evaluate information on as many measures of performance as you can. It will give you confidence that your results are real and are likely to be repeated in the future. If you focus your efforts on fine tuning the model to maximize some measure of its performance you will surely overfit it. If you make small changes to the model or to the simulation parameters and see large changes in the results — you have overfit the model. The real world doesn't behave that way.

Keep your out-of-sample test honest. If you run a backtest, analyze the results, including the out-of-sample period, adjust the model, and rerun the backtest, your second test is no longer really out-of-sample. What does this say about the independence of the third, fourth, and fifth rounds of adjustments and simulations?

All backtesting is affected by biases. Be honest with yourself about how much of the performance of the backtest is due to real world opportunities and how much was created by overfitting the models. Test the simulation's robustness by stressing it. Try changes such as:

- Put in a one or two week delay in implementing your models.
- Double the transactions costs.
- Assume that you can't always get all of your trades done.
- Change the number of stocks in the portfolio.
- Change the amount of turnover.

If you still get good results, you should have more confidence that the results are real and robust and are likely to be repeated in the future.

OPTIMIZATION

This section describes portfolio optimization. It relates both to backtesting and the construction of "real" portfolios. Portfolio optimization is a mathematical process that takes a number of data items and parameters and uses them to construct an "optimal" portfolio. The portfolio is called optimal because it best balances all of your (sometimes conflicting) preferences and requirements. The objective functions in modern optimizers can be very complex. They are limited only by the investors' ability to describe and quantify their preferences and the necessary inputs. Elements that are commonly used in optimizers include items such as:

- Maximize the portfolio's alpha — Purchasing the most attractive stocks.
- Maintain a dividend yield of 0.50% more than the S&P 500.
- Maintain a tracking error of 3.5% relative to the benchmark.
- Permit no more than 2% over or underweighting of any stock relative to its weight in the benchmark portfolio.
- Permit no more than 5% of the portfolio to be invested in any stock.
- Permit no more than 5% overweighting or underweighting of any industry.
- Minimize transactions costs.

Why Use an Optimizer?

"Traditional" portfolio managers that purchase a small number of heavily researched stocks and don't worry about risk control other than keeping a reasonable level of sector diversification don't need an optimizer. They just purchase the most attractive stocks, and if the portfolio gets too overweighted in a sector, they sell off the least attractive stocks in that sector.

On the other hand, portfolio managers using quantitative investment strategies cannot treat risk control or portfolio construction lightly. They are forced to use an optimizer because the problem is too complex and they cannot manage all of the multiple dimensions of portfolio characteristics effectively without one. A relatively simple portfolio construction problem might be to build the portfolio with the highest possible alpha, while maintaining a beta between 1.05 and 1.10 and having no more than a 5% overweight in any economic sector. Often the problem is much more complex and includes parameters such as minimizing tracking error and more constraints. As long as you can quantify all of your expectations and preferences, optimization will allow you to construct the portfolio that best fits your needs.

Optimization Inputs

A partial list of the data that optimizers need includes:

Alphas, expected returns or another measures of stocks relative attractiveness: You will need to rate each stock that is eligible for purchase in a way that is consistent. If you rate them from 1 (most attractive) to 5 (least attractive), the optimizer will assume that all of the 1's are equally attractive. Also the ranks must be provided in such a way that the difference in the attractiveness of two stocks is proportional to the difference in their alphas. For example a stock with an alpha of 2.1 is treated as equally more attractive than a stock with an alpha of 2.3 as is a stock alpha 3.5 versus one of 3.7. Also, if you will accept 25 basis points of tracking risk to increase your alpha by 50 basis points, the optimizer will trade off 50 basis points of tracking risk for an increase in alpha of 1%.

Risk estimates: The two most important terms in the optimizer are expected returns and risks. Estimates of portfolio risk are typically produced using a fundamental risk model. The risk model is an estimate of the future covariance matrix of stock returns. It captures the risks of the stocks and the correlations between stocks. It is used because it provides more reliable estimates of risk than those calculated using historical standard deviations and correlations.

Investor preferences: You will need to describe all of your preferences to the optimizer in such a way that it can balance them appropriately. It needs to quantify how you make tradeoffs such as: How much "alpha" are you willing to give up to reduce your tracking risk? How much tracking risk are you willing to accept to meet your target dividend yield?

Investment constraints: The optimizer needs to incorporate all of your investment constraints and policy restrictions. These may be rules on diversification, economic sector weights or policy targets.

Transactions costs: The optimizer needs estimates of how much it will cost to trade. They should be expressed in the same units as the alphas used to rank the stocks. In this way, trades will be made only when they are justified after transactions costs. Ideally you should make your transactions costs estimates a function of the liquidity of the stock and the size of the trade.

Problems with Optimization

There are several reasons why portfolio optimization may produce poor portfolios. Most relate to the quality of the data. The optimizer can only incorporate the data provided to it. The most obvious potential problems are those in the rankings from your stock selection models. We addressed this issue in an earlier section. But even if you have identified and eliminated all of the problems in your "alphas," other types of data errors can cause poor optimization results. Typically the result is that the tracking error risk that you experience will be much larger than you expected. There is also an opportunity cost. You may end up holding stocks with lower alphas in order to compensate for the data problems. Examples of potential pitfalls include:

Misestimated Stock Attributes: Assume that you are trying to construct a portfolio with both an above average dividend yield and an above average beta. This is difficult because most stocks with high betas have low yields and stocks with high yields have low betas. At the end of February 1998, there was an exception. RJR Nabisco's (RN) historical beta versus the S&P 500 was 1.19 and its dividend yield was 5.94%. One way for the optimizer to get the desired beta and yield would be to "load up" on RN. The downside of that is that it introduces a lot of unnecessary risk into the portfolio. This is the risk that RN will underperform. Another effect is that RN will displace other stocks with higher alphas. When you spotted this problem, you would ask yourself if you believe that RN will continue to have an above average beta and an above average yield. If not you should make an adjustment to its beta or its yield and reoptimize the portfolio.

Tracking Error Bias: All agree that statistical estimates of risk for portfolios constructed using optimizers are always too low. This is due to the combination of unavoidable errors in a risk model and the optimization process. An optimizer will overweight positions where the risk estimates and correlations are too low and underweight positions where the risk estimates and correlations are too high. Therefore your estimates of tracking error (the standard deviation of the difference between the portfolio's return and the benchmark return) will be too low. The amount of bias will depend on the risk model and the investment strategy, but the bias will always exist. Your backtests may give you insights into the size of the bias.

Overreliance on your Risk Model: Don't trust your risk model to the exclusion of your intuition. Each risk model was developed by applying a specific structure to returns for a specific time period. If you rely too much on the estimates of volatility and correlations in the risk model, you will be surprised when things change.

In addition to the fact that risk models are statistical estimates of risks and correlations and unavoidably contain errors, there are other causes of problems in using risk models to the exclusion of other measures of risk and diversification. These problems include:

Omitted Risk Factors: All risk sources are not captured in a statistical risk model. The following is an example of a risk that risk models will not capture. Assume that your strategy is based on a DDM. For the last several years, the multinational export driven companies have had the fastest growing earnings. If your models project these growth rates into the future, when you optimize your portfolio you will have a significant exposure to these companies. If the dollar were to strengthen and the U.S. economy outperform the rest of the world, the export driven companies that you own will underperform the rest of the market. It is unlikely that your risk model will have warned you about this risk, and your underperformance will be much larger than you could have expected from looking at the estimates of your portfolio's risk. To guard against omitted risk factors, be aware of them and manage your portfolio's exposure to factors such as economic sectors and industries.

Risk Models are Linear, the Real World is Not: Most risk models only look at the portfolio's average factor exposures rather than the distribution of the factors across the portfolio. Consider two portfolios, both of which have betas of 1.00. The betas of the stocks in first portfolio are smoothly distributed between 0.85 and 1.15. All of the stocks in the second portfolio have either very high or very low betas, although they average to 1.00. Clearly the two portfolios do not have the same risks. The optimization process should reflect this. To do this, it should manage the distribution of risk factors rather than just looking at a single statistic such as the exposure to the market risk factor.

By adding constraints and additional terms to the optimizer's objective function, you can reduce your susceptibility to these problems and the tracking error bias. If you do this, the model estimated tracking error may rise, but the "true" tracking error will fall.

The other commonly voiced complaint about portfolio optimization is that the portfolio manager cannot quantify all of the required data and preferences. The result is that the optimized portfolio does not fit with the portfolio manager's expectations in some dimension. For example, portfolio managers may not be able to rank stocks in such a way that the rankings accurately reflect their opinions. One solution would be to only allow the optimizer to purchase stocks from a "buy list." They cannot describe how they trade off risk and return or express their investment policy constraints and they have desired portfolio characteristics which they cannot describe or quantify for the optimizer.

How to Best Use an Optimizer

Use optimization as an iterative process. Optimize the portfolio, look at the results, modify the optimization parameters, and re-optimize. Continue the process until you reach a satisfactory solution. This allows you to construct a portfolio that meets your preferences without having to quantify all of them in advance. It also helps you to understand the effects of changing the parameters.

The optimization process should be designed to maximize the process' information and manage the level of risk while minimizing the intrusion of undesired sources of risk and variability. Some risks are unavoidable. For example, a low P/E strategy will underperform when growth stocks outperform value stocks. If you can't accept this risk, adjust the strategy. Rather than a pure value strategy such as low P/E, you may want to develop a "growth at a reasonable price" (GARP) strategy that doesn't force the systematic bet against growth stocks.

Often the process is set up so that the optimizer selects stocks for purchase only from a preestablished universe of stocks — stocks that are ranked above a threshold. Conversely, portfolios are often pre-screened for sell candidates — stocks that violate a sell discipline such as ranking poorly on the composite model or very poorly on one of the components.

Remember that the forecast tracking error for an optimized portfolio has a downward bias and the true tracking error will be higher than that predicted by the risk model. The extent of the bias will be determined by the quality of the risk model, and how closely the desired portfolio characteristics align with the factors in the risk model. The importance of the bias will depend on the strategy. A portfolio with a forecast tracking error of 3% and an experienced tracking error of 3.5% is probably not too much of a problem. In contrast, a core strategy with a forecast tracking error of 1% and an experience tracking error of 1.5% may be viewed as out of control. In that case the optimization can be modified to reduce the forecast tracking error, but a better solution is to modify the parameters to reduce the bias.

You will have to decide how you are going to balance risk, turnover, and performance. Given that you can control the level of portfolio risk and portfolio turnover with precision, and you know the least about your forecasts of relative returns, I recommend that you target acceptable levels of risk and turnover and then maximize your alpha given that limitation.

PORTFOLIO ANALYSIS

Once you have optimized the portfolio, you still need to fully understand its structure and manage its risk exposures. To do this, you should examine the portfolio from as many different angles as possible. Exhibit 5 is a partial example of a *Portfolio Profile Report*. It shows several characteristics for the portfolio and compares them to the Russell 2000. From the report you can observe that the portfolio has a value tilt relative to the Russell. It has lower P/E and Price/Book ratios and a slightly higher dividend yield. These exposures are not surprising given that the portfolio was constructed using the DDM. A full *Portfolio Profile Report* should include as many of the characteristics of the portfolio that you think are relevant. Don't just use the reports and graphs to make sure that the portfolio has the desired characteristics; also use them to make sure that inadvertent "bets" do not slip in.

Exhibit 5: Portfolio Profile Report
Model Portfolio as of 12/31/97

	Portfolio	Russell 2000	Difference
Portfolio Value	$49,996,009		
Number of Holdings	117	1897	−1780
Median Capitalization	$703.6	$729.6	−$26.0
Dividend Yield	1.44	1.28	0.16
P/E Ratio	15.99	28.28	−12.29
Price/Book Ratio	3.18	3.88	−0.70
S&P Beta	1.09	1.13	−0.04
EPS Growth — Last 5 Years	25.00	22.38	2.62
EPS Growth — Next 5 Years	19.37	19.41	−0.04
Beta vs. Russell 2000	0.93	1.00	−0.07
R-Square	0.95	1.00	−0.05
Tracking Error	3.48	0.00	3.48

Exhibit 6: Multifactor Profile Report
Model Portfolio as of 12/31/97

Multifactor Model	Portfolio	Russell 2000	Difference
Earnings Estimate Revision	0.40	−0.06	0.46
Dividend Discount Model	1.96	−0.02	1.98
Earnings Yield	1.51	0.10	1.40
Cash Flow/Price	0.94	−0.21	1.15
Sales/Price	1.04	0.39	0.65
Book/Price	0.89	0.49	0.40
Dividend Yield	−0.05	−0.19	0.09
Return on Equity	0.11	−0.88	0.99
Forecast Earnings Growth	0.54	0.61	−0.07
Historical Earnings Growth	0.13	0.03	0.10
5 Year Relative Strength	0.28	0.42	−0.14
3 Month Relative Return	−1.08	−0.25	−0.83
18 Month Relative Return	−0.38	−0.18	−0.20
Monthly Volatility	1.58	1.24	0.34
Specific Risk	1.66	1.16	0.50
Earnings Dispersion	0.97	0.68	0.29
Leverage	−0.09	−0.30	0.21
Fundamental Beta	0.25	0.38	−0.13
Log of Capitalization	−3.45	−3.40	−0.05
Adjusted Analyst Coverage	−0.82	−0.69	−0.13

Exhibit 6 is a partial example of a different *Portfolio Profile Report*, once again comparing the portfolio to the Russell 2000. It includes several of the models in Vestek's MultiFactor System. On the first two lines, you can see the positive exposure to the Erev Model and the DDM. On the next several lines, you can see the positive exposure to other value models such as earnings yield and cash flow yield. These are in line with what would be expected for a portfolio constructed using a DDM. Looking further down the report, notice that the stocks in the port-folio have underperformed the average stock in the Russell 2000 for 3 months, 18 months, and 5 years. Again, given the portfolio's value tilt, this should not be a surprise. However you should keep these exposures in mind and make sure that you are comfortable with them.

Looking at the volatility measures such as monthly volatility and specific risk, you can see that the portfolio is overweighted in risky stocks. Again, as long as you are aware of the exposures and are comfortable with them, they are not a problem. If you do not want these exposures, you should reoptimize the portfolio and see if you can eliminate them without significantly reducing your alpha, increasing your risk or introducing other unwanted characteristics. You may also want to investigate the con-struction of your stock selection models to eliminate their exposure to these factors.

In addition to looking at average factor exposures, you should examine the distribution of the exposures. Exhibits 7a and 7b are bar charts that compare distri-butions of P/E ratios and growth rates for the portfolio and the Russell 2000. Look-ing at Exhibit 7a, you can see that the portfolio is overweighted relative to the Russell in low P/E stocks and underweighted in high P/E stocks. This is expected given the strategy's concentration on the DDM, and no corrective action is required.

Looking at Exhibit 7b, you can see that the portfolio is overweighted in both low growth and high growth stocks and is underweighted in stocks with average growth rates. This is because a stock will be attractive on the DDM either because it has a low P/E and not too low of a growth rate or a high growth rate and not too high of a P/E. In this case, the portfolio's exposures probably do not intro-duce significant risk. However, if the chart showed that the portfolio was over-weighted in low growth stocks and significantly underweighted in high growth stocks, you would have to decide if the risk introduced by that bet was acceptable.

All of the *Portfolio Profile* tables and charts should be used to understand the structure and risks of the portfolio. If they show that the portfolio has the desired characteristics, you should continue. If not, you should reoptimize the portfolio and see if you can reduce the undesired risks while maintaining the desired characteristics. You may also want to adjust the models to eliminate the root cause of the risks. In the end, you will have to compromise. You will have to sacrifice some exposure to desired factors in order to reduce exposures to undes-ired risks, and you will have to take some risk to get the alpha.

Performance Attribution

Performance attribution needs to be performed both during the backtesting and on the live portfolio. Often the results diverge. The difference may be due to bias, may be because the environment changed or due to other causes. Your goal is to know the contributors to the performance. Were your models working or were you lucky? Did you add value by overweighing the attractive stocks? Were you able to identify the better performing stocks on the "buy list"? You should evaluate your portfolios' performance from as many angles as possible.

Exhibit 7: Distribution of Portfolio by P/E and Growth Sectors
a: Distribution of Portfolio by P/E Sector

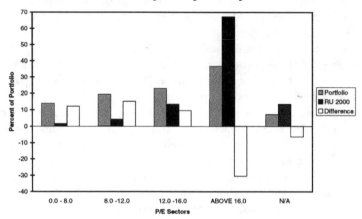

b: Distribution of Portfolio by Growth Sector

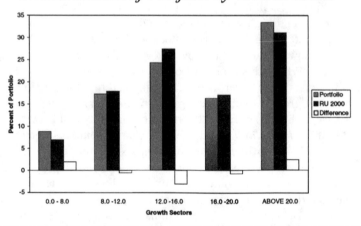

Exhibit 8 is an example of a *Performance Attribution by Sector Report* (PSEC). It groups the stocks using the DDM and examines how it affected the portfolio's performance. It divides the portfolio's relative performance into contribution from the DDM (how overweighting and underweighting the DDM contributed) and contribution from "Other Models" (how much value was added by factors other than the DDM). Each row on the table shows the impact of stocks grouped on the DDM. The first three columns show the portfolio's and the benchmark portfolio's weights and the difference in weight. The next three columns show the portfolio and benchmark portfolio returns and the difference in return for each group. The last three columns show how the weights and returns contributed to the portfolio's performance for the month. The interpretation of the report is as follows.

Exhibit 8: Attribution of the DDM's Contribution to Portfolio Performance

DDM	Weights			Returns			Contribution to Rel. Perf.		
Percentile	Portfolio	Bench	Diff	Portfolio	Bench	Diff	Other Models	DDM	Total
> 90	40.4%	21.1%	19.4%	-0.38	-0.16	-0.22	-0.09	0.29	0.20
65-90	50.7%	20.6%	30.1%	0.74	-0.37	1.11	0.57	0.39	0.95
35-65	5.0%	29.0%	-24.0%	0.75	-2.42	3.17	0.16	0.18	0.34
10-35	3.7%	20.8%	-17.1%	3.46	-2.67	6.13	0.22	0.17	0.40
< 10	0.1%	8.5%	-8.4%	5.43	-3.32	8.75	0.01	0.14	0.15
Total	100.0%	100.0%	0.0%	0.40	-1.65	2.05	0.87	1.17	2.05

- The portfolio outperformed the benchmark portfolio by 2.05% for the month. This number is in the lower right hand corner of the table.
- The portfolio was significantly overweighted relative to the benchmark portfolio for stocks that were attractive on the DDM. You can observe this looking at the difference column
- The DDM worked well during the month. This can be seen by examining the column for the benchmark portfolio return. As you go down the column (more lowly ranked stocks), the returns get worse.
- The portfolio's overweighting of stocks that were attractive on the DDM contributed 1.17% to the performance. For example, the 19% over-weighting of stocks in the top 10% on the DDM, combined with the 1.47% (−0.16% minus −1.65%) outperformance of those stocks relative to the Russell 2000 contributed 0.29% to the portfolio's performance.
- In aggregate, the other models contributed 0.87% to the performance. Note that in four of the five DDM groups, the stocks in the portfolio outperformed the similarly ranked stocks in the benchmark. Also note that the stocks in the portfolio that were in the bottom 35% of the universe on the DDM were the best performing group of stocks in the portfolio. This suggests that where the Erev model was in conflict with the DDM and the combined model was attractive enough to purchase the stock, the combination added value.

WHAT DO YOU DO WHEN THE MODEL STOPS WORKING?

All models and investment strategies go through periods of poor performance. The risk of constantly modifying your models is that you will make unnecessary or ill-advised changes based on a short period of underperformance. The question that you must answer is will this behavior persist or will the performance return to what you expect? There may be cycles or what appears to be a forecastable cycle may be an illusion. The cycles may be tied to the market's behavior or macroeconomic events and potentially forecastable, or the fluctuations in performance may be random.

When the model appears to have stopped working, you should return to basics. Revisit the rationale that you had for constructing the model and expecting it to provide excess returns. You should ask questions such as:

Are the results in terms of length or magnitude out of line with what you could expect from the strategy's past performance or what was experienced in the backtest?

Have any of the premises of the original theory changed? Has your model "caught on" with the public at large and the anomalies that you were able to capture before are now too quickly embedded in the stocks' prices for you to be able to profit from them?

Is the model correlated with some other factor that provided the returns and now that factor is no longer working? For example did your model put you into small cap stocks at the right time, but was unable to discriminate among small cap stocks? If that was the case, the small cap bet that helped in earlier periods may now be coming back to haunt you. Performance attribution should give you insights into the sources of your performance. Portfolio profiles should help you determine if you are making inadvertent factor bets that may be working against you.

It may be that the market has changed. Has some exogenous factor slipped into the investment process? For example, it may be that many of the stocks in your portfolio are highly exposed to currency fluctuations during a period when the dollar has been very strong. If so, see if you can eliminate the unintended risk exposure and still maintain your desired portfolio characteristics?

While the model was working, did all of the performance come from one sector? If so, did the model stop working in that sector? If you are using a multiple factor model, which of the factors are still working, and which have stopped?

With a thorough analysis of these and related questions, you should be able to see if there is truly a problem. If there is, you should have some insights into how it may be fixed. These questions are also good topics to consider when the model is working. If the model is working too well, your luck is likely to change.

What Do You Do When the Model Works but Your Portfolios Don't?

Ideally, you should be able to look at three measures of the performance of your models' performance.

- Statistical model tests — For each model and for the composite.
- Backtests — Simulated performance of the model portfolio.
- Real portfolios.

The first question that needs to be addressed is: Are your models working in a statistical sense? Look at all of the results and attributions. Ask questions such as:

- Are the models' performance concentrated in just a few stocks?
- Has the time frame that the models add value become shorter?
- Are the models working in all sectors?

If those questions don't spot a problem, move on to the performance of your paper portfolios and focus on issues such as:

- Do your paper portfolios continue to perform? If so, what are the differences between the paper portfolios and the real portfolios?
- Is there a look ahead bias? Do you update the model portfolios faster than the real ones?
- Are the portfolio managers making subjective overrides to the model rankings? Are they changing the portfolio construction methodology?
- Are client requirements making the real portfolios diverge from the model portfolios?

If you cannot identify any reasons why the portfolio construction process is different, the difference in performance may due to trading and transactions costs.

Slippage in performance from trading can come from two sources. You may be buying the stocks at higher prices than you expected, or you may not be buying "attractive" stocks because their prices have "run away" from you. The same thing may be happening on the sell side. You may be selling the stocks at lower prices than you expected, or you may hanging on to unattractive stocks because you don't want to sell at depressed prices. In both cases, the performance of your funds will suffer relative to your model portfolios. You can do several things:

- Adjust the forecasts of transactions costs in your simulations.
- Adjust your optimization process to purchase more liquid stocks and take smaller positions in the less liquid stocks. Also recognize that stocks that are liquid when you purchase them may not be as liquid when you want to sell them. This is especially true for momentum stocks.
- Adjust your models and weights in the composite model so that you have more time to trade before the models' value added disappears. — Look for slower alphas.
- Investigate alternative trading strategies.
- Develop new investment strategies and products to increase your capacity.

CONCLUSION

I have described the quantitative research and investment process as a sequential process: construct your models, test the models individually, combine the models and test the combination, backtest the strategy, optimize the portfolio, and analyze the results. In reality, the process should be circular and continuous.

- Look for ways to improve the models. Improvements may come from new data sets, improved statistical techniques or better insights. At the same time, be wary of overfitting the models.
- Develop new models.
- The backtests should be updated on an ongoing basis. Be sure to evaluate the more recent periods, as well as looking at cumulative performance.
- Experiment with changes in the optimization process.

Remember, stock prices are very volatile and quantitative models can explain only a small amount of the volatility. Your modeling, model testing and portfolio construction procedures should be developed so that your portfolio's reflect as much of the models' predictive power as possible while minimizing the intrusion of other factors and random events. Your models and investment strategy should be based on robust theories as to the behavior of stock prices. Do not overfit your models or your investment process; rather use your research to develop evidence to prove or disprove your theories. Do not run just one test or calculate one statistic, but look at as many tests and statistics as possible. Examine your portfolio's structure and performance from many dimensions. Lastly, use the performance of your "live" portfolios as an opportunity for further research and refinement. The better you do these things, the more likely that your performance will be determined by your models and methods rather than by luck.

Chapter 5

Factor-Based Approach to Equity Portfolio Management

Frank J. Fabozzi, Ph.D., CFA
Adjunct Professor of Finance
School of Management
Yale University

INTRODUCTION

The theory of asset pricing in terms of factors is well developed in the academic literature and is explained in every textbook on investment management. In this chapter, we will show how factor models can be used to construct equity portfolios and control portfolio risk

TYPES OF FACTOR MODELS

There are three types of factor models being used today to manage equity portfolios: statistical factor models, macroeconomic factor models, and fundamental factor models.[1] We describe these three factor models below.

Statistical Factor Models

In a *statistical factor model,* historical and cross-sectional data on stock returns are tossed into a statistical model. The statistical model used is *principal components analysis* which is a special case of a statistical technique called *factor analysis.* The goal of the statistical model is to best explain the observed stock returns with "factors" that are linear return combinations and uncorrelated with each other.

For example, suppose that monthly returns for 1,500 companies for ten years are computed. The goal of principal components analysis is to produce "factors" that best explain the observed stock returns. Let's suppose that there are six "factors" that do this. These "factors" are statistical artifacts. The objective in a

---

[1] Gregory Connor, "The Three Types of Factor Models: A Comparison of Their Explanatory Power," *Financial Analysts Journal* (May-June 1995), pp. 42-57.

I wish to thank Bruce Jacobs and Kenneth Levy of Jacobs Levy for their helpful comments on an earlier draft of this chapter.

statistical factor model then becomes to determine the economic meaning of each of these statistically derived factors.

Because of the problem of interpretation, it is difficult to use the factors from a statistical factor model for valuation and risk control. Instead, practitioners prefer the two other models described below, which allow them to prespecify meaningful factors, and thus produce a more intuitive model.

Macroeconomic Factor Models

In a *macroeconomic factor model*, the inputs to the model are historical stock returns and observable macroeconomic variables. That is, the raw descriptors are macroeconomic variables. The goal is to determine which macroeconomic variables are pervasive in explaining historical stock returns. Those variables that are pervasive in explaining the returns are then the factors and included in the model. The responsiveness of a stock to these factors is estimated using historical time series data.

Two examples of proprietary macroeconomic factor models are the Burmeister, Ibbotson, Roll, and Ross (BIRR) model[2] and the Salomon Brothers model.[3] Salomon Brothers refers to its model as the "Risk Attribute Model" or RAM. A RAM is built for the United States and other countries

In the BIRR model, there are five macroeconomic factors that reflect unanticipated changes in the following macroeconomic variables:

- Investor confidence (confidence risk)
- Interest rates (time horizon risk)
- Inflation (inflation risk)
- Real business activity (business cycle risk)
- A market index (market timing risk)

Exhibit 1 explains each of these macroeconomic factor risks

In the U.S. version of the Salomon Brothers RAM model, the following six macroeconomic factors have been found to best describe the financial environment and are therefore the factors used:

- change in expected long-run economic growth
- short-run business cycle risk
- long-term bond yield changes
- short-term Treasury bill changes
- inflation shock
- dollar changes versus trading partner currencies

---

[2] Edwin Burmeister, Roger Ibbotson, Richard Roll, and Stephen A. Ross, "Using Macroeconomic Factors to Control Portfolio Risk," unpublished paper. The information used in this chapter regarding the BIRR model is obtained from various pages of the BIRR website (*www.birr.com*).

[3] This model is described in Eric H. Sorensen, Joseph J. Mezrich, and Chee Thum, *The Salomon Brothers U.S. Risk Attribute Model, Salomon Brothers*, Quantitative Strategy, October 1989, and Joseph J. Mezrich, Mark O'Donnell, and Vele Samak, *U.S. RAM Model: Model Update*, Salomon Brothers, Equity Portfolio Analysis, April 8, 1997.

Exhibit 1: Macroeconomic Factor Risks in the BIRR Factor Model

Confidence Risk

Confidence Risk exposure reflects a stock's sensitivity to unexpected changes in investor confidence. Investors always demand a higher return for making relatively riskier investments. When their confidence is high, they are willing to accept a smaller reward than when their confidence is low. Most assets have a positive exposure to Confidence Risk. An unexpected increase in investor confidence will put more investors in the market for these stocks, increasing their price and producing a positive return for those who already held them. Similarly, a drop in investor confidence leads to a drop in the value of these investments. Some stocks have a negative exposure to the Confidence Risk factor, however, suggesting that investors tend to treat them as "safe haven" when their confidence is shaken.

Time Horizon Risk

Time Horizon Risk exposure reflects a stock's sensitivity to unexpected changes in investors' willingness to invest for the long term. An increase in time horizon tends to benefit growth stocks, while a decrease tends to benefit income stocks. Exposures can be positive or negative, but growth stocks as a rule have a higher (more positive) exposure than income stocks.

Inflation Risk

Inflation Risk exposure reflects a stock's sensitivity to unexpected changes in the inflation rate. Unexpected increases in the inflation rate put a downward pressure on stock prices, so most stocks have a negative exposure to Inflation Risk. Consumer demand for luxuries declines when real income is eroded by inflation. Thus, retailer, eating places, hotels, resorts, and other "luxuries" are harmed by inflation, and their stocks therefore tend to be more sensitive to inflation surprises and, as a result, have a more negative exposure to Inflation Risk. Conversely, providers of necessary goods and services (agricultural products, tire and rubber goods, etc.) are relatively less harmed by inflation surprises, and their stocks have a smaller (less negative) exposure. A few stocks attract investors in times of inflation surprise and have a positive Inflation Risk exposure.

Market Timing Risk

Market Timing Risk exposure reflects a stock's sensitivity to moves in the stock market as a whole that cannot be attributed to the other factors. Sensitivity to this factor provides information similar to that of the CAPM Beta about how a stock tends to respond to changes in the broad market. It differs in that the Market Timing factor reflects only those surprises that are not explained by the other four factors.

Business Cycle Risk

Business Cycle Risk exposure reflects a stock's sensitivity to unexpected changes in the growth rate of business activity. Stocks of companies such as retail stores that do well in times of economic growth have a higher exposure to Business Cycle Risk than those that are less affected by the business cycle, such as utilities or government contractors. Stocks can have a negative exposure to this factor if investors tend to shift their funds toward those stocks when news about the growth rate for the economy is not good.

Source: Reproduced from pages of the BIRR website (*www.birr.com*).

Exhibit 2: Macroeconomic Factors in the Salomon Brothers U.S. Risk Attribute Model

Economic Growth[a]
Monthly change in industrial production as measured concurrently with stock returns.

Business Cycle[b]
The change in the spread between the yield on 20-year investment-grade corporate bonds and 20-year Treasury bonds is used as a proxy for the shorter-term cyclical behavior of the economy. Changes in the spread capture the risk of default resulting from the interaction of earnings cyclicality and existing debt structure.

Long-Term Interest Rates[b]
The change in interest rates is measured by the change in the 10-year Treasury yield. Changes in this yield alters the relative attractiveness of financial assets and therefore induces a change in the portfolio mix.

Short-Term Interest Rates[b]
The change in short-term interest rates is measured by changes in the 1-month Treasury bill rate.

Inflation Shock[a]
Inflation is measured by the Consumer Price Index. The inflation shock component is found by subtracting expected inflation from realized inflation. Expected inflation is measured using a proprietary econometric model.

U.S. Dollar[b]
The impact of currency fluctuations on the market is measured by changes in the basket of currencies. Specifically, a 15-country, trade-weighted basket of currencies is used.

a. Adapted from Joseph J. Mezrich, Mark O'Donnell, and Vele Samak, *U.S. RAM Model: Model Update*, Salomon Brothers, Equity Portfolio Analysis, April 8, 1997, p. 1.
b. Adapted from the discussion on page 4 of Eric H. Sorensen, Joseph J. Mezrich, and Chee Thum, *The Salomon Brothers U.S. Risk Attribute Model*, Salomon Brothers, Quantitative Strategy, October 1989.

In addition, there is another factor called "residual market beta" which is included to capture macroeconomic factors after controlling for the other six macroeconomic factors. Exhibit 2 provides a brief description of each macroeconomic factor.

We'll use the RAM model to explain the procedure for estimating the parameters of the model. For each stock in the universe used by Salomon Brothers (about 3,500) a multiple regression is estimated. The dependent variable is the stock's monthly return. The independent variables are the six macroeconomic factors, the residual market factor, and other market factors. The size and statistical significance of the regression coefficients of each of the macroeconomic factors is examined. Then for all stocks in the universe the regression coefficient for each of the macroeconomic factors is standardized. The purpose of standardizing the estimated regression coefficients is that it makes a comparison of the relative sensitivity of a stock to each macroeconomic factor easier.

The standardization methodology is as follows. For a given macroeconomic factor, the average value and standard deviation of the estimated regression coefficient from all the stocks in the universe are computed. The standardized regression coefficient for a stock with respect to a given macroeconomic factor is then found by calculating the difference between the estimated regression coefficient and the average value and then dividing this value by the standard deviation. The standardized regression coefficient is restricted to a value between −5 and +5.

A stock's standardized regression coefficient for a given macroeconomic factor is then the measure of the sensitivity of that stock to that risk factor. The standardized regression coefficient is therefore the factor sensitivity. If a stock has a factor sensitivity for a specific macroeconomic factor of zero, this means that it has average response to that macroeconomic factor. The more the factor sensitivity deviates from zero, the more responsive the stock is to that risk factor. For example, consider the economic growth factor. A positive value for this macroeconomic factor means that if all other factors are unchanged, a company is likely to outperform market returns if the economy improves. A negative value for the economic growth factor means that if all other factors are unchanged, a company is likely to underperform market returns if the economy improves.

The sensitivity for the factors are estimated so that they are statistically independent. This means that there will be no double counting the influence of a factor.

Fundamental Factor Models

Fundamental factor models use company and industry attributes and market data as raw descriptors. Examples are price/earnings ratios, book/price ratios, estimated economic growth, and trading activity. The inputs into a fundamental factor model are stock returns and the raw descriptors about a company. Those fundamental variables about a company that are pervasive in explaining stock returns are then the raw descriptors retained in the model. Using cross-sectional analysis the sensitivity of a stock's return to a raw descriptor is estimated.

As determined by Jacobs and Levy,[4] many of these descriptors are highly correlated. Adding highly correlated factors to a model neither enhances returns nor lowers risk. Factors that by themselves seem to be important may be unimportant when combined with other factors; factors that by themselves seem not to be important may be important when combined with other factors. A manager must be able to untangle these relationships.

Two commercially available fundamental factor models are the BARRA and the Wilshire models. The BARRA E2 model begins with raw descriptors.[5] It then combines raw descriptors to obtain risk indexes to capture related company attributes. For example, raw descriptors such as debt-to-asset ratio, debt-to-equity ratio, and fixed-rate coverage are measures that capture a company's financial leverage. These measures would be combined to obtain a risk index for financial leverage.

---

[4] Bruce I. Jacobs and Kenneth N. Levy, "Disentangling Equity Return Regularities: New Insights and Investment Opportunities," *Financial Analyst Journal* (May-June 1988), pp. 18-43.

[5] The BARRA E2 model is BARRA's second generation U.S. equity model. In 1997, BARRA released its third generation U.S. equity model (BARRA E3). The discussion in this chapter and the information provided in Exhibits 3 and 4 are based on the BARRA E2 model. The E3 model closely resembles the E2 model in structure, but with improved industry and risk index definitions.

The BARRA E2 fundamental factor model has 13 risk indexes and 55 industry groups. For 12 of the risk indexes and the 55 industry groups, the model is estimated for BARRA's HICAP universe (1,000 of the largest-capitalization companies plus selected slightly smaller companies to fill underrepresented industry groups) using statistical techniques. The universe has varied from 1,170 to 1,300 companies.

Exhibit 3 reproduces the information about the 13 risk indexes as published by BARRA. Also shown in the exhibit are the raw descriptors used to construct each risk index. For example, the earnings-to-price ratio is a combination of the following raw descriptors: current earnings-to-price ratio, earnings-to-price ratio for the past five years, and IBES earnings-to-price ratio projection. Before each raw descriptor in Exhibit 3 is a plus or minus sign. The sign indicates how the raw descriptor influences a risk index. The 55 industry classifications are shown in Exhibit 4.

Exhibit 3: BARRA E2 Model Risk Index Definitions*

1. Variability In Markets (VIM)
This risk index is a predictor of the volatility of a stock based on its behavior and the behavior of its options in the capital markets. Unlike beta, which measures only the response of a stock to the market, Variability in Markets measures a stock's overall volatility, including its response to the market. A high beta stock will necessarily have a high Variability in Markets exposure. However, a high exposure will not necessarily imply a high beta; the stock may be responding to factors other than changes in the market.

This index uses measures such as the cumulative trading range and daily stock price standard deviation to identify stocks with highly variable prices. BARRA uses different formulas for three categories of stocks.

a. Optioned stocks — all stocks having listed options.
b. Listed stocks — all stocks in the HICAP universe that are listed on an exchange but do not have listed options.
c. Thin stocks — all stocks that are traded over the counter or are outside the HICAP universe, except those with listed options.

Optioned stocks are distinct for several reasons. First, the option price provides an implicit forecast of the total standard deviation of the stock itself. Second, optioned stocks tend to be those with greatest investor interest and with the most effective trading volume. Stock trading volume descriptors understate the effective volume because they omit option volume.

Thin stocks, about ten percent of the basic sample, are broken out because they tend to trade differently from other stocks. Over-the-counter stocks and other thinly traded securities show price behavior inconsistent with efficient and timely prices. Thin stocks are less synchronized with market movements, and exhibit frequent periods in which no meaningful price changes occur as well as occasional outlying price changes that are promptly reversed. These influences cause some indicators of stock price variability to be biased.

In calculating this index, BARRA standardizes the formulas for the three stock categories relative to one another to provide one index for the total population.

A. Optioned Stock Descriptors
+ Cumulative Range, 12 months
+ Beta * Sigma
+ Option Standard Deviation
+ Daily Standard Deviation

Exhibit 3 (Continued)

B. Listed Stock Descriptors
+ Beta * Sigma
+ Cumulative Range, 12 months
+ Daily Standard Deviation
+ Trading Volume to Variance
− Log of Common Stock Price
+ Serial Dependence
− Annual Share Turnover

C. Thin Stock Descriptors
+ Beta * Sigma
+ Cumulative Range, 12 months
+ Annual Share Turnover
− Log of Common Stock Price
− Serial Dependence

2. Success (SCS)

The Success index identifies recently successful stocks using price behavior in the market (measured by historical alpha and relative strength) and, to a lesser degree, earnings growth information. The relative strength of a stock is significant in explaining its volatility.

+ Relative Strength
+ Historical Alpha
+ Recent Earnings Change
+ IBES Earnings Growth
− Dividend Cuts, 5 years
+ Growth in Earnings per Share

3. Size (SIZ)

The Size index values total assets and market capitalization to differentiate large stocks from small stocks. This index has been a major determinant of performance over the years as well as an important source of risk.

+ Log of Capitalization
+ Log of Total Assets
+ Indicator of Earnings History

4. Trading Activity (TRA)

Trading activity measures the relative activity of a firm's shares in the market, or the "institutional popularity" of a company. The most important descriptors are the share turnover variables. In addition, this index includes the ratio of trading volume to price variability, the logarithm of price, and the number of analysts following the stock, as reported in the IBES database. The stocks with more rapid share turnover, lower price, and signs of greater trading activity are generally the higher risk stocks.

+ Annual Share Turnover
+ Quarterly Share Turnover
+ Share Turnover, 5 years
+ Log of Common Stock Price
+ IBES Number of Analysts
+ Trading Volume to Variance

Exhibit 3 (Continued)

5. Growth (GRO)

The Growth index is primarily a predictor of a company's future growth but also reflects its historical growth. BARRA estimates earnings growth for the next five years using regression techniques on a comprehensive collection of descriptors, all of which are distinct elements of the growth concept. The Growth index includes descriptors of payout, asset growth and historical growth in earnings, the level of earnings to price, and variability in capital structure.

- − Payout, 5 years
- − Earnings to Price Ratio, 5 years
- + Earnings Growth
- + Capital Structure Change
- − Normalized Earnings to Price Ratio
- + Recent Earnings Change
- − Dividend Yield, 5 years
- + IBES Earnings Change
- − Yield Forecast
- + Indicator of Zero Yield
- − Earnings to Price Ratio
- − IBES Earnings to Price Ratio
- + Growth in Total Assets

6. Earnings to Price Ratio (EPR)

The Earnings to Price Ratio measures the relationship between company earnings and market valuation. To compute the Earnings to Price Ratio, BARRA combines measures of past, current, and estimated future earnings.

- + Current Earnings to Price Ratio
- + Earnings to Price Ratio, 5 years
- + IBES Earnings to Price Ratio Projection

7. Book to Price Ratio (BPR)

This index is simply the book value of common equity divided by the market capitalization of a firm.

8. Earnings Variability (EVR)

The Earnings Variability index measures a company's historical earnings variability and cash flow fluctuations. In addition to variance in earnings over five years, it includes the relative variability of earnings forecasts taken from the IBES database, and the industry concentration of a firm's activities.

- + Variance in Earnings
- + IBES Standard Deviation to Price Ratio
- + Earnings Covariability
- + Concentration
- + Variance of Cash Flow
- + Extraordinary Items

9. Financial Leverage (FLV)

The Financial Leverage index captures the financial structure of a firm as well as its sensitivity to interest rates using the debt to assets ratio, the leverage at book value, and the probability of fixed charges not being covered. Bond market sensitivity is included only for financial companies.

Exhibit 3 (Continued)

- Bond Market Sensitivity
+ Debt to Assets Ratio
+ Leverage at Book (Debt to Equity)
+ Uncovered Fixed Charges

10. Foreign Income (FOR)
This index reflects the fraction of operating income earned outside the United States. It is a measure of sensitivity to currency exchange rate changes.

11. Labor Intensity (LBI)
This index estimates the importance of labor, relative to capital, in the operations of a firm. It is based on ratios of labor expense to assets, fixed plant and equipment to equity, and depreciated plant value to total plant cost. A higher exposure to Labor Intensity indicates a larger ratio of labor expense to capital costs and can be a gauge of sensitivity to cost-push inflation.

+ Labor Share
- Inflation-adjusted Plant to Equity Ratio
- Net Plant to Gross Plant

12. Yield (YLD)
The Yield index is simply a relative measure of the company's annual dividend yield.

13. LOCAP
The LOCAP characteristic indicates those companies that are not in the HICAP universe. It permits the factors in the model to be applied across a broader universe of assets than that used to estimate the model. The LOCAP factor is, in part, an extension of the Size index, allowing the returns of approximately 4500 smaller companies to deviate from an exact linear relationship with the Size index.

*In 1997, BARRA released its E3 model which closely resembles the E2 model but with improved risk index definitions.
Source: *United States Equity Model Handbook* (Berkeley, CA: BARRA, 1996), pp. 19-23.

Exhibit 4: BARRA E2 Model Industry Classifications*

The industry classifications in the U.S. Model are:			
Aluminum	15. Liquor	29. Photographic, Optical	43. Retail (All Other)
Iron & Steel	16. Tobacco	30. Consumer Durables	44. Telephone, Telegraph
Precious Metals	17. Construction	31. Motor Vehicles	45. Electric Utilities
Misc. Mining, Metals	18. Chemicals	32. Leisure, Luxury	46. Gas Utilities
Coal & Uranium	19. Tires & Rubber	33. Health Care (Non-drug)	47. Banks
International Oil	20. Containers	34. Drugs, Medicine	48. Thrift Institutions
Dom. Petroleum Reserves	21. Producer Goods	35. Publishing	49. Miscellaneous Finance
For. Petroleum Reserves	22. Pollution Control	36. Media	50. Life Insurance
Oil Refining, Distribution	23. Electronics	37. Hotels, Restaurants	51. Other Insurance
. Oil Service	24. Aerospace	38. Trucking, Freight	52. Real Property
. Forest Products	25. Business Machines	39. Railroads, Transit	53. Mortgage Financing
. Paper	26. Soaps, Housewares	40. Air Transport	54. Services
. Agriculture, Food	27. Cosmetics	41. Transport by Water	55. Miscellaneous
. Beverages	28. Apparel, Textiles	42. Retail (Food)	

* In 1997, BARRA released its E3 model which has improved industry classifications.
Source: *United States Equity Model Handbook* (Berkeley, CA: BARRA, 1996), pp. 32.

Exhibit 5: Fundamental Factors and Market Sensitive Factor Definitions for Wilshire Atlas Factor Model

1.Earnings/price ratio	Sum of the most recent four quarters' earnings per share divided by the closing price.
2. Book value/price ratio	Book value divided by common equity shares outstanding.
3. Market capitalization	The natural logarithm of the product of a security's price multiplied by the number of shares outstanding.
4. Net earnings revision	Analysts momentum measure: Net earnings revision, based on I/B/E/S data, measures analysts' optimism of earnings. Net earnings revision is the percentage of analysts who are feeling more optimistic about earnings in the next period. The higher the net earnings revision number, the more optimistic analysts are about an increase in that company's earnings.
5. Reversal	Price momentum measure: Reversal captures the mean reversion tendencies of stocks. It is a measure of the difference between a security's actual return in the last period and the expected return with respect to its beta. If a stock has a positive reversal this means that it had a higher than expected return in the last period given its beta. Thus, this security is expected to have a lower than expected return in the next period so that the returns for this security will conform to the norm expectations over the long run.
6. Earnings torpedo	Earnings momentum measure: Earnings torpedo, based on I/B/E/S data, is a measure of the estimated growth in earnings for a security relative to historical earnings. Earnings torpedo is based on the ratio of next years estimated earnings per share versus its historical earnings per share. The securities in the universe are then ranked by the estimate and given an earnings torpedo score. A security with a high earnings torpedo score is considered to be vulnerable to a large drop in price if earnings do not meet the higher earnings estimates forecasted by analysts in the next period.
7. Historical beta	Classic measure of security volatility. Measured for each security by regressing the past 60 months worth of excess returns against the S&P500. A minimum of 38 months are required for the data to be valid.

Source: Adapted from *U.S. Equity Risk Model* (Santa Monica, CA: Wilshire Associates, July 1997 draft).

As with the macroeconomic factor model, the raw descriptors are standardized or normalized. The risk indices are in turn standardized. The sensitivity of each company to each risk index is standardized.

The Wilshire Atlas model uses six fundamental factors, one market factor sensitivity, and 39 industry factors to explain stock returns. The six fundamental factors and the market factor sensitivity are listed in Exhibit 5, along with their definitions.

The BARRA and Wilshire factor models are commercially available. Now we'll look at a proprietary model developed by a firm for its own use in managing client equity portfolios — Goldman Sachs Asset Management (GSAM). This firm is the investment management subsidiary of Goldman Sachs & Co., a broker/dealer firm. There are nine descriptors used in the GSAM factor model. These descriptors which are the factors in the model are described in Exhibit 6. The factors fall into three categories: (1) value measures, (2) growth and momentum measures, and (3) risk measures.

Exhibit 6: Factor Definitions for the Goldman Sachs Asset Management Factor Model

Factor	Definition
Book/Price	Common equity per share divided by price
Retained EPS/Price	Year-ahead consensus EPS forecast less indicated annual dividend divided by price. One-year forecast EPS is a weighted average of the forecasts for the current and next fiscal years.
EBITD/Enterprise Value	Earnings before interest, taxes and depreciation divided by total capital. Total capital is equity at market plus long-term debt at book.
Estimate Revisions	The number of estimates raised in the past three months, less the number lowered, divided by the total number of estimates.
Price Momentum	Total return over the last 12 months, less the return for the latest month (to adjust for short-term reversals).
Sustainable Growth	The consensus long-term growth forecast.
Beta	The regression coefficient from a 60-month regression of the stock's excess returns (above the T-bill rate) against the market's excess returns.
Residual Risk	The "unexplained" variation from the above regression; the standard error of the regression.
Disappointment Risk	The risk that actual earnings will not meet projections. Stocks with high expected one-year earnings growth have high disappointment potential; stocks with low expectations have less disappointment risk.

Source: Table 4 in *Select Equity Investment Strategy*, Goldman Sachs Asset Management, February 1997, p. 4.

THE OUTPUT AND INPUTS OF A FACTOR MODEL

Now that we have identified the types of factor models, let's look at the output of the model and the inputs to the model after the estimation has taken place. The output of a factor model is found by first multiplying a factor sensitivity by the assumed value for the factor measure (assumed risk factor).[6] This gives the contribution to the model's output from a given risk factor exposure. Summing up over all risk factors gives the output. For a K-factor model this is expressed mathematically as follows:

$$\text{Output} = \text{Beta}_1 \times (\text{Factor}_1 \text{ measure}) + \text{Beta}_2 \times (\text{Factor}_2 \text{ measure}) + \dots + \text{Beta}_K \times (\text{Factor}_K \text{ measure})$$

Let's look first at the Beta's. These are the factor sensitivities and are estimated statistically. As explained earlier, they are commonly standardized or normalized.

The output varies by model. For example, in the BIRR macroeconomic factor model, the output is the *expected excess return* given the estimated factor sensitivities and the assumed values for the factor measures. The expected excess return is the expected return above the risk-free rate. In contrast, in the Salomon

[6] For an example of quantitative estimation of returns to the size factor using economic variables, see Bruce I. Jacobs and Kenneth N. Levy, "Forecasting the Size Effect," *Financial Analysts Journal* (May-June 1989), pp.61-78.

Brothers RAM factor model, the output is a score that is used to rank the outcome given the estimated factor sensitivities and assumed values for the factor measures.

The factor measures vary by model. In the BIRR macroeconomic factor model, for example, a factor measure is the estimated market price of the risk factor expressed in percent per year. For the Salomon Brothers RAM factor model, a factor measure is the normalized value for the factor.

Let's use the two macroeconomic models described earlier to show how the output is obtained. First, the BIRR model. The estimated risk exposure profile for Reebok International Limited and the assumed values for the risk factors (expressed in percent per year) are shown below:

Risk factor	Estimated factor sensitivity	Estimated market price of risk (%)
Confidence risk	0.73	2.59
Time horizon risk	0.77	−0.66
Inflation risk	−0.48	−4.32
Business cycle risk	4.59	1.49
Market timing risk	1.50	3.61

The expected excess return is then found as follows:

Expected excess return for Reebok = 0.73 (2.59) + 0.77 (−0.66) + (−0.48) (−4.32) + 4.59 (1.49) + 1.50 (3.61) = 15.71%

To obtain the expected return, the risk-free rate must be added. For example, if the risk-free rate is 5%, then the expected return is 20.71% (15.71% plus 5%).

In the Salomon Brothers RAM model, the set of forecasts for the factor measures are called *scenario factors*. Based on scenario factors, the sensitivity of a stock to each factor can be calculated. Adding up the sensitivity of a stock to each factor gives a stock's *scenario score*. Recall that in this factor model there are six macroeconomic factors (described in Exhibit 2) and the residual beta. Each factor is expressed in normalized or standardized form. For Pepsico (in October 1989) the factor betas and a factor scenario for a weakening economy are given below:[7]

Risk factor	Estimated factor sensitivity	Factor scenario (Weakening economy)
Economic growth	−1.8	−1.0
Business cycle	−0.9	−0.5
Long rate	0.0	0.5
Short rate	0.1	0.3
Inflation rate	−0.3	0.1
U.S. dollar	0.1	0.3
Residual beta	−1.1	−0.5

---

[7] Sorensen, Mezrich, and Thum, "The Salomon Brothers U.S. Stock Risk Attribute Model," p. 6.

The scenario score for Pepsico is then:

Pepsico scenario score = -1.8 (-1.0) + (-0.9) (-0.5) + 0 (0.5) + 0.1 (0.3)
+ (-0.3) (0.1) + 0.1 (0.3) + (-1.1) (-0.5) = 1.7

This scenario score is then compared to the scenario score of other stocks in the universe of purchase or short-sale candidates of a portfolio manager.

PORTFOLIO CONSTRUCTION WITH FACTOR MODELS

Now let's see how factor models are used in portfolio construction. Specifically, based on expectations about the future outcomes of the factors, an active equity manager can construct a portfolio to add value relative to some benchmark should those outcomes be realized.

Portfolio Expected Excess Returns and Risk Exposure Profiles

In factor models in which the output is an expected excess return for a stock, the expected excess return for a portfolio can be easily computed. This is the weighted average of the expected excess return for each stock in the portfolio. The weights are the percentage of a stock value in the portfolio relative to the market value of the portfolio. Similarly, a portfolio's sensitivity to a given factor risk is a weighted average of the factor sensitivity of the stocks in the portfolio. The set of factor sensitivities is then the portfolio's risk exposure profile. Consequently, the expected excess return and the risk exposure profile can be obtained from the stocks comprising the portfolio.

Since a stock market index is nothing more than a portfolio that includes the universe of stocks making up the index, an expected excess return and risk exposure profile can be determined for an index. This allows a manager to compare the expected excess return and the risk profile of a stock and/or a portfolio to that of a stock market index whose performance the portfolio manager is measured against. For example, in the BIRR model, the risk exposure profile for the S&P 500 is shown below, as well as that of Reebok for comparative purposes:

	Estimated factor sensitivity for	
Risk factor	S&P 500	Reebok
Confidence risk	0.27	0.73
Time horizon risk	0.56	0.77
Inflation risk	−0.37	−0.48
Business cycle risk	1.71	4.59
Market timing risk	1.00	1.50

By comparing the risk exposure profile of Reebok to the S&P 500, a portfolio manager can see the relative risk exposure. Using the same assumed values for the risk factors as used earlier for Reebok, the expected excess return for the S&P 500 is 8.09% compared to 15.71% for Reebok.

Exhibit 7: Portfolio Holdings for Manager X

BARRA Microcomputer Products:		Interactive PORCH					Page 1
Portfolio: SAMPLE		Market: SAP500				Pricing Date: 07-31-90	

IDENT	NAME	SHARES	PRICE	%WGT	BETA	%YLD	IND
1 FDX	FEDERAL EXPRESS CORP	80700	41.625	3.00	1.15	0.00	AIR
2 NEM	NEWMONT MNG CORP	67500	49.500	2.98	0.76	1.21	GOLD
3 I	FIRST INTST BANCORP	167700	33.000	4.94	1.32	9.09	BANKS
4 HWP	HEWLETT PACKARD CO	126900	43.125	4.89	1.15	0.97	BUS MN
5 IBM	INTERNATIONAL BUS MACH	141400	111.500	14.08	1.01	4.34	BUS MN
6 F	FORD MTR CO DEL	273100	41.500	10.12	0.98	7.17	MOT VH
7 HCSG	HEALTHCARE SVCS GRP IN	93000	24.250	2.01	1.29	0.28	SERVCS
8 TXN	TEXAS INSTRS INC	81500	32.000	2.33	1.41	2.25	ELCTRN
9 S	SEARS ROEBUCK & CO	342900	33.625	10.30	1.09	5.94	RET OT
10 AXP	AMERICAN EXPRESS CO	291900	29.125	7.59	1.20	3.15	FINANC
11 JNJ	JOHNSON & JOHNSON	205800	70.625	12.98	1.02	1.92	HEALTH
12 EK	EASTMAN KODAK CO	324800	38.125	11.06	1.10	5.24	PHOTOG
13 WMX	WASTE MGMT INC	185900	41.375	6.87	1.24	0.86	POLL C
14 PCI	PARAMOUNT COMMUNICATIO	118900	39.500	4.20	1.14	1.77	PUBLSH
15 TAN	TANDY CORP	79800	36.750	2.62	1.26	1.63	RET OT

Source: The information in this exhibit is adapted from Figure VI-1 of *United States Equity Model Handbook* (Berkeley, CA: BARRA, 1996), p. 40.

In factor models such as the Salomon Brothers RAM model where the output is a *scenario score*, the risk exposure profile of a portfolio and market index is calculated in the same manner as when the model's output is the expected excess return. However, in scenario score models the portfolio's and market index's output is a ranking.

The power of a factor model regardless of the type of output is that given the risk factors and the factor sensitivities, a portfolio's risk exposure profile can be quantified and controlled. The examples below show how this can be done with a fundamental factor model. This allows managers to avoid making unintended bets.

Assessing the Exposure of a Portfolio

A fundamental factor model can be used to assess whether the current portfolio is consistent with a manager's strengths. In this application of factor models and the one that follows, we will use the BARRA factor model.[8] Exhibit 7 is a list of the holdings of manager X as of July 31, 1990.[9] There are 15 stocks held with a total market value of $111.9 million.

Exhibit 8 assesses the risk exposure of manager X's portfolio relative to the risk exposure of the S&P 500. The boxes in the second column of the exhibit indicate the significant differences in the exposure of manager X's portfolio relative to the S&P 500. There are two risk indices boxed — success and foreign

---

[8] The illustrations are adapted from Chapter VI of *United States Equity Model Handbook* (Berkeley, CA: BARRA, 1996).

[9] This was an actual portfolio of a BARRA client.

income — and two industry groupings boxed — business machines and miscellaneous finance. Exhibit 3 describes the risk indices. The -0.45 exposure to the success risk index reveals that manager X's portfolio exhibits low relative strength as measured by stock price and earnings momentum — a style characteristic. Consequently, the success risk index indicates an exposure to style. Thus, we can see that manager X is making a style bet. The 0.62 exposure to the foreign income risk index tells manager X that the companies in the portfolio tend to earn a significant portion of their operating income abroad. Consequently, manager X is making an international bet. In terms of industry exposure, manager X is extremely more aggressive in his or her holdings of business machine stocks and miscellaneous finance stocks.

Notice in this example how the manager is able to identify where the bets are made. Manager X has made a style bet, an international bet, and a bet on two industries. If the manager did not intend to make these bets, the portfolio can be rebalanced to eliminate any unintended bets.

Tilting a Portfolio

Now let's look at how an active manager can construct a portfolio to make intentional bets. Suppose that manager Y seeks to construct a portfolio that generates superior returns relative to the S&P 500 by tilting it toward high-success stocks. At the same time, the manager does not want to increase tracking error risk significantly. An obvious approach may seem to be to identify all the stocks in the universe that have a higher than average success risk index. The problem with this approach is that it introduces unintentional bets with respect to the other risk indices.

Instead, an optimization method combined with a factor model can be used to construct the desired portfolio. The input to this process is the tilt exposure sought, the benchmark stock market index, and the number of stocks to be included in the portfolio. The BARRA optimization model also requires a specification of the excess return sought. In our illustration, the tilt exposure sought is high success stocks, the benchmark is the S&P 500, and the number of stocks to be included in the portfolio is 50. While we do not report the holdings of the optimal portfolio here, Exhibit 9 provides an analysis of that portfolio by comparing the risk exposure of the 50-stock optimal portfolio to that of the S&P 500.

Fundamental Factor Models and Equity Style Management

The factors used in fundamental factor models such as the BARRA factor model (Exhibit 3), Wilshire factor model (Exhibit 5), and the GSAM factor model (Exhibit 6) are the same characteristics used in style management. Since the factors can be used to add value and control risk, this suggests that factor models can be used in style management for the same purposes.

Exhibit 8: Analysis of Manager X Portfolio's Exposure Relative to the S&P 500

```
Comparison Summary Report                          Date: 07-31-90

Portfolio            SAMPLE
Comparison Port.     SAP500
Market               SAP500

Number of Assets            15
Port. Value      111,940,087.50
Predicted Yield           3.78
Alpha                     0.00
Utility                  -0.36
Tracking Error            7.25
```

FACTORS	SAMPLE	SAP500	DIFF	MCTE
VARIABILITY IN MARKETS	0.02	-0.06	0.09	0.010
SUCCESS	-0.45	0.01	-0.47	-0.021
SIZE	0.54	0.29	0.26	0.004
TRADING ACTIVITY	0.22	0.00	0.22	-0.002
GROWTH	-0.12	-0.05	-0.07	0.016
EARNINGS/PRICE	0.08	0.01	0.08	0.007
BOOK/PRICE	0.18	-0.02	0.20	0.001
EARNINGS VARIATION	0.00	-0.05	0.05	0.003
FINANCIAL LEVERAGE	0.28	0.03	0.25	-0.001
FOREIGN INCOME	0.62	0.12	0.51	-0.001
LABOR INTENSITY	0.30	0.01	0.29	-0.003
YIELD	0.16	0.02	0.14	0.007
LOCAP	0.02	0.00	0.02	-0.005
ALUMINUM	0.00	0.60	-0.60	0.099
IRON AND STEEL	0.00	0.30	-0.30	0.081
PRECIOUS METALS	1.25	0.42	0.83	0.071
MISC. MINING, METALS	0.54	0.61	-0.07	0.073
COAL AND URANIUM	0.00	0.40	-0.40	0.013
INTERNATIONAL OIL	0.00	4.49	-4.49	-0.033
DOM PETROLEUM RESERVES	0.51	3.46	-2.96	-0.047
FOR PETROLEUM RESERVES	0.69	2.25	-1.56	-0.037
OIL REFINING, DISTRIBUTN	0.00	1.29	-1.29	-0.011
OIL SERVICE	0.00	1.02	-1.02	-0.017
FOREST PRODUCTS	0.00	0.30	-0.30	0.120
PAPER	0.00	2.06	-2.06	0.082
AGRICULTURE, FOOD	0.00	4.99	-4.99	0.047
BEVERAGES	0.00	1.41	-1.41	0.066
LIQUOR	0.00	1.05	-1.05	0.050
TOBACCO	0.00	1.38	-1.38	0.067
CONSTRUCTION	0.00	0.88	-0.88	0.098
CHEMICALS	1.99	3.44	-1.45	0.083
TIRE & RUBBER	0.00	0.10	-0.10	0.101
CONTAINERS	0.00	0.17	-0.17	0.069
PRODUCERS GOODS	0.02	4.49	-4.47	0.086
POLLUTION CONTROL	6.87	1.13	5.75	0.124
ELECTRONICS	2.21	2.39	-0.18	0.126
AEROSPACE	0.00	2.47	-2.47	0.089
BUSINESS MACHINES	19.07	4.80	14.26	0.130
SOAPS, HOUSEWARE	0.00	1.99	-1.99	0.084
COSMETICS	4.54	0.94	3.60	0.096
APPAREL, TEXTILES	0.00	0.77	-0.77	0.080
PHOTOGRAPHIC, OPTICAL	6.75	0.55	6.20	0.114
CONSUMER DURABLES	0.00	0.99	-0.99	0.104
MOTOR VEHICLES	8.91	2.42	6.49	0.114
LEISURE, LUXURY	0.00	0.18	-0.18	0.096
HEALTH CARE (NON-DRUG)	5.06	1.85	3.21	0.070
DRUGS, MEDICINE	5.70	6.81	-1.12	0.066
PUBLISHING	2.10	1.48	0.62	0.090
MEDIA	2.10	1.67	0.43	0.079
HOTELS, RESTAURANTS	0.00	1.75	-1.75	0.094
TRUCKING, FREIGHT	0.00	0.13	-0.13	0.098
RAILROADS, TRANSIT	0.00	0.92	-0.92	0.046
AIR TRANSPORT	3.00	0.59	2.41	0.139
TRANSPORT BY WATER	0.00	0.03	-0.03	0.039
RETAIL (FOOD)	0.00	0.85	-0.85	0.062
RETAIL (ALL OTHER)	6.12	5.19	0.93	0.098
TELEPHONE, TELEGRAPH	0.00	8.26	-8.26	0.036
ELECTRIC UTILITIES	0.00	4.37	-4.37	0.024
GAS UTILITIES	0.00	1.17	-1.17	0.019
BANKS	6.49	2.93	3.56	0.063
THRIFT INSTITUTIONS	0.00	0.28	-0.28	0.073
MISC. FINANCE	10.87	2.20	8.67	0.094
LIFE INSURANCE	0.00	0.92	-0.92	0.061
OTHER INSURANCE	2.37	2.24	0.13	0.059
REAL PROPERTY	0.82	0.19	0.63	0.107
MORTGAGE FINANCING	0.00	0.00	-0.00	0.068
SERVICES	2.01	1.89	0.12	0.070
MISCELLANEOUS	0.00	0.56	-0.56	0.053

Source: The information in this exhibit is adapted from Figure VI-3 of *United States Equity Model Handbook* (Berkeley, CA: BARRA, 1996), p. 42.

Exhibit 9: Analysis of a 50-Stock Portfolio Constructed to be Tilted Toward High Success Stocks

```
Comparison Summary Report                    Date: 07-31-90

Portfolio            SUCCESS
Comparison Port.     SAP500
Market               SAP500

Number of Assets           50
Port. Value        99,999,723.50
Predicted Yield          3.04
Alpha                    0.31
Utility                  0.18
Tracking Error          [4.19]
```

FACTORS	US50	SAP500	DIFF
VARIABILITY IN MARKETS	0.10	-0.06	0.16
SUCCESS	0.77	0.01	0.76
SIZE	0.24	0.29	-0.05
TRADING ACTIVITY	-0.06	0.00	-0.07
GROWTH	0.10	-0.05	0.15
EARNINGS/PRICE	-0.00	0.01	-0.01
BOOK/PRICE	-0.16	-0.02	-0.14
EARNINGS VARIATION	0.00	-0.05	0.05
FINANCIAL LEVERAGE	-0.16	0.03	-0.19
FOREIGN INCOME	-0.10	0.12	-0.21
LABOR INTENSITY	-0.04	0.01	-0.05
YIELD	-0.11	0.02	-0.13
LOCAP	0.00	0.00	-0.00
ALUMINUM	1.98	0.60	1.38
IRON AND STEEL	0.00	0.30	-0.30
PRECIOUS METALS	0.50	0.42	0.07
MISC. MINING, METALS	0.47	0.61	-0.14
COAL AND URANIUM	0.42	0.40	0.02
INTERNATIONAL OIL	4.36	4.49	-0.13
DOM PETROLEUM RESERVES	2.45	3.46	-1.01
FOR PETROLEUM RESERVES	3.19	2.25	0.94
OIL REFINING, DISTRIBUTN	1.44	1.29	0.15
OIL SERVICE	1.79	1.02	0.77
FOREST PRODUCTS	0.03	0.30	-0.27
PAPER	1.07	2.06	-0.99
AGRICULTURE, FOOD	5.29	4.99	0.30
BEVERAGES	0.00	1.41	-1.41
LIQUOR	0.37	1.05	-0.68
TOBACCO	3.13	1.38	1.75
CONSTRUCTION	2.27	0.88	1.39
CHEMICALS	3.39	3.44	-0.05
TIRE & RUBBER	0.00	0.10	-0.10
CONTAINERS	0.00	0.17	-0.17
PRODUCERS GOODS	4.36	4.49	-0.14
POLLUTION CONTROL	2.38	1.13	1.25
ELECTRONICS	4.24	2.39	1.84
AEROSPACE	3.11	2.47	0.64
BUSINESS MACHINES	1.39	4.80	-3.42
SOAPS, HOUSEWARE	4.79	1.99	2.80
COSMETICS	0.29	0.94	-0.66
APPAREL, TEXTILES	0.98	0.77	0.21
PHOTOGRAPHIC, OPTICAL	0.00	0.55	-0.55
CONSUMER DURABLES	0.73	0.99	-0.27
MOTOR VEHICLES	4.35	2.42	1.94
LEISURE, LUXURY	0.00	0.18	-0.18
HEALTH CARE (NON-DRUG)	2.10	1.85	0.25
DRUGS, MEDICINE	4.60	6.81	-2.21
PUBLISHING	0.00	1.48	-1.48
MEDIA	0.16	1.67	-1.51
HOTELS, RESTAURANTS	0.59	1.75	-1.16
TRUCKING, FREIGHT	0.00	0.13	-0.13
RAILROADS, TRANSIT	0.00	0.92	-0.92
AIR TRANSPORT	0.00	0.59	-0.59
TRANSPORT BY WATER	0.00	0.03	-0.03
RETAIL (FOOD)	4.78	0.85	3.93
RETAIL (ALL OTHER)	9.80	5.19	4.62
TELEPHONE, TELEGRAPH	0.00	8.26	-8.26
ELECTRIC UTILITIES	12.31	4.37	7.95
GAS UTILITIES	1.03	1.17	-0.14
BANKS	0.00	2.93	-2.93
THRIFT INSTITUTIONS	0.00	0.28	-0.28
MISC. FINANCE	2.10	2.20	-0.10
LIFE INSURANCE	1.67	0.92	0.75
OTHER INSURANCE	1.55	2.24	-0.69
REAL PROPERTY	0.23	0.19	0.04
MORTGAGE FINANCING	0.00	0.00	-0.00
SERVICES	0.19	1.89	-1.70
MISCELLANEOUS	0.15	0.56	-0.42

Source: The information in this exhibit is adapted from Figure VI-7 of *United States Equity Model Handbook* (Berkeley, CA: BARRA, 1996), p. 47.

Exhibit 10: Summary of Perfect Foresight Tests Two Strategies Using Factor Models: 12-Month Rolling Value Added (%) from January 1987 to July 1995

Country	Long Stock Strategy			Market Neutral Strategy		
	High	Low	Average	High	Low	Average
United States	82%	39%	55%	195%	75%	138%
United Kingdom	131	52	82	326	50	155
Japan	106	56	74	236	66	121
Canada	91	63	77	—	—	—

Source: Table 15 from David J. Leinweber, Robert D. Arnott, and Christopher G. Luck, "The Many Sides of Equity Style," Chapter 11 in T. Daniel Coggin, Frank J. Fabozzi, and Robert D. Arnott (eds.), *The Handbook of Equity Style Management* (New Hope, PA: Frank J. Fabozzi Associates, 1997).

RETURN PERFORMANCE POTENTIAL OF FACTOR MODELS

It is interesting to see how well a portfolio constructed using a factor model would have performed with perfect foresight. For example, suppose we are examining monthly returns. We look at the actual factor return for the month and use that as our expectation at the beginning of the month. Given the forecasts an optimization model can be used to design the optimal portfolio.

Leinweber, Arnott, and Luck performed this experiment for several countries using the BARRA factor model for those countries — United States, United Kingdom, Japan, and Canada — for the period January 1987 to July 1995.[10] Transaction costs for rebalancing a portfolio each month were incorporated. A 12-month rolling value added return was calculated. A value added return is the return above a broad-based stock index for the country.

Two strategies were followed. One was simply a long position in the stocks. The second was a market neutral long-short strategy.[11] Exhibit 10 reports the results of the perfect foresight tests. With perfect foresight, the BARRA factor model would have added significant value for each country stock portfolio. For example, in the United States even in the worst 12-month rolling period the factor-based model added 39% for the long stock strategy and 75% for the market neutral long-short strategy.

Eric Sorensen, Joseph Mezrich, and Chee Thum performed two backtests of the Salomon Brothers RAM (a macroeconomic factor model) to assess the model. The tests were basically event studies.[12] In the first backtest, these

[10] David J. Leinweber, Robert D. Arnott, and Christopher G. Luck, "The Many Sides of Equity Style," Chapter 11 in T. Daniel Coggin, Frank J. Fabozzi, and Robert D. Arnott (eds.), *The Handbook of Equity Style Management* (New Hope, PA: Frank J. Fabozzi, 1997).
[11] See Bruce I. Jacobs and Kenneth N. Levy, "The Long and Short on Long-Short," *Journal of Investing* (Spring 1997), pp. 73-86.
[12] Sorensen, Mezrich, and Thum, *The Salomon Brothers U.S. Risk Attribute Model.*

researchers looked at daily returns following an unexpected announcement regarding an inflation measure. Specifically, on July 14, 1989 the Producer Price Index that was announced was sharply less than anticipated. As a result, the yield on Treasury bills with one month to maturity fell on that day from 8.6% to 8.4%. An optimized portfolio that had a high sensitivity to inflation was constructed. The inflation sensitive tilted portfolio outperformed the S&P 500 by 46 basis points from the day prior to the event (July 13, 1989) through the day after the event (July 15, 1989). This result supports the position that the factor model was an important tool for constructing a portfolio based on expectations.

The second backtest was based on a longer period of time. The event in this case was the movement of the U.S. dollar during the spring of 1989. Specifically, there was an unexpected strengthening (i.e., appreciation) of the U.S. dollar relative to the German mark from May 12 to June 2, 1989. An optimized portfolio was constructed that was tilted towards stocks that benefited from a stronger U.S. dollar. The RAM-based portfolio tilted with this bias outperformed the S&P 500 by 62 basis points.

DIVIDEND DISCOUNT MODELS VERSUS FACTOR MODELS

Another approach used to value common stock is a dividend discount model (DDM). Based on certain assumptions, a DDM gives the expected return for a stock. As explained in this chapter, a factor model also gives the expected return for a stock. Thus both a factor model and a DDM are valuation models. The DDM can be either a stand-alone model or one of several inputs to a factor model.

A study by Bruce Jacobs and Kenneth Levy suggests that simple factor models can outperform a traditional dividend discount model.[13] Specifically, when they compared the contribution of a simple factor model with a traditional dividend discount model they found that less than one-half of 1% of the quarterly average actual returns is explained by the DDM. In contrast, about 43% of the average actual returns is explained by a factor model which includes the DDM and other factors. Thus, in their study the factor model outperformed the DDM hands down.

SUMMARY

There are three types of factor models: statistical factor models, macroeconomic factor models, and fundamental factor models. Statistical factor models use a statistical technique called principal components analysis to identify which raw descriptors best explain stock returns. The resulting factors are statistical artifacts

---

[13] Jacobs and Levy, "On the Value of 'Value'," *Financial Analysts Journal* (July/August 1988).

and are therefore difficult to interpret. Consequently, a statistical factor model is rarely used in practice. The more common factor models are the macroeconomic factor model and the fundamental factor model.

In a factor model, the sensitivity of a stock to a factor is estimated. The risk exposure profile of a stock is identified by a set of factor sensitivities. The risk exposure profile of a portfolio is the weighted average of the risk exposure profile of the stocks in the portfolio. Similarly, the risk exposure profile of a market index can be obtained.

The output of a factor model can be either the expected excess return or a scenario score. The expected excess return of a stock is found by multiplying each factor sensitivity by the assumed value for the risk factor and summing over all risk factors. The expected return is the expected excess return plus the risk-free rate. The expected excess return for a portfolio and a market index is just the weighted average of the expected excess return of the stocks comprising the portfolio or the market index.

The power of a factor model is that given the risk factors and the factor sensitivities, a portfolio's risk exposure profile can be quantified and controlled. Applications of factor models include the ability to assess whether or not the current portfolio is consistent with a manager's strengths and to construct a portfolio with a specific tilt without making unintentional bets. Since many factors in a fundamental model are the same characteristics used in style management, factor models can be used in controlling risk in a style management strategy.

Both dividend discount models and factor models can be used to value common stock. The output of a dividend discount model can be used as a factor in a factor model. One study suggests that factor models have significantly outperformed dividend discount models.

Chapter 6

Relative Predictive Power of the *Ad Hoc* Expected Return Factor Model and Asset Pricing Models

Robert A. Haugen, Ph.D.
President
Haugen Custom Financial Systems

INTRODUCTION

The two premier asset-pricing models of modern finance are the *Capital Asset Pricing Model* (CAPM) and the *Arbitrage Pricing Theory* (APT). The power of CAPM in explaining differences in return among the cross-section of U.S. stocks has been recently called into question.[1] In addition it has been shown that APT betas have relatively low power in explaining cross-sectional differences in return.[2] Since predictive models rooted in financial theory have limited power, it may be more fruitful to turn to models that are more comprehensive in terms of the variables that they employ, even though they are *ad hoc*, in the sense that they are not based on a rigorous theoretical framework.

In an expected return factor model, a comprehensive list of factors that describe the profile of a company going into a particular month are interfaced with projections of the payoffs to each element of the profile. By multiplying the projected payoff by the particular factor exposure, you obtain the component of the stock's total expected return for the month stemming from the factor. By aggregating over all factors, the analyst obtains an estimate of the expected total monthly return for the stock.

Similar predictions can be made with CAPM and APT. With CAPM there is only one relevant element of the profile — the stocks beta relative to the returns to the market. The projected payoff is the monthly-expected risk premium to the market. In the case of the APT there may be multiple elements — the betas with respect to the various factors that account for the stock's systematic risk. It should

---

[1] See for example Fama, E. and K. French, "The Cross-Section of Expected Stock Returns," *The Journal of Finance* (June 1992), and R. Haugen, *The New Finance: The Case for an Over-reactive Stock Market* (Upper Saddle River, NJ: Prentice Hall, 1999, Second Edition).
[2] See R. Haugen and N. Baker, "Commonality in the Determinants of Expected Stock Returns," *The Journal of Financial Economics* (July 1996).

prove interesting to examine the relative predictive power of *ad hoc* and theoretical models. This chapter reports the results of such a test. The three contestants in the race will be CAPM, APT, and an expected return factor model. All will be run over the same time period of 1980 to mid-year 1997, and over the same stock population — roughly the largest 3,000 stocks in the U.S.

MODELS OF EXPECTED RETURNS

The Expected Return Factor Model

The expected return factor model (ERFM) will require fundamental accounting data. Its run will assume a 3-month reporting lag from the start through 1987. After 1987 the actual data files that were available at the time will be used to compute the exposures needed for the corporate profile to calculate expected rates of return.

The model examined here is very similar to that of Haugen and Baker.[3] Six classes of factors are employed. *Risk variables* include market and APT type betas, volatility of stock return, the unexplained component of stock volatility, as well as debt-to-equity and interest coverage. *Measures of liquidity* include total capitalization, the number of times capitalization turns over annually, and price per share. *Measures of profitability* include profit margin, capital turnover, and the return on assets and equity. Five-year trend for each of these measures is also included, as is the trailing 5-year growth in earnings per share. *Measures of cheapness* in stock price include the ratios of sales, cash flow, earnings, dividends, and book value to market price. *Technical variables* include the trailing returns to the stock over the last month, two months, three months, six months, the trailing year, three years and five years. *Measures of earnings revision and surprise* include revisions in consensus forecasts in earnings over various horizons, as well as trailing differences between these consensus forecasts and earnings actually reported. Finally ten sector variables are included which take a value of one if a stock is in a particular sector and zero otherwise.

Expected returns are calculated as the sum of the products of the projected factor payoffs (the mean of the trailing 12 months) and the factor exposures going into the month. The stock population is then ranked by expected return and formed into deciles. The deciles are re-formed monthly. As with the runs for the other two contestants, transaction costs will not be accounted for. This is purely a test of predictive power. The results for ERFM are presented in Exhibit 1. It shows the log of the cumulative rates of return for the 10 deciles.

The average annual returns to the deciles are plotted in Exhibit 2. The spread between one end of the line-of-best-fit through the ten plot points is 37.17%. And the percentage of the differences in the overall returns to the deciles explained by decile number is 94%. All in all, an impressive display of predictive power.

---

[3] See Haugen and Baker, "Commonality in the Determinants of Expected Stock Returns."

Exhibit 1: Logarithm of Cumulative Decile Performance Ad Hoc Expected Return Factor Model

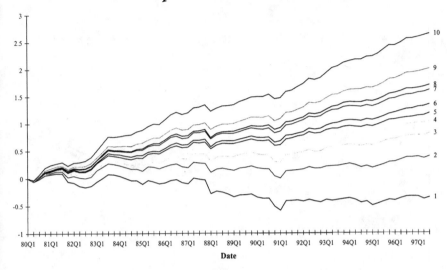

Exhibit 2: Decile Returns for the Ad Hoc Factor Model

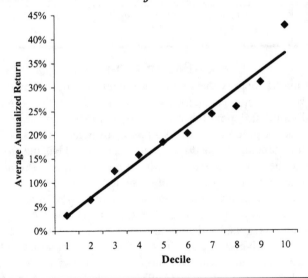

Exhibit 3: Logarithm of Cumulative Decile Performance CAPM

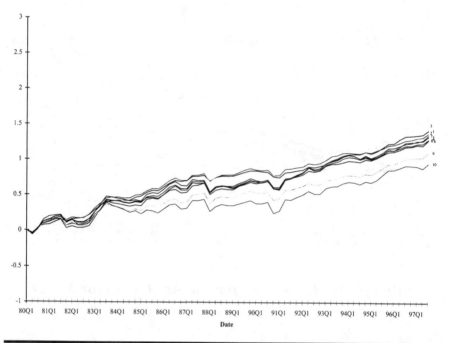

The CAPM and the APT
=====================

Under CAPM market beta is the sole determinant of expected stock return. We compute beta by regressing each stock's return on the S&P 500's return over the trailing 48-60 months, depending on data availability. Betas are recalculated every month. CAPM predicts a positive payoff to beta so the 3,000 stocks are ranked by trailing beta and formed into deciles. Decile 10 has the stocks with the largest beta, and, therefore, the stocks with the highest expected returns. Decile 1 the lowest. The results for the CAPM are presented in Exhibit 3.

The perverted nature of the predictions of CAPM rears its head once again. Decile 10 has the lowest cumulative return and Decile 1 nearly the highest. The average annual returns, by decile, are shown in Exhibit 4. The slope of the line of best fit is negative with a spread of −5.67% between one end of the line and the other. For individual years, the slope is negative in 13 years and positive in only 5. The 1980s weren't good to CAPM. It had 10 years of successive negative spreads from 1981 through 1990, averaging −11.6%.

Perhaps we can find significantly better results with the APT. There are, of course, many possible versions of the APT. Here is a description of the one entered in this race:

Exhibit 4: Decile Returns for CAPM Model

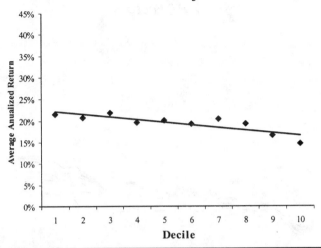

Macroeconomic factors:

- The monthly return on Treasury bills.
- The difference in the monthly return on long- and short-term Treasury securities.
- The difference in the monthly return on Treasury bonds and low-grade corporate bonds of the same maturity.
- The monthly change in the consumer price index.
- The monthly change in industrial production.
- The beginning-of-month dividend-to-price ratio for the S&P 500.

Beta estimation:

- Regress each stock's monthly return on the six macroeconomic factors over the trailing 48-60 months depending on data availability. Betas are re-estimated monthly.

Payoff estimation:

- The payoff to each macroeconomic beta is projected as the mean of the trailing 12 monthly payoffs.

We are ready to examine APT's predictive prowess in Exhibit 5. APT doesn't perform nearly as well as ERFM, but at least its predictions are not perverse. Decile 5 comes in first, but Decile 10 finishes second, and Decile 1 last. But the spreads are not nearly as impressive as those of ERFM. The average annualized rates of return to the deciles are plotted in Exhibit 6. APT shows a spread between one end of the line-of-best-fit and the other of 4.68%.

Exhibit 5: Logarithm of Cumulative Decile Performance APT Factors

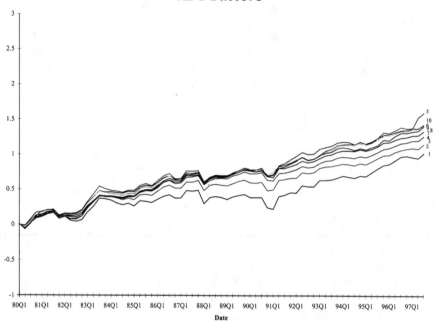

Exhibit 6: Average Returns for APT Model

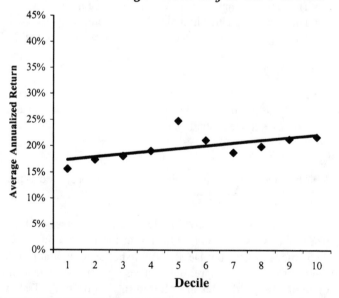

Exhibit 7: Results of the Race

Ad Hoc Expected Return Factor Model:
Average Annualized Spread Between Deciles 1 & 10:   46.04%
Years with Negative Spreads   0 years

Capital Asset Pricing Model:
Average Annualized Spread Between Deciles 1 & 10:   -6.94%
Years with Negative Spreads: 13 years

Arbitrage Pricing Theory:
Average Annualized Spread Between Deciles 1 & 10:   6.06%
Years with Negative Spreads: 6 years

In assessing these results, we should keep in mind that the APT had an inherent advantage over the CAPM in the race. In ranking the deciles by beta, we forced the CAPM to project forward its prediction — a *positive* payoff to risk. Its dismal performance can be attributed to the fact that it was forced to run the race on a track where the payoff to risk is actually negative. CAPM would have done considerably better if we had estimated the monthly payoff to market beta, and then projected forward the average of the trailing 12 payoffs, as we did with the APT. The overall results can be seen in Exhibit 7.

SUMMARY

Models based on financial theory have perverted to modest power in explaining or predicting the cross-section of stock returns. More comprehensive models, although *ad hoc* in nature, do a much better job of predicting stock returns. These models should be given serious consideration for building stock portfolios and for estimating the cost of external equity capital.

Chapter 7

Quantitative Tools in Equity Valuation and Portfolio Management: Applying the DDM

Steven Pisarkiewicz
Senior Portfolio Manager
Sanford C. Bernstein & Co., Inc.

Mark R. Gordon
Director of Quantitative Research
Sanford C. Bernstein & Co., Inc.

INTRODUCTION

When Steven Pisarkiewicz was a young man growing up in St. Louis, one of the rites of passage to manhood was to learn to play poker and blackjack from his father. Because he had four brothers, the games were always an occasion for teasing, jokes, and wisecracks. He learned the fundamentals of winning these games as well as the anguish of losing, but he'll never forget one comment his father made: "Be patient. Luck will come if your money holds out."

All the boys thought this was very funny. The statement was true, but it was no prescription for success in blackjack for someone with limited time and money. Furthermore, the corollary to his remark was also true: taking on too much risk can be permanently damaging, i.e. one's money may run out before luck comes along. Over time, however, Steve learned that if played consistently well, the game was nearly a fair one, with a slight advantage to the dealer. But it was intriguing to observe that with "extra" information, the advantage could swing in the player's favor. But what "extra" information is relevant? And given what's relevant, what's the best play in each situation? How much should one bet? What risks does the player bear in the process? What are the probabilities and expected returns of winning?

Viewing blackjack from this perspective, the similarities between the card game and investment management emerge: both involve risk and return, both admit that advantage occurs from time to time, both are rife with the possibility of misinterpreting information, and both can fall victim to emotional or superstitious responses.

Counting cards in blackjack has proven to be the best way to gain an advantage. That is, when an excess of tens and aces remain in the deck, the advantage shifts to the player. Similarly, quantitative investment management tools can help swing the advantage in equity portfolio management. Quantitative approaches start with the assumption that relevant information does indeed exist. Well-crafted tools are capable of sorting and organizing germane information upon which you can act. Optimizers can trade off risk and return, reacting to new relevant information and guiding the selection and allocation decisions. The best of these tools restrict your attention to theoretically credible and empirically supported hypotheses, treating the data as evidence, rather than proof. In this way, the tools can serve to shield the investor from emotional or superstitious responses, thereby enhancing our performance as portfolio managers.

RATIONALE FOR QUANTITATIVE INVESTMENT TOOLS

The goal of all equity portfolio managers, regardless of investment style or technique, is to add value; that is, to exploit differences between the current prices of stocks and their intrinsic or realistic value. Implicit in this mission statement is that the stock market is not completely efficient: that there are peaks and troughs in corporate performance and that uncertainty about future profitability and growth can, at times, be highly exaggerated, creating mispricing. To understand security valuation and identify mispricing is, therefore, an essential task in managing money.

Classical investment theory posits that the valuation of a stream of future cash flows should be done by present value discounting. For a buy-and-hold stock investor, the value of a stock is the present value of the stock's future cash flows (mostly dividends). The mathematical expression for this is known as the *Dividend Discount Model* (DDM) and is described by the equation:

$$V_0 = D_1/[1 + k] + D_2/[1 + k]^2 + D_3/[1 + k]^3 + \ldots$$

where V_0 is the stock value, D_n are the dividends, and k is the discount rate. By supplying this equation with the values of D_n and k, we can estimate V_0.

Whenever a stock's market price falls below this estimate of value V_0, the stock is considered undervalued. Alternatively, solving for the discount rate that equilibrates the present value of the cash flows with the stock's current market price gives us the *internal rate of return* (IRR) for the stock. If our forecasts of the cash flows are accurate, the return to a buy-and-hold investor *is* the IRR.

It is our belief, therefore, that the DDM represents an excellent foundation upon which to build a valuation tool to identify mispricing. It's rooted in the universally-accepted finance theory of discounted cash flow analysis, its focus on long-term cash flows captures the economic earnings power of the company, and it is unaffected by labels of value or growth: the DDM user is interested only in the most lucrative combinations of current prices and future earnings power.

The challenge of putting the DDM to work is forecasting with accuracy the future earnings power and dividend-paying capability of a company. Some investment firms have chosen to face this challenge head on, and have built large research staffs to develop proprietary forecasts. Some use Wall Street earnings estimates. Others use value metrics such as current dividend yield or book value-to-price as a means to sort stocks, identify the cheapest ones, and build portfolios. But cheapness compared to other stocks, which is the essence of these approaches, doesn't address the question of whether the stock price is low enough to compensate the investor for the future growth characteristics of the company (which is usually subpar — otherwise the stock wouldn't be cheap!). The DDM does this.

The limitations of dividend yield and book value as valuation tools are important only if they result in inferior performance. The next section of this chapter will compare these valuation approaches to the DDM. It will also address the important issue of how to construct a portfolio. If all the stocks in a given sector of the market are attractively valued, how much should you buy? Convinced of the mispricing of these stocks, is it prudent to buy them all and dramatically overweight the sector relative to the market weight? And once you have identified a stock as mispriced by these measures, when do you buy it? Stock market history is replete with instances where bargain stocks have fallen further in price. How can one avoid the pitfall of buying too early? Likewise, once a successful stock idea has risen in price, when do you sell?

All of these concerns call for a portfolio management framework that not only encompasses expected return, risk, performance objectives, and utility, but a framework that utilizes quantitative tools — tools that exploit information in a proven way and that can be used together in a complementary manner. Most importantly, the tools must address three important concerns:

1. Timely management of the securities data.
2. Quality control of the inputs and decision making process.
3. Control of both security specific risk and portfolio risk.

The first concern refers to the need to organize price data, earnings forecasts, and stock characteristics in a way that allows for cross-sector comparisons. The second refers to the imperfect nature of forecasting company earnings and dividends, as well as the need to prevent ourselves from letting our emotions distort our decisions. That is to say, it is critical to stay true to one's investing beliefs and practice the same investment disciplines over time. The third concern refers to the need to guide portfolio construction by measuring concentration risk and to guide the timing of purchases and sales. We at Bernstein have combined fundamental stock research with quantitative tools for more than 20 years. Below we share with you what we've learned over these years.

IDENTIFYING MISPRICED STOCKS

The cornerstone of Bernstein's valuation process is a multistage DDM that capitalizes on our proprietary fundamental research. As with all DDM approaches, it is based on a discounted cash flow analysis. For each security in our universe, we derive expected returns as follows:

Expected Return = Dividend Yield + Rate of Dividend Growth

where dividend yield refers to the maximum amount (not necessarily the current yield) a firm could pay out without depleting its productive capacity. Our estimate of this is free cash flow divided by current stock price. Dividend growth rates are derived from our analysts' forecast of earnings power and free cash flow growth.

Because corporate earnings grow at different rates as companies mature, it is important to use a multistage model to heighten the accuracy of the forecasting process. We have identified four distinct phases of the total forecast period in which to input growth and payout rates. This allows rapidly growing companies with little or no free cash flow to "compete" in the DDM with mature companies. The four phases are presented in Exhibit 1 and described as follows:

Exhibit 1: Earnings Behavior: Growth Company

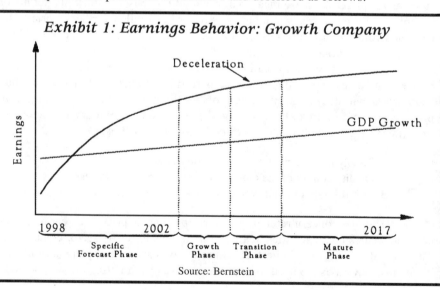

Source: Bernstein

Exhibit 2: Earnings Behavior: Cyclical Company

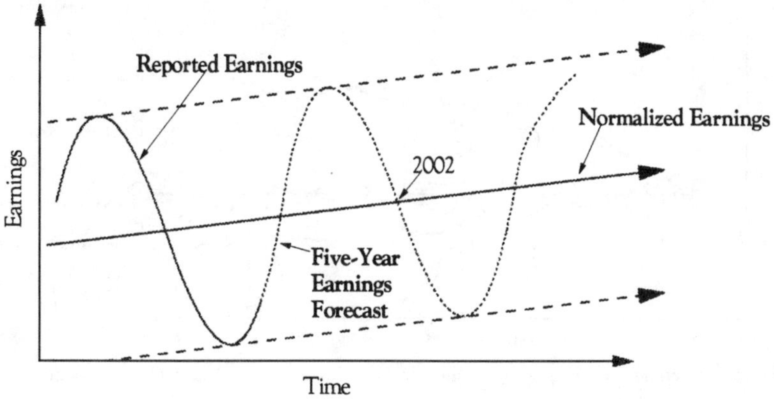

Source: Bernstein

Phase 1: The explicit forecast phase for which our analysts develop estimates of earnings and free cash flow for each of the next five years.

Phase 2: The growth phase (relative to GDP) where we forecast the growth
rate of earnings and free cash flow over the next 2 to 6 years depending
on the company and the served industry.

Phase 3: The transition phase, where above-average growth companies see
their earnings power ratchet down to more sustainable levels. We forecast this slowing rate of growth over the next 5 to 9 years depending on
the company and the served industry.

Phase 4: The terminal phase, which reflects a mature company growing at
the or near the rate of the overall economy.

Companies with cyclical earnings streams, as shown in Exhibit 2, regularly exhibit peaks and troughs in reported earnings. The key to a successful forecast is, therefore, to determine their normalized earnings power and input this
forecast in Phase 2. This avoids distortions that result from extrapolating peak or
trough earnings into the future. In addition, we modify the multistage model for
cyclical companies by eliminating Phase 3 and moving directly to the terminal
phase, where payout rates are adjusted to 48%, and cyclical stocks, by our definition, grow in line with the overall economy.

For each stock in our universe, the DDM solves for the IRR that equates
our forecast of free cash flow yield with current stock prices. We run these calculations daily to reflect changes in stock prices and adjustments in analysts' forecasts.
We compare the resulting IRRs to the IRR of the S&P 500 and the premiums or def-
icits are translated into expectations of outperformance or underperformance using
proprietary adjustments. We refer to this adjusted expected return premium as the
"DDM edge." We rank "edges" daily from highest to lowest and construct a prelim-
inary model portfolio from the top (most attractive) two quintiles of the rank order.

Exhibit 3: Dividend-Discount Model: January 1971-January 1998

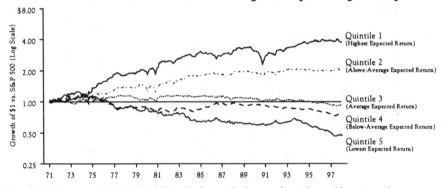

Note: Stocks are equal weighted within quintiles; quintiles are formed monthly; transaction costs not included

Source: Bernstein

Exhibit 4: Dividend-Discount Model Results

Quintile	January 1971-January 1998 Annualized Relative Return (%)
Quintile 1 (Highest Expected Return)	5.7
Quintile 2 (Above-Average Expected Return)	3.0
Quintile 3 (Average Expected Return)	−0.3
Quintile 4 (Below-Average Expected Return)	−1.2
Quintile 5 (Lowest Expected Return)	−3.1

Source: Bernstein

The key investment question is: Does this DDM rank order produce a portfolio that delivers results superior to the S&P 500 Index over time? Further, does the research effort that we undertake to develop forecasts for the DDM yield results superior to a naive rank-ordering of book value-to-price, or simple dividend yield? We regularly test the efficacy of our DDM by evaluating the relative performance of each quintile in the valuation ranking. At the end of each month, we build a capitalization-weighted portfolio of the stocks in each quintile and measure each portfolio's performance relative to the S&P 500 over the next month. Exhibit 3 depicts the cumulative growth of $1 (relative to the S&P 500) for each quintile from 1/1/71 through 1/1/98.

The best performing portfolio in Exhibit 3 was formed from the first quintile stocks, those with the highest expected return. Exhibit 4 summarizes the annualized performance (relative to the S&P 500) for each of the quintiles.

The results in Exhibit 4 support the prediction that the DDM produces superior performance relative to the S&P 500. The return premiums for quintiles 1 and 2 are highly competitive, and the monotonic pattern of results from quintile 1 to quintile 5 lend credibility to the predictive power of the DDM as a valuation tool. But these results must be evaluated relative to the performance of portfolios ranked by other valuation methods, such as book value-to-price and dividend yield. These value measures are, after all, structurally related to the DDM. In the case of dividend yield:

Exhibit 5: Book Value/Price: January 1971-January 1998

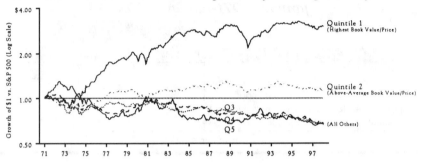

Note: Stocks are equal weighted within quintiles; quintiles are formed monthly; transaction costs not included

Source: Bernstein

Exhibit 6: Dividend Yield: January 1971-January 1998

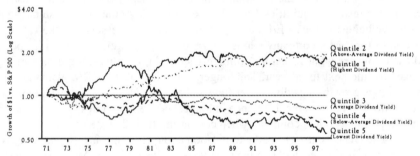

Note: Stocks are equal weighted within quintiles; quintiles are formed monthly; transaction costs not included

Source: Bernstein

IRR = Current Yield/Price + Growth Rate of Yield

where the IRR differences between stocks would be the yield differences, assuming the same rate of dividend growth for all companies.

Similarly, using more severe assumptions, IRR differences are proportional to differences in book-to-price ratios:

IRR = [Payout Rate × ROE × B/P] + [(1 − Payout Rate) × ROE]

where ROEs and payouts are constant and uniform for all companies. Exhibits 5 and 6 display the relative performance results of these valuation tools, and Exhibit 7 compares the relative results of all three methodologies.

It's clear from Exhibit 7 that the DDM has delivered results superior to the other valuation tools: the DDM's first and second quintiles have higher relative performance; the spread between quintile 1 and quintile 5 is wider with the DDM methodology; and the relative returns are more monotonic in character.

Exhibit 7: Comparison of Valuation Methodologies: January 1971-January 1998

Quintile	Annualized Relative Returns (%)		
	Dividend-Discount Model	Book Value/Price	Dividend Yield
Quintile 1 (Highest Expected Return)	5.7	4.7	2.4
Quintile 2 (Above-Average Expected Return)	3.0	0.4	2.7
Quintile 3 (Average Expected Return)	−0.3	−1.7	−0.8
Quintile 4 (Below-Average Expected Return)	−1.2	−1.7	−1.8
Quintile 5 (Lowest Expected Return)	−3.1	−1.6	−2.5

Source: Bernstein

The efficacy of the DDM is challenged, however, when you examine the historic performance results of portfolios ranked by forecast consensus earnings (next fiscal year) divided by current prices. The results of this analysis begin in 1976 (the inception of I/B/E/S estimates), and are shown in Exhibits 8 and 9.

Notwithstanding the differences in measurement periods, the forecast E/P performance results of quintiles 1 and 2 are comparable to the DDM results. Nonetheless, we believe forecast E/P falls short of capturing the essence of the valuation process: to forecast a company's longer term earnings power. This earnings power and cash flow are what investors ultimately share in, not the accounting earnings forecast for the next fiscal year. The longer term view of the DDM also addresses how earnings growth rates differ over time and across industries. For example, forecast E/P doesn't address the difference in longer-term growth rates of a electric utility and a pharmaceutical company when comparing their E/P statistics.

The DDM is, therefore, the foundation upon which our investment process is built. We consider those stocks in the top two quintiles of the DDM rank order to be our buy candidates. As these stocks fall in ranking past the midpoint of the rank order due to price appreciation or forecast revision, they become candidates for sale. We have applied this valuation approach consistently for two decades and found it highly effective in identifying broad value themes as well as individual stock valuation distortions. However, it has not been consistently effective in identifying when a stock has reached a valuation extreme and therefore cannot necessarily predict the most opportune time to initiate an investment action. For that decision, we rely on two sentiment indicators to guide us. We describe these in the next two sections.

Timing of Purchases and Sales

One of the risks of value investing is buying and selling too soon. The risk of underperformance can be meaningful if you buy stocks under price pressure in a market of heightened anxiety and stress. After all, there is no one who will "ring the bell" to signify that the stock has bottomed. To minimize this risk, you must therefore find coincident or leading indicators of near-term stock price behavior. We at Bernstein have settled on two: consensus earnings revisions and recent stock performance trends. To date, we have found them to be the most powerful quantitative tools to assist in the timing of purchases and sales.

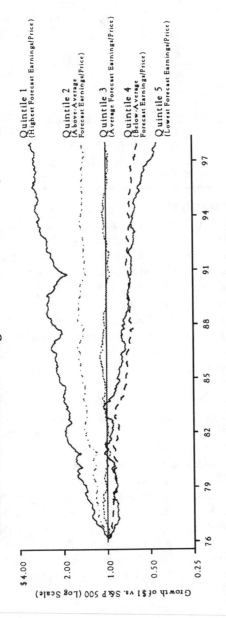

Exhibit 8: Forecast Earnings/Price: March 1976-January 1998

Note: Stocks are equal weighted within quintiles; quintiles are formed monthly; transaction costs not included

Source: Bernstein

Exhibit 9: Forecast Earnings/Price

Quintile	March 1976-January 1998 Annualized Relative Return (%)
Quintile 1 (Highest Expected Return)	6.4
Quintile 2 (Above-Average Expected Return)	2.0
Quintile 3 (Average Expected Return)	0.0
Quintile 4 (Below-Average Expected Return)	−2.8
Quintile 5 (Lowest Expected Return)	−4.2

Source: Bernstein

Exhibit 10: Impact of Consensus Earnings Revisions

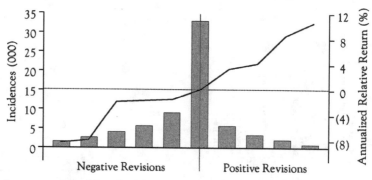

Note: Performance annualized from the three-month returns subsequent to the earnings revision.
Source: Bernstein

Consensus Earnings Revisions

It's quite intuitive to believe that if Wall Street analysts are revising next quarter's earnings downward for a given company, the stock's price is likely to decline. What's not widely known is that the full impact of the decline is not always immediate, but more likely to occur over the next three months. The psychological underpinnings for this observation lie in the fact that analysts don't fully adjust to new information immediately, however provocative it may be. People react with a lag because their impressions are often anchored in the past. In addition, the reactions are often serial in nature, as they progressively decouple from their older impressions. So can we as portfolio managers exploit this behavior? Can earnings revision analysis be integrated into an investment management framework to add value reliably?

We sought to answer these questions by first analyzing the S&P 500 stocks from 1977 to the present. We ranked these stocks on a monthly basis by the degree to which I/B/E/S estimates of the subsequent quarter's earnings were revised up or down. We grouped the stocks into deciles by the magnitude of the revisions. We then calculated each stock's relative performance in the quarter following the revision and computed the average annualized performance for each decile. The results shown in Exhibit 10 plot the frequency of revisions in the histogram, and the subsequent relative performance of each decile plotted in the line chart. As you can see, the stocks with the largest downward revisions underperformed the market by 8% on average, while the stocks with the largest upward revisions outperformed the market by 10.5%, on average, following the revision. Clearly, earnings revisions can be a powerful tool for predicting short-term stock price movements, both up and down. As such, we can use it to accelerate or delay the buys and sells identified by our DDM valuation model.

In order to integrate consensus earnings revisions into the expected return framework of the DDM, we must convert the revisions data as follows:

$$\text{Revisions Index} = [(\text{Estimate}_{now} - \text{Estimate}_{1\ month\ ago})/\text{Stock Price}]$$
$$- \text{Revision Index for S\&P 500}$$

The revisions are now in a form similar to a relative dividend yield and can be used as a penalty (if negative) or increment (if positive) in the expected return framework of the DDM. That is, we can add it to or subtract it from the DDM edge.

Relative Performance Trends

To complement the information provided by the consensus earnings revisions data, we also considered the influence of recent relative performance trends (momentum, if you will) on a stock's near-term price behavior. To test its influence, we studied the performance patterns of the stocks in S&P 500 Index. For each quarter since 1926, we computed the trailing 12-month relative return for each stock and grouped the stocks into quintiles of performance. We then computed the relative return for the subsequent three months and determined the average for each quintile. The results in Exhibit 11 list the average quarterly return (annualized) for each quintile over the entire history of the S&P 500, from 1926 to 1996. Clearly, the stocks with the strongest recent performance (quintile 1) had the strongest subsequent performance, on average. Conversely, quintile 5 delivered the weakest subsequent performance. Like the consensus earnings revision work, the results argue strongly for using this tool to encourage the acceleration or delay of trades.

In backtesting the power of this momentum indicator, we learned that incorporating a 1-month lag in the calculation for all sectors (other than technology) produced better results. Therefore, our calculation formula is:

$$\text{Relative Return Trend} = [\text{11-mos. return(1-mo. lag)}]_{stock}$$
$$- [\text{11-mos. return(1-mo. lag)}]_{market}$$

Both consensus earnings revisions and relative return trends guide the timing of our investment decisions, but they provide no insight into understanding concentration risk, or the risk of placing an outsized wager (overweight or underweight) against the benchmark. To understand this, we use both a factor risk model and a mean-variance optimizer. These are discussed in the remainder of this chapter.

Exhibit 11: Impact of Recent Performance Trends: 1926-1997

S&P 500 Ranked Annually by Last 12-Month Performance	Subsequent Relative Quarterly Performance (Annualized) (%)
Quintile 1 (Highest Expected Return)	+3.5
Quintile 2 (Above-Average Expected Return)	1.3
Quintile 3 (Average Expected Return)	0
Quintile 4 (Below-Average Expected Return)	−0.8
Quintile 5 (Lowest Expected Return)	−1.8

Source: Bernstein

Exhibit 12: Impact of Market Cap on Relative Returns: An Illustration

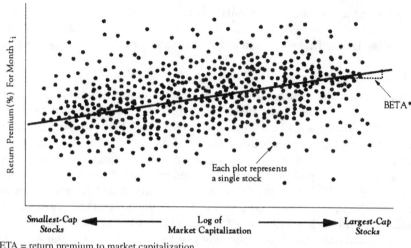

* BETA = return premium to market capitalization

IDENTIFYING RISK

Factor Risk Model

For the purposes of this discussion, we define risk as the variability of the portfolio's returns relative to the portfolio's benchmark, i.e. tracking error, measured as the standard deviation of the relative returns. We seek to accept risk only if we receive adequate additional relative return. This type of portfolio risk is an aggregation of the risks of the individual stocks, using the appropriate variance-covariance computation to reflect how those risks are altered when the stocks are placed together in the portfolio. Therefore, the risks of the individual stocks and the covariance of the stocks in the portfolio are the inputs for the total portfolio risk calculation. The key question is, then, how do you determine the risk associated with an individual stock?

One traditional method to measure stock risk was to analyze their individual historic returns relative to the benchmark and develop a very large covariance matrix of stock-pair combinations. The difficulty with this approach is that the historical data reflect the riskiness of the stocks in the past. The current business of a restructured company, for example, may have a very different risk profile today. As such, this method may not fully reflect the future variability of a stock's relative performance. In addition, new stocks have no historical data.

Factor risk models help solve these problems. Instead of trying to quantify the risk of each stock using historic performance data, these models quantify the risk of a set of factors to which each stock is exposed. The factors we use include industry sectors; stock characteristics such as market capitalization and earnings variability; and fundamental valuation measures such as book value-to-price, earnings-to-price, and dividend-to-price. Although these factors have relatively constant risks, each stock's exposure to the factors is different, and each stock's exposure may vary over time. Thus, each stock has a unique level of risk, and the risk of new stocks can be determined by measuring their exposure to the factors.

We measure factor risk by calculating the variability of the slopes of the monthly regressions of individual stock returns against the factor. For example, to determine the risk of a factor such as market capitalization, we regress the individual monthly returns of each of the S&P 500 stocks onto their capitalizations. The illustration in Exhibit 12 shows that, for the sample month selected, larger cap stocks tend to have a greater return premium than smaller cap stocks.

Regression slopes (betas) are determined for each month's returns from December 1972 through the most recent month end. The standard deviation of the monthly regression betas is the risk of the factor. In other words, if the risk of the factor is high, it reflects the historical evidence that the betas (the sensitivity of return to the factor) were highly variable over a long history (26 years) of performance data.

Once we have determined the risk of the factors, the stock's exposure to risk from a factor is simply the value of the factor for the stock. So a utility stock's exposure to the capitalization factor is simply the log of the stock's capitalization. The utility stock's exposure to the utility sector factor we define as "one," or 100%, while the same stock's exposure to all other sector factors is zero.

Covariance analyses are simplified (compared to the historical, performance risk calculation method) because we need only measure the correlation of the factors, not the correlation of the stocks in the universe. Once we establish the covariance matrix, we can determine the overall variance of a sample portfolio by combining the following elements:

1. The weights of each stock in the portfolio.
2. The *relative* exposure of each stock to the risk factors.
3. The volatility of each risk factor.
4. The correlation of the risk factors to each other.
5. The stock-specific (non-factor) residual risk.

We are now ready to bring all of the quantitative tools together in the expected return framework to build a portfolio. Our goal is to establish a means of maximizing the risk-adjusted return with a methodology that can be used to adjust the portfolio over time to maintain optimality.

Portfolio Optimization

The goal of optimization is to select stocks from a universe of stocks with the highest risk-adjusted expected returns and weight them to maximize the portfolio's utility, or risk-adjusted expected return. At Bernstein, we define utility as follows:

$$\text{Utility} = \text{Expected Reward} - \text{Expected Variance} \times \text{Risk Aversion Coefficient}$$

where the Risk Aversion Coefficient reflects the risk tolerance the investment service is seeking to maintain. A value of 0.5 reflects a desire for the fastest asset growth and maximum risk tolerance. A value of 2.5 is still very aggressive. A value of 10 is considered very conservative.

To estimate the Expected Reward component in the Utility equation, we combine the following elements in a proprietary regression model for expected return.

Expected Return = β_1(DDM Edge) + β_2(Earnings Revision Index)
+ β_3(Relative Performance Trends) + ε

where the β values reflect the best fit regression of the independent variables with the historical performance of a model portfolio (ε is a random error term). The Expected Variance term in the Utility equation is the portfolio variance as calculated by the multifactor risk model.

We maximize the portfolio's risk-adjusted return by taking the first derivative of the Utility equation with respect to each stock in our universe. The constraint that we be fully invested is the familiar "budget constraint" found in classical economic theory. The solution to such optimization problems is arrived at when the marginal values (derivatives) are equal. In the case of a new portfolio, the optimizer works in a step-wise fashion, using up cash to buy stock positions starting with the most attractive risk-adjusted stocks in the universe. The optimizer recalculates the portfolio's expected return and expected risk with each iteration before seeking the next investment idea. In the case of an ongoing portfolio, the optimizer trades off the potential benefit of a new addition to the portfolio with the cost of selling a mature investment idea. That is, the risk-adjusted expected return of the "buy" must be sufficiently attractive to overcome both a performance hurdle we impose (to reduce excessive turnover) and the transaction costs of both the "buy" and the "sell." This process continues in a step-wise fashion until no extant, unexploited opportunity remains.

Exhibit 13 presents an example of how all these tools act in concert. Suppose we were managing a pension account and needed to invest cash received from dividends. In this hypothetical example, the DDM has served up two stocks for the optimizer to evaluate. Both are attractive from a valuation perspective, with expected outperformance (DDM edge) that ranks the stocks in the top two quintiles of value. If the optimizer were to stop at this point, it would prefer Central & Southwest because of its higher edge. However, Wall Street analysts have recently cut their estimates of Central & Southwest's earnings to a significantly greater degree than Amoco, and the stock has underperformed. Negative earnings revisions are not unusual for buy candidates in the value domain; the lower penalty for Amoco suggests a stabilization of the bad earnings news that caused Amoco to rank highly in the DDM in the first place. Furthermore, the factor risk model indicates that Central & Southwest's mid-capitalization size and sector designation tend to concentrate the current portfolio along these lines. That is, the current portfolio presently holds a modest overweight in utility stocks, as well as a overweight in select mid-cap stocks. To add Central & Southwest would move the risk profile of the portfolio further away from the benchmark.

The factor risk model and the optimizer sense this and penalize Central & Southwest. Amoco, by contrast, would diversify the portfolio. When the optimizer takes these considerations into account, it judges Amoco's risk-adjusted return superior and recommends we buy Amoco. If Central & Southwest were to fall further in price and therefore offer higher expected returns, or if its relative performance trends level off, the stock could become a candidate for purchase. But not at this time. In this way, the optimizer brings all the tools together, comparing the expected return and marginal risk of the candidate stock to the current portfolio and assessing the trade based on its attractiveness in the current portfolio.

SUMMARY

If the true test of the efficacy of these tools is their performance with "live" portfolios, then we are proud to report that we have delivered a premium of 2.7% per year over the five years ending 1997, with an annualized standard deviation of the quarterly premia (tracking error) of 6.0%. The tools also satisfy the important criteria established at the beginning of this chapter: they provide a systemic way to organize a very large quantity of securities data and they provide an effective way to manage timing risk and concentration risk. They provide explicit measures of expected return and expected risk, allowing us to quality control and fine tune the process using the daily measurements the tools provide. In short, they have made us more effective and efficient, allowing us to manage the process, rather than the process manage us.

Exhibit 13: Combining Return and Risk: An Example
Risk-Adjusted Return Analysis

	Rank	Expected Outperformance	Earnings Revision	Relative Return Trend	Concentration Risk	Risk-Adjusted Return
Central & Southwest	#35	495 bp	(39) bp	(200) bp	(141) bp	115 bp
Amoco	141	232	(5)	(14)	43	256

Concentration-Risk Analysis

	Cheap Sector	Cheap Sector	Cheap Company	Earnings Variability	Cap	Dividend/ Price	Book/ Price	Earnings/ Price	Residual Risk	Concentration Risk
Central & Southwest	(81) bp	(3) bp	(6) bp	14 bp	(26) bp	(25) bp	(2) bp	(11) bp	(1) bp	(141) bp
Amoco	28	0	(5)	7	12	(2)	(1)	(4)	8	43

As of 8/8/97, Strategic Value

Chapter 8

Value-Based Equity Strategies

Gary G. Schlarbaum
Partner
Miller, Anderson & Sherrerd, LLP

INTRODUCTION

As equity investors, we have certain bedrock beliefs that guide our investment decisions. These beliefs are based on our experience, that of our predecessors, and on findings from continuing research. In fact, one of our bedrock beliefs is that careful research is a major contributor to investment success.[1] To test our long-held belief that focusing on measures of value is very important in the investment process, we measured value using price/earnings ratios (P/E's). We also looked at the importance of near-term business dynamics, as measured by earnings-estimate revisions, and how those might affect the performance of value stocks. Then we looked at a combination of the two to see how that would have worked. As it turned out, a combination of the two — a value score — worked better than either by itself.

Our research has practical application. When we construct equity portfolios, we begin by looking for stocks with low expectations — measured by low-P/E's. Second, we look for stocks that have rising expectations — measured by positive earnings-estimate revisions.[2] Third, we subject the resulting candidate stocks to rigorous fundamental analysis by our experienced analysts and portfolio managers. Finally, we build diversified portfolios — in keeping with our experience that broadly diversified value portfolios are less volatile but provide comparable excess returns. This is a continuing process. We screen our database every week in search of inexpensive stocks whose fundamentals are turning. Screening is central to our stock-selection process.

Our research focused on the 500 largest U.S. companies over the period 1977 through 1994. We formed various 100-stock portfolios and examined the

---

[1] The research reported in this chapter was conducted at Miller, Anderson & Sherrerd in the fall of 1994. It is best viewed as an extension of research that was conducted by Paul Miller and Jay Sherrerd (two of our founding partners) back in the mid-1960's — even before our firm began. This work was continued by Robert Hagin, who did extensive work on value investing in the 1980's. Our 1994 results show, as did the earlier work, that investing in value stocks gives an investor an important edge, reaffirming one of the basic principles that lie at the heart of our equity-investment process.

[2] It is, of course, preferable to detect stocks for which expectations are about to rise by thoroughly analyzing inexpensive stocks. Our analysts spend much of their time looking for such stocks.

market-relative returns of those portfolios. The market-relative return is the difference between the return on a particular portfolio and the average return on the universe. For the purpose of this research, we assumed that we rebalanced those portfolios quarterly. We developed results for portfolios of various types — equal-weighted, value-weighted, diversified, and nondiversified. The best results were obtained from equal-weighted diversified portfolios.

The results for portfolios formed using P/E ratios are reported first. Results for portfolios formed using estimate revisions and value scores are presented in the subsequent two sections. An examination of results within individual economic sectors is then presented. Finally, we look at the differences in results between diversified and nondiversified portfolios.

RETURNS FOR PORTFOLIOS
CONSTRUCTED USING P/E RATIOS

We have long believed that value is the central consideration in a sensible investment process. Although the P/E ratio is not the only possible measure of value, we believe it is the most effective. We have not undertaken a comparative evaluation of different measures of value in this study. Rather, we have focused on P/E ratios. We have found them to be a very effective tool for selecting stock portfolios over the period of the study.[3]

The effectiveness of value investing reflects the mispricing of financial assets at either end of the spectrum. Investors overvalue the prospects of the stocks they consider to be the best and undervalue the prospects of those they view as the worst. There is a tendency to project positive or negative developments of the past into the future. As a result, prices are pushed too far in the direction of recent events. Ultimately, however, there is reversion to the mean as the perceptions of investors change. The reversion to the mean can be more or less rapid, but overvalued (high-P/E) securities will tend to underperform on average, while undervalued (low-P/E) securities will, on average, deliver superior returns. The implosion of stock price when a high-multiple stock misses the consensus estimate by a penny or two in the reporting of quarterly results is a vivid example of a rapid change in perception and movement toward the mean.

The price/earnings ratios used to form portfolios for this study were based on current price and consensus estimates of earnings for the next 12 months. This choice is based on our view that the market focuses on and capitalizes earnings 12 months ahead. We did not do any tests to determine whether estimates of future earnings provide better results than trailing earnings. We consider estimates of future earnings preferable from a conceptual point of view. Furthermore, the estimates are clean and not clouded by extraordinary items.

---

[3] The findings are consistent with those developed by Paul Miller and Jay Sherrerd in the 1960's and with those obtained by various academic researchers in later years.

Exhibit 1: P/E Strategy — Using Sector-Neutral Equal-Weighted Portfolios *

	P/E Quintile	Annual Rate of Return (%)	Market-Relative Return (%)	Quarters of Outperformance
Lowest	1	17.6	3.1	46
	2	16.3	1.8	43
	3	14.0	-0.4	35
	4	12.6	-1.8	29
Highest	5	11.2	-3.3	25
Universe:		14.4		

* Period included 69 calendar quarters from the first quarter of 1977 through the third quarter of 1994.

Exhibit 2: P/E Strategy — Using Sector-Neutral Equal-Weighted Portfolios

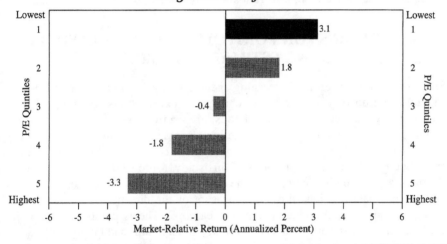

Absolute returns, market-relative returns, and a count of the number of the quarters of outperformance are shown for five portfolios in Exhibit 1. The market-relative returns are depicted in Exhibit 2 as well. The results for the lowest-P/E portfolio are shown on the top line of the table, those for the second-lowest-P/E portfolio are shown on the second line, etc. The bars in Exhibit 2 are shown in the same order.

The results included in Exhibits 1 and 2 are for equal-weighted, sector-neutral portfolios. The portfolios were formed in two steps. First, the stocks were grouped into 12 economic sectors. Then the lowest quintile of P/E's from each sector was selected for inclusion in the low-P/E portfolio. The same procedure with the appropriate quintiles was used to form the rest of the portfolios. The returns, then, are those of very well diversified value-based portfolios. (A comparison of the results for diversified and nondiversified portfolios is contained in a later section of this chapter.)

We found that, over this period, being sector neutral and picking the lowest-P/E portfolio from each economic sector led to 3.1% a year additional return relative to the 14.4% return for the universe. In contrast, the high-P/E portfolio had an annual return of 3.3% below that of the universe. Moreover, the low-P/E portfolio outperformed in 46 out of 69 quarters included in the study while the high-P/E portfolio outperformed in only 25 of the quarters. In other words, the low-P/E portfolio outperformed two thirds of the time, and the high-P/E portfolio underperformed about two thirds of the time.

The results reported in this section are consistent with our belief that value is the central consideration in a well designed investment process. P/E ratios were very effective tools for selecting stocks over the period studied here. Concentrating on low-P/E stocks and avoiding high-P/E stocks provided an important advantage for investors. We believe that focus on stocks with low expectations as measured by P/E ratios will continue to provide an advantage.

RETURNS FOR PORTFOLIOS CONSTRUCTED USING ESTIMATE REVISIONS

Stock prices are driven by the earnings generated by the underlying businesses. The question posed here is whether changes in expectations about earnings, as measured by analysts' estimate revisions, are useful in selecting a portfolio of common stocks.[4] Estimate revisions are important as representations of the near-term business dynamics of the companies being considered. We used 3-month smoothed revisions for the purposes of this study. More weighting is assigned to the most recent month in computing the estimate revision used for ranking stocks.

Estimate revisions provide a measure of the direction and magnitude of change in expectations about a company's earnings. The assumption is that rising expectations are associated with above-average stock returns and falling expectations are associated with below-average returns. Revisions tend to be positively serially correlated. Positive revisions tend to be followed by positive revisions, and negative revisions tend to be followed by negative revisions. It is difficult for analysts to judge how far a positive or negative trend may go once it has begun. Recent academic studies have shown that investors and analysts tend to respond sluggishly to new information (i.e., that markets are not totally efficient). Analysts react slowly to a change in the direction of the underlying fundamentals because of a natural unwillingness to believe the change. These studies opine that the effect may be stronger on the downside because of the reluctance of analysts to make negative comments about companies with which they have investment-banking relationships. As a result, the analysts issue frequent, minor revisions instead of marking their estimates down all at once.

---

[4] I/B/E/S collects the earnings estimates of analysts and, in addition to reporting them, aggregates the estimates into summary measures such as the mean and median. A revision is a change in the mean estimate for a company. Changes for the three most recent months are combined to obtain the measure of estimate revisions used here.

Exhibit 3: Estimate-Revision Strategy — Using Sector-Neutral Equal-Weighted Portfolios*

	Estimate-Revision Quintile	Annual Rate of Return (%)	Market-Relative Return (%)	Quarters of Outperformance
Best	1	18.6	4.2	51
	2	15.8	1.4	39
	3	14.7	0.3	36
	4	11.9	−2.5	28
Worst	5	10.2	−4.3	23
Universe:		14.4		

* Period included 69 calendar quarters from the first quarter of 1977 through the third quarter of 1994.

There is also a strong relationship between estimate revisions and earnings surprises.[5] Positive estimate revisions are frequently followed by a positive earnings surprise. The positive earnings surprise will often be followed by subsequent positive estimate revisions. There is a kind of virtuous cycle when the fundamentals of a company are improving. Of course, the opposite is true when the underlying fundamentals are deteriorating. Disappointing earnings lead to negative revisions, which are followed by more disappointments, and so on.

We again formed five portfolios of 100 stocks each to ascertain the relationship between returns and estimate revisions. The stocks were grouped into 12 economic sectors. Then the stocks were divided into quintiles within the sectors on the basis of estimate revisions. The stocks from the highest quintile within each economic sector formed the first portfolio. The same procedures with the appropriate quintiles were used to form the rest of the portfolios.

Absolute returns, market-relative returns, and a count of the number of quarters of outperformance are shown for the five portfolios in Exhibit 3. Market-relative returns are also shown in Exhibit 4. The results for the best-revision portfolio are shown in the top line of the table, those for the second-best-revision portfolio are shown in the second line, and so on. The bars in Exhibit 4 are shown in the same order.

The sector-neutral portfolios with the best-revision stocks provided an extra 4.2% a year relative to the 14.4% return for the universe. The worst-revision portfolio, on the other hand, underperformed the universe by 4.3%. The returns were perfectly rank ordered by the revisions. Moreover, the best-revision portfolio outperformed the universe in 51 out of 69 quarters — nearly 75% of the time. Meanwhile, the worst-revision portfolio was nearly as consistent, trailing in 46 of 69 quarters.

These results show the strong relationship between near-term business dynamics and equity returns. The results are consistent and powerful. (We should note that the extra returns based on near-term business dynamics are harder to capture than those based on measures of value because of the greater trading

---

[5] An earnings surprise is the difference between the actual quarterly earnings of a company and the consensus estimate at the time of the report.

activity required.) It is clear that the direction of expectations is a powerful influence on stock performance.

We saw in the previous section that portfolios of low-expectation stocks outperform. This section demonstrated that portfolios of stocks with rising expectations also outperform.

RETURNS FOR PORTFOLIOS
CONSTRUCTED USING VALUE SCORES

We have demonstrated in the previous two sections that both value as measured by P/E and fundamental business dynamics as measured by estimate revisions are effective as portfolio selectors. Stocks with low expectations, on average, outperform the market. Stocks with high expectations lag. Stocks with rising expectations, on average, outperform the market. Stocks with falling expectations lag. Seemingly a combination of good value and positive dynamics would be more powerful than either by itself in forming a portfolio. The question addressed in this section is whether this is in fact the case.

Each stock in the universe of the largest 500 stocks was assigned a percentile ranking based on P/E and a percentile ranking based on estimate revision. A value score was then computed for each stock by determining a weighted average of the percentile rankings. We assigned 70% of the weight to P/E and 30% to estimate revision. This was the only set of weightings that we tried. In fact, other combinations are undoubtedly very effective as well; investors with a stronger growth orientation might well choose to place more weight on estimate revisions.

Exhibit 4: Estimate Revision Strategy — Using Sector-Neutral Equal-Weighted Portfolios

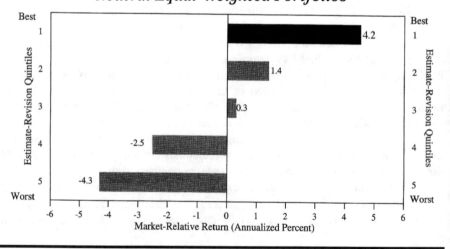

Exhibit 5: Value Score Strategy — Using Sector-Neutral Equal-Weighted Portfolios*

	Value Score Quintile	Annual Rate of Return (%)	Market-Relative Return (%)	Quarters of Outperformance
Best	1	19.0	4.6	49
	2	16.3	1.9	45
	3	14.5	0.0	34
	4	12.8	-1.6	25
Worst	5	9.0	-5.4	14
Universe:		14.4		

* Period included 69 calendar quarters from the first quarter of 1977 through the third quarter of 1994.

Exhibit 6: Value Score Strategy — Using Sector-Neutral Equal-Weighted Portfolios

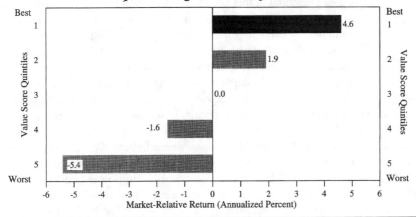

We again formed five portfolios of 100 stocks each to discern the relationship between returns and value scores (combinations of P/E and estimate revisions). Stocks were divided among 12 economic sectors and ordered from high to low on the basis of the value scores. Those with the best (highest) value scores were assigned to the first portfolio, and those with the worst (lowest) value scores were assigned to the fifth portfolio. Equal weightings were used in forming the portfolios. The results shown below are, as a result, for equal-weighted sector-neutral portfolios.

Absolute returns, market-relative returns, and a count of the number of quarters of outperformance are shown for the five portfolios in Exhibit 5. Market-relative returns are shown again in Exhibit 6. The results for the best-value-score portfolio are shown in the top line of Exhibit 5. Those for the second-best-value-score portfolio are shown in the second line, and so on. The bars in Exhibit 6 are shown in the same order. The sector-neutral portfolio of stocks with the best value scores earned an extra 4.6% a year relative to the universe. The sector-neutral portfolio of the lowest-value-score stocks lagged the universe by 5.4%. The portfolio returns were perfectly rank-ordered. The best-value-score portfolio consistently outperformed the universe; the count was 49 out of 69 quarters, more than 70% of the time. The worst-value-score portfolio was even more consistent, lagging in 55 of 69 quarters.

A comparison of the results included in this section with those in the previous two reveals that the value score is a better selector than either P/E or estimate revision. The top-quintile portfolio's relative return was more than one and a half percent higher than that of the top-quintile-P/E portfolio and moderately higher than that of the top-quintile-estimate-revision portfolio. At the opposite end of the spectrum, the bottom-quintile-value-score portfolio lagged the universe by 5.4%, whereas the bottom-quintile-estimate-revision portfolio trailed by 4.3% and the worst-quintile-P/E portfolio by 3.3%. The advantage of the value score is most pronounced at the least attractive end of the range. Simply avoiding stocks in the fifth quintile of the value scores should significantly enhance performance. The comparisons of top- and bottom-quintile performance for the three selectors is shown in Exhibit 7.

The results presented in this section (and the previous sections) do not take trading costs into account. The impact of trading costs is to mitigate the positive excess returns obtained by investing in the most attractive stocks. The question is by how much. The answer depends on both the cost of trading and the amount of portfolio turnover required to be continuously invested in the more attractive stocks.

The cost of trading will depend on trading skills and on the kind of stock deemed attractive by the selector. It is reasonable to presume that both turnover and trading costs would be higher for an approach based on estimate revisions than for one based on P/E ratios. It is also reasonable to conclude that the value-score approach combining the two would fall somewhere in between. As long as the last statement is true, the value-score approach will be better than an approach based on revisions alone because of the superior discrimination power and lower trading costs of the value-score system. The value-score approach would be superior to one based on P/E ratios unless the turnover were much higher for the former.

Exhibit 7: Performance Comparisons Using Three Strategies

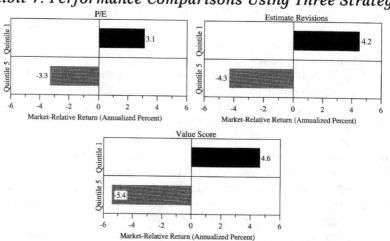

Exhibit 8: Quarterly Turnover Using the Value Score

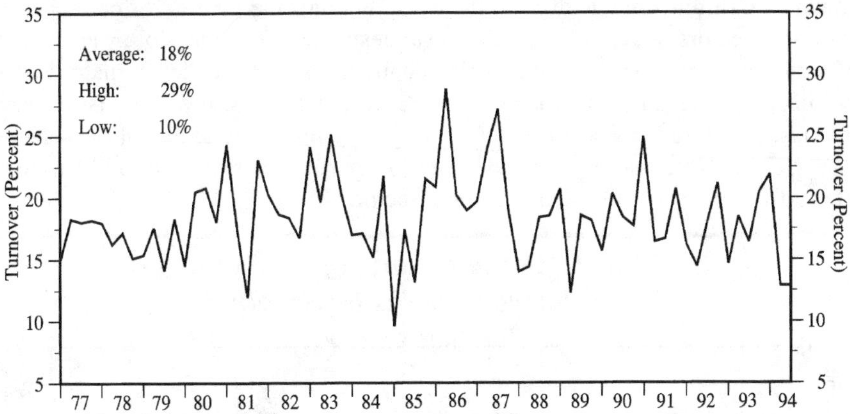

We have examined turnover percentages for the value-score approach for the entire period of our study. Quarterly turnover percentages for a strategy that involved buying quintile-one stocks and holding them until they became quintile-three stocks are shown in Exhibit 8. Using the value-score, the average quarterly turnover was 18%. The highest turnover for any quarter was 29%, and the lowest was 10%. The average of 18% implies an annual turnover of 72%. This is not an extraordinarily high turnover ratio for an active manager. And the strategy should allow the investor to capture a combination of quintile-one and quintile-two returns with an emphasis on the quintile-one stocks.

The turnover ratio for the low-P/E approach was 12% — implying a 48% annual turnover. Assuming that transaction costs amount to two percent for a round trip, the difference in turnover ratios between the value-score approach and the low-P/E approach reduces the advantage of the value-score approach by 48 basis points — just about one half of 1%. This reduces the advantage from approximately 1.5% to 1.0% for first-quintile stocks. Nonetheless, the value-score approach retains a significant advantage. And it retains that advantage so long as round-trip costs are 6% or less.

COMPARISON OF SELECTION STRATEGIES ON A SECTOR-BY-SECTOR BASIS

This section focuses on how well the three selectors considered in this study — P/E ratio, estimate revision, and value score (a combination of P/E's and revisions) — work within each of the 12 economic sectors employed in the study. Previous results cause us to expect that the value score will work most effectively in most sectors. However, there is no reason to believe that the same selector will work best in every sector. Furthermore, there is no reason for an investor to use the same approach in every sector of the stock market.

The within-sector relative returns for all quintiles for each selection are shown in Exhibit 9. Each chart in the exhibit shows the results for one of the 12 economic sectors. Review of the charts suggests that the value score was the most effective selector in eight of the twelve economic sectors while estimate revision was best in three and P/E was best in one. In most cases, the conclusions seem obvious, but there are several sectors in which performance of two of the selectors is very close. Note that the vertical scales in Chart 6 were selected to illustrate the return differences within each economic sector.

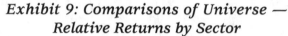

Exhibit 9: Comparisons of Universe — Relative Returns by Sector

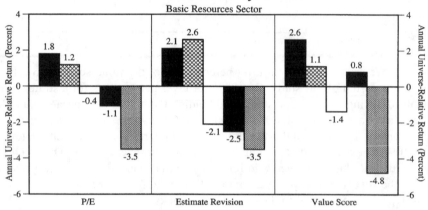

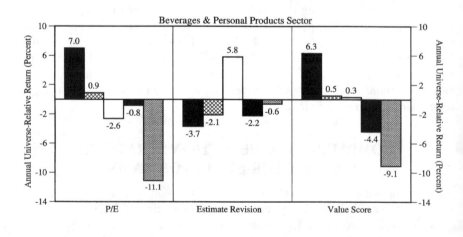

Exhibit 9: (Continued)

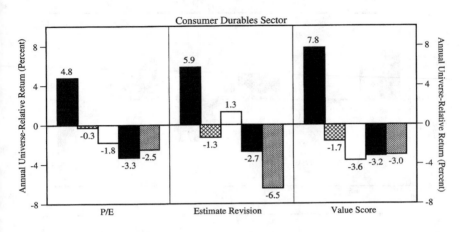

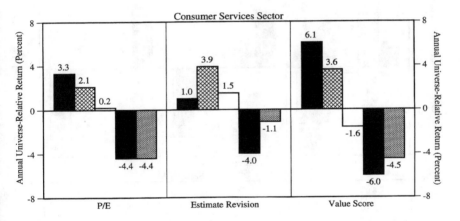

Exhibit 9: (Continued)

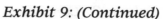

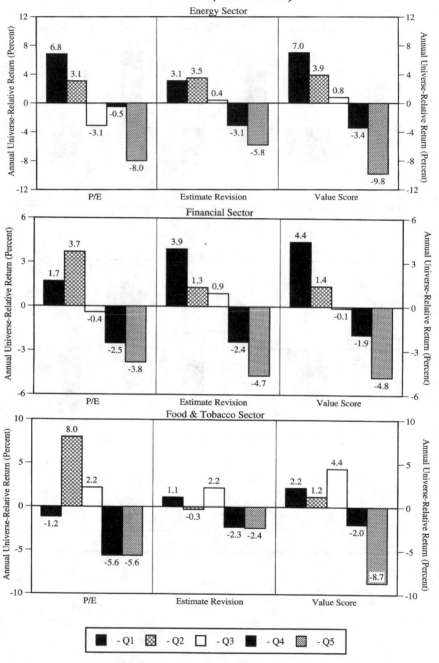

Exhibit 9: (Continued)

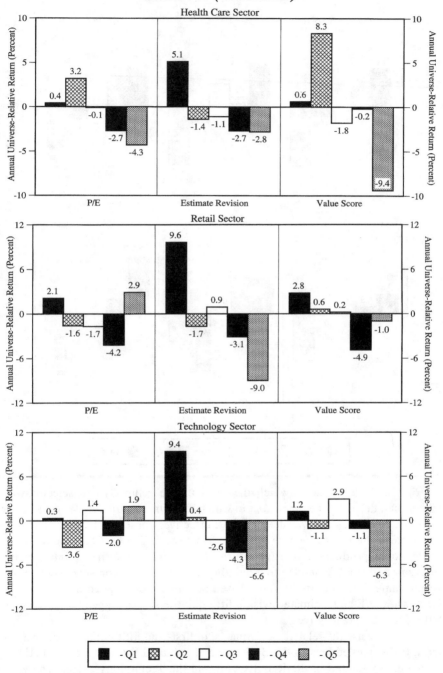

Exhibit 9: (Continued)

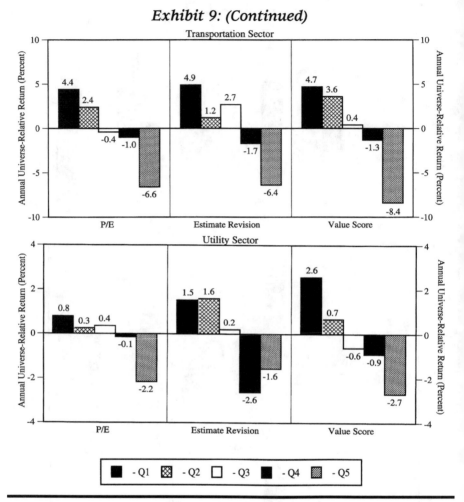

In those cases in which the first-quintile returns for a selector were higher than those for the others *and* in which the fifth-quintile returns were lower, the selector in question was deemed most effective. For example, the value score was clearly the most effective in the energy sector. The first quintile of value-score stocks produced a relative return of 7.0% while the first quintile of P/E stocks provided 6.8% and the first quintile of estimate-revision stocks only 3.4%. At the same time, the fifth quintile based on value score lagged the universe by 9.8% while P/E and estimate-revision fifth-quintile stocks lagged the universe by 8.0% and 5.8%, respectively.

If we use the relative performance of first- and fifth-quintile stocks as criteria, P/E's worked best in the Beverage and Personal Products sector. Estimate revisions dominated in the Retail sector and the Technology sector. The value score was clearly most effective in Basic Resources, Consumer Services, Energy, Financials, Food and Tobacco, Transportation, and Utilities sectors. The Consumer Durables sector yielded mixed results; the value score was most effective on the upside, but revisions were relatively close on the upside and clearly were most effective in identifying laggards. On balance, we conclude that estimate revisions are most effective. The other controversial sector is Health Care. Estimate revisions best identified superior performers. But the value score was clearly dominant in identifying laggards. This fact — and the good performance of the first two quintiles based on value score — led to the conclusion that the value score is most effective.

Caution is warranted in interpreting the results contained in this section of the chapter. Too much weight should not be placed on empirical results for a specific period of time. One could argue, for example, that value scores should be used in all sectors because of their conceptual soundness and the power of the overall cross-sectional results. We have, in fact, chosen to sort stocks into quintiles by value score in 10 of the 12 sectors in our continuing analytical work on the stock market. Nonetheless, we do place more emphasis on estimate revisions in the Retail and Technology Sectors. The empirical results supporting this decision are very strong, as shown above.

Moreover, there are sound conceptual reasons for believing that near-term business dynamics will dominate in determining the winners and losers in the Retail and Technology sectors. Value is elusive in both cases. Take Technology, for example. The rate of change and obsolescence in Technology is very rapid. Once a product is obsolete, the equipment used to produce it has little, if any, value. As a result, stocks in the technology sector that appear cheap are not necessarily inexpensive at all. Often the companies are simply in a declining stage, and the usual measures of value provide no help in determining where stock prices might go. In Retail, too, it is not so much the value of the fixtures and physical space as the concept that counts. When a concept is working, the fundamentals move in a positive direction. When it is not, a decline in price and an apparently attractive measure of value do not mean that the stock is likely to do well in the future. Rather, when a concept is not working, the fundamentals move in a negative direction; that is the signal to avoid the stock.

DIVERSIFIED VERSUS
NONDIVERSIFIED PORTFOLIOS

Throughout this chapter, we have presented returns from diversified portfolios. The purpose of this section is to compare the returns and risks of *diversified* portfolios and *nondiversified* portfolios. Each portfolio contains 100 securities. Diversified portfolios, are those that are spread across economic sectors so that the weighting of each economic sector in the portfolio is the same as the weighting of the sector in the universe. These portfolios are "sector-neutral." For example, the low-P/E diversified portfolio includes the low-P/E quintile of stocks *from each economic sector.*

Nondiversified portfolios are formed without regard to economic sector membership. The low-P/E, nondiversified portfolio contains the 100 stocks with the lowest P/E ratios in the whole universe. This low-P/E portfolio would typically have a larger weight in banks and utilities than the universe.

The focus of our attention is always the best portfolio — the top-quintile portfolio. We examined returns and risks for the best diversified and the best nondiversified portfolio in every instance. We found that diversified portfolios provided higher relative returns on average, and, at the same time, protected the investor on the downside in those instances in which the returns from the best portfolios lagged those of the universe. This was true regardless of the selector used in forming the portfolios.

The average relative returns and the worst annual relative return for diversified and nondiversified portfolios are shown in Exhibits 10, 11, and 12. Exhibit 10 shows the results for portfolios based on P/E ratios; Exhibit 11 shows the results for estimate revisions; and Exhibit 12 shows the results for the value score. The average relative return was always higher for the diversified portfolios' and it was nearly one percent higher in the case of the value-score portfolios. Similarly, the worst annual return was always lower for nondiversified portfolios than for diversified portfolios. The difference was not large in the case of the estimate-revision portfolios. But it was dramatic for the low-P/E portfolios and the value-score portfolios; in each case the difference was over 16%.

The results reported in this section suggest that a diversified value approach is preferable to one that is highly concentrated. Diversifying across economic sectors does not reduce the extra returns provided by value portfolios. In fact, over the period of this study, diversification actually enhanced returns. More importantly, diversified portfolios provided significant protection against years of dramatic underperformance.[6] Clients may question their commitment to value investing after a year in which their portfolio trailed the universe by 1,000 basis points. It is easier to maintain their commitment after a year in which performance lagged by 100 to 200 basis points.

---

[6] We believe that broad diversification is desirable much of the time. Furthermore, we believe that systematic approaches must work within sectors to be effective overall. Nonetheless, these results do not imply that it is not possible to add value through making sector overweighting and underweighting decisions. In fact, our own experience has shown that it is possible to augment returns through sector-weighting decisions. Our results suggest that either (1) other tools are more valuable for making sector decisions than the selectors used to pick stocks within sectors here or (2) there were few opportunities to add value through sector selection over the time period of the study because sectors were fairly priced relative to one another most of the time. There is probably a degree of truth in both of these possibilities.

Exhibit 10: Lowest P/E Strategy

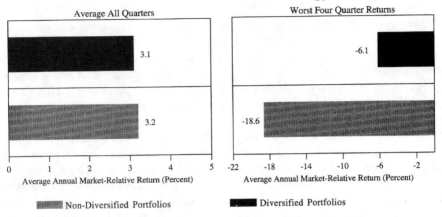

Exhibit 11: Highest Estimate-Revision Strategy

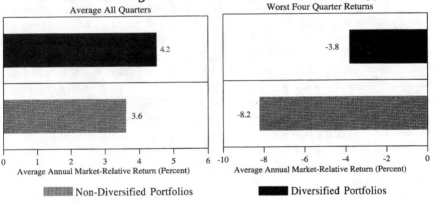

Exhibit 12: Highest Value-Score Strategy

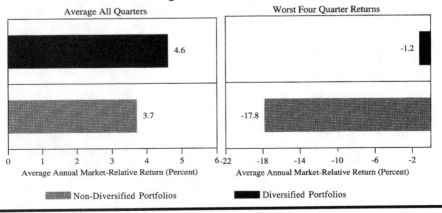

CONCLUSION

The research reported here has confirmed the bedrock beliefs upon which we construct equity portfolios. We have once again found that value investing leads to higher returns. We have shown that a value approach can be enhanced by judicious use of a measure of the underlying business's dynamics. We have further shown that a diversified approach to value investing is particularly effective at controlling portfolio risk — while not detracting from the benefit of the value-only approach.

Hence, when we build equity portfolios, we begin by looking for stocks with low expectations — measured by low-P/E's. Second, we look for stocks that have rising expectations — measured by positive earnings-estimate revisions. Third, we subject the resulting candidate stocks to rigorous fundamental analysis by our experienced analysts and portfolio managers. Finally, we build diversified portfolios — in keeping with our research findings that broadly diversified value portfolios are less volatile but provide comparable excess returns.

Our approach employs a systematic component wherein stocks are ranked within each economic sector according to our value score. The stocks are sorted into quintiles. Each economic-sector portfolio is the responsibility of a portfolio manager who devotes his research time and the research resources of his team to investigating those stocks ranked highest within the sector. Stocks within the first two quintiles are selected for the portfolios. Fourth- and fifth-quintile stocks are eliminated. In the end, we believe, the systematic elements of our approach, combined with the judgment of our experienced portfolio managers, constitute a very attractive approach to managing large equity portfolios.

We believe that a focused approach to stock selection built around this effective ranking system will produce superior investment results over the long haul.

Chapter 9

Equity Analysis Using Value-Based Metrics

James A. Abate, CPA, CFA
Senior Vice President, Portfolio Manager
BEA Associates

Frank J. Fabozzi, Ph.D., CFA
Adjunct Professor of Finance
School of Management
Yale University

James L. Grant, Ph.D.
Professor of Finance
Graduate School of Management
Simmons College

INTRODUCTION

Value-based metrics of corporate financial success such as *economic value added* and *cash flow return on investment* are now making significant inroads into the realm of equity analysis.[1] These metrics are also paving the way for a "modern" school of equity fundamental analysis that departs from the traditional method, with its prior focus on accounting-based measures like earnings per share and return on equity.

Although competing measures exist, value-based metrics emphasize the importance of giving *shareholders* their due. The theory behind these measures of corporate financial success is quite simple and compelling: when investors contribute moneys to a firm, they expect to earn a return on those contributed funds which is commensurate with the risk. The firm's managers are thereby charged to invest in real assets (both physical and human) having a return on invested capital that exceeds the overall cost of capital. In this chapter we discuss the two main value-based metrics (economic value-added and cash flow return on investment), the issues

---

[1] EVA® is a registered trademark of Stern Stewart & Co. For an insightful discussion of their commercial economic profit measure along with many applications of how this metric can be used in a corporate finance setting, see G. Bennett Stewart III, *The Quest for Value* (New York: Harper Collins, 1991). CFROI is the investment and financial advisory product of Holt Value Associates, LP, and the Boston Consulting Group (BCG), respectively.

associated with measuring these metrics, and the application of a value-based metric to equity analysis and construction by one asset management firm (BEA Associates).

THE EVA MEASURE OF CORPORATE SUCCESS

Perhaps the best known value-based metric among today's corporate and investment players is a measure called EVA® — for Economic Value Added.[2] Hatched commercially in 1982 by Joel Stern and G. Bennett Stewart, this economic profit measure gained early acceptance among the corporate financial community because of its innovative way of looking at profitability *net* of the dollar weighted cost of debt *and* equity capital. Indeed, many firms — including corporate giants like AT&T and Coca-Cola — have used EVA to design incentive payment schemes that lead managers to make wealth-enhancing investment decisions in the interest of shareholders.

EVA is also gaining popularity in the investment community. Introduced most notably by CS First Boston a few years ago, it is now also being spearheaded by renowned equity strategists like Abby Joseph Cohen and Stephen Einhorn throughout the U.S. Equity Research Group at Goldman Sachs where EVA is used to evaluate the performance potential of many sectors of the economy. On the investment management side, the active equity team at BEA Associates uses real economic profit concepts to manage investment portfolios. We will discuss BEA Associates' approach at the end of this chapter.[3]

The financial significance of using a value-based metric like EVA from a corporate valuation perspective is crystal clear. As explained (and demonstrated empirically) by one of the authors, wealth-creating firms have positive EVA because their expected net after-tax operating profit exceeds the dollar weighted average cost of debt and equity capital.[4] On the other hand, wealth wasters lose market value *and* incur share price declines because their corporate profitability falls short of their overall capital costs. This wealth loss can occur even though the firm's profitability is sufficiently high enough to cover its cost of debt financing. Moreover, it shows how to select individual companies and industries by examining the quantitative relationship between the NPV-to-Capital and EVA-to-Capital ratios in the marketplace.

---

[2] Stern-Stewart's financial metric is a practitioner's tool for measuring the firm's economic profit or economic value added. Stewart-Stern refers to the present value equivalent of this profit measure as the firm's *market value added* (MVA).

[3] A growing number of investment firms now look at companies, industries and/or the macro-economy in an economic profit context. For examples, see Al Jackson, Michael J. Mauboussin, and Charles R. Wolf, "EVA Primer," *Equity-Research Americas* (CS First Boston: February 20, 1996); Steven G. Einhorn, Gabrielle Napolitano, and Abby Joseph Cohen, "EVA: A Primer," *U.S. Research* (Goldman Sachs, September 10, 1997); and, James A. Abate, "Select Economic Value Portfolios," *U.S. Equity Product Overview* (BEA Associates, January 1998). BEA Associates, a member of Credit Suisse Asset Management, is a multi-product global asset management firm. This chapter's discussion covers BEA's U.S. Active Equity Group.

[4] James L. Grant, *Foundations of Economic Value Added* (New Hope, PA: Frank J. Fabozzi Associates, 1997).

The Basic EVA Formulation

Central to the EVA (and therefore, NPV) calculation is the distinction between levered and unlevered firms.[5] A *levered* firm, like most real-world firms, is one that partly finances its growth with long-term debt. In contrast, equivalent business-risk *unlevered* firms are, in principle, 100% equity financed. This firm-type classification is helpful because EVA is calculated by subtracting the firm's dollar weighted average cost of debt *and* equity financing from its *unlevered* net operating profit after tax, UNOPAT.

$$EVA = UNOPAT - \$COC$$

UNOPAT is used in the EVA formulation for two reasons. First, emphasis on this unlevered term serves as a modern-day reminder that the firm largely receives its profitability from the desirability (or lack thereof) of its overall products and services. Second, since most firms have some form of debt outstanding, they receive a yearly interest tax subsidy — measured by the corporate tax rate times the firm's interest expense — that is already reflected in the dollar cost of capital ($COC) calculation.

This latter distinction is important. An incorrect focus by corporate managers on the levered firm's net operating profit after taxes, LNOPAT, rather than its equivalent business risk profit measure, UNOPAT, would lead to an *upward* bias in the firm's reported economic value added. By avoiding the "double counting" of the firm's yearly debt-interest tax subsidy, an equity analyst avoids imparting a *positive* bias in not only the firm's real corporate profitability but also its overall corporate valuation and underlying stock price.

In simple terms, the firm's unlevered net operating profit after tax, UNOPAT, can be expressed in terms of its tax-adjusted earnings before interest and taxes, EBIT, according to:[6]

$$UNOPAT = EBIT \times (1 - t)$$
$$= [S - CGS - SGA - D] \times (1 - t)$$

---

[5] The concept of levered and unlevered firms is central to the development of the Modigliani-Miller principles of corporation finance. These firm-type classifications were also used extensively by Eugene F. Fama and Merton H. Miller in their pioneering book, *The Theory of Finance* (New York: Holt, Rinehart, and Winston, 1972).

[6] The UNOPAT simplification shown in the text omits the depreciation tax subsidy received by the unlevered firm. In principle, UNOPAT can be expressed as:

$$UNOPAT = EBITD(1 - t) + tD$$
$$= EBIT(1 - t) + D$$

For a formal discussion of the unlevered firm's net operating cash flow, UNOPAT, see Grant, *Foundations of Economic Value Added.*

A basic discussion of the EVA model is also provided by Thomas P. Jones, "The Economic Value Added Approach to Corporate Investment," in *Corporate Financial Decision Making and Equity Analysis* (Charlottesville, VA: AIMR, The Research Foundation of the ICFA, 1995).

where, in the first expression, EBIT $\times (1 - t)$ is the unlevered firm's net operating profit after tax. This profit term is a reflection of the firm's earnings before interest and taxes, EBIT, less its *unlevered* corporate taxes; namely, EBIT less t times EBIT. Likewise, the terms, S, CGS, and SGA in the UNOPAT specification refer to the firm's sales, cost of goods sold, and selling, general and administrative expenses, respectively. In principle, the depreciation term, D, should be a charge that reflects the *economic* obsolescence of the firm's assets.

In turn, the firm's *dollar* cost of capital, $COC, can be expressed as:

$$\$COC = [COC\%/100] \times TC$$

where %COC is its weighted-average percentage cost of debt *and* equity capital, while TC is the firm's total operating capital. The weighted capital cost percentage, %COC, is given by:

$$\%COC = \% \text{ After-tax Debt Cost} \times \text{Debt Weight}$$
$$+ \% \text{ Equity Cost} \times \text{Equity Weight}$$

Taken together, these financial developments show that the firm's "economic value added" for any given year can be expressed as:

$$EVA = UNOPAT - \$COC$$
$$= EBIT \times (1 - t) - COC \times TC$$
$$= [S - CGS - SGA - D] \times (1 - t) - COC \times TC$$

This expression shows that the firm's EVA is equal to its *unlevered* net operating profit after tax less the dollar cost of all capital employed in the firm.[7]

EVA Measurement Challenges

A value-based metric like EVA differs from a traditional measure of profit such as accounting net income. However, the economic profit calculation is not simple in practice. This is sometimes missed by EVA proponents. Specifically, Goldman Sachs U.S. Equity Research Group and David Young of INSEAD point out that there are some 160 accounting adjustments that can be made to a firm's accounting statements to convert them to a *value-based* format emphasizing cash operating profit and asset replacement cost considerations.[8] Many of the potential adjustments can have a material impact on the analyst's estimate of a company's after-tax return on capital through their *joint* impact on the firm's unlevered net operating profit after tax and the dollar-based capital estimate. Additionally, there are significant empirical anomalies and academic issues involved when estimating the firm's weighted average cost of debt *and* equity capital.

Additionally, the firm's after-tax return on capital (ROC) is calculated by dividing its *unlevered* net operating profit after tax by the *economic* capital

---

[7] For an illustration of these concepts using a simple income statement and balance sheet, see Frank J. Fabozzi and James Grant, *Equity Management* (New Hope, PA: Frank J. Fabozzi Associates, 1998).

[8] See Einhorn, Napolitano, and Cohen, "EVA: A Primer," and S. David Young's graduate school teaching note, "Economic Value Added," INSEAD, Fontainebleau, France, 1998.

employed in the business. In practice, however, there are numerous accounting items that *jointly* impact the numerator and the denominator of the ROC ratio. These potential distortions arise from the accounting-versus-economic treatment of depreciation, intangibles (including research and development expenditures and goodwill arising from corporate acquisitions), deferred taxes, and inventory and other reserves. Such measurement issues are important because they impact the analyst's estimate of cash operating profit in the numerator of the after-tax return on capital ratio (e.g., profit impact of accounting depreciation versus economic obsolescence) and the economic capital estimate used in the denominator (e.g., impact of net fixed assets on the balance sheet versus economic replacement cost of assets).[9]

Estimating UNOPAT in Practice

The major EVA players — including CS First Boston and Goldman Sachs on the Wall Street research side, BEA Associates on the investment management side, and Stern Stewart & Co. on the corporate advisory side — have narrowed the list of accounting adjustments to a firm's financial statements. In this context, Exhibit 1 shows Stern Stewart's "bottom up" and "top down" income statement approaches to calculating a firm's unlevered net operating profit after tax while Exhibit 2 shows how capital can be estimated in practice with some key balance sheet adjustments based on the equivalent "asset approach" and "financing sources of assets" approaches to measuring the firm's economic capital.[10]

The Stern Stewart Approach In Stern Stewart's "bottom up" approach to estimating UNOPAT, the equity analyst begins with a firm's operating profit after depreciation and amortization. Accounting items that get added back to this figure include the increase in LIFO reserve, goodwill amortization, and the change in *net* capitalized research and development. Two other accounting figures that are shown in Exhibit 1 include the *implied* interest expense on operating leases as well as the increase in bad-debt reserve.

The rise in LIFO reserve is added back to the firm's accounting-based operating profit to give the analyst a better gauge of the actual cost of inventory units used to manufacture the firm's product. In a period of rising prices (inflation), LIFO inventory cost understates corporate profit due to the higher cost of goods sold figure resulting from inventory costing (last in, first out) of newly produced product at near-to-current market prices. Coincidentally, current assets on the firm's balance sheet are understated due to an *incorrect* assumption about the replacement cost of inventory — namely, those units still in inventory having an assumed purchase cost based on the initial inventory units.

---

[9] Goldman Sachs and Stern Stewart do not make any explicit cash adjustments to accounting depreciation on the income statement and (therefore) accumulated depreciation on the balance sheet. This approach to handling accounting depreciation seems at odds with the long established view that managers can manipulate earnings by the judicious use of accounting depreciation policies.

[10] Numerous EVA-based accounting adjustments can be found in Stewart, *The Quest for Value*. The distinction between *levered* and *unlevered* firms in an economic profit context is emphasized by Grant, *Foundations of Economic Value Added*.

Exhibit 1: Calculation of NOPAT from Financial Statement Data

A. Bottom-up approach
Begin:
    Operating profit after depreciation and amortization
Add:
    Implied interest expense on operating leases
    Increase in LIFO reserve
    Goodwill amortization
    Increase in bad-debt reserve
    Increase in net capitalized research and development
Equals:
    Adjusted operating profit before taxes
Subtract:
    Cash operating taxes
Equals:
    NOPAT

B. Top-down approach
Begin:
    Sales
Add:
    Increase in LIFO reserve
    Implied interest expense on operating leases
    Other income
Subtract:
    Cost of goods sold
    Selling, general, and administrative expenses
    Depreciation
Equals:
    Adjusted operating profit before taxes
Subtract:
    Cash operating taxes
Equals:
    NOPAT

Note: Exhibit based on information in G. Bennett Stewart III, *The Quest for Value* (New York: Harper Collins, 1991).

Also, the goodwill amortization on the income statement is added back to the operating profit because the companion accumulated figure on the firm's balance sheet — arising from patents, copyrights, internal software, and even corporate acquisitions (price paid for target firm in excess of underlying value of target's *physical* assets) — is viewed as a form of economic capital or asset investment. Since research and development are also viewed as capital investment, the value-based convention is to "capitalize" it on the balance sheet while slowly writing it off over an extended period of time (typically 40 years) on the income statement — rather than "expense" all R&D expenditures in the year incurred. With these adjustments, the analyst arrives at UNOPAT by subtracting "cash taxes" from the firm's estimated pretax cash operating profit. In practice, this means that the accrual-based "income tax expense" item on the income statement needs to be increased by (1) the interest tax subsidy on debt (as well as debt equivalents like leases), and (2) the tax on the firm's *non*-recurring income sources.

Exhibit 2: Calculation of Capital Using Accounting Financial Statements

A. Asset approach

Begin:

　　Net operating assets

Add:

　　LIFO reserve
　　Net plant and equipment
　　Other assets
　　Goodwill
　　Accumulated goodwill amortization
　　Present value of operating leases
　　Bad-debt reserve
　　Capitalized research and development
　　Cumulative write-offs of special items

Equals:

　　Capital

B. Source of financing approach

Begin:

　　Book value of common equity

Add equity equivalents:

　　Preferred stock
　　Minority interest
　　Deferred income tax reserve
　　LIFO reserve
　　Accumulated goodwill amortization

Add debt and debt equivalents:

　　Interest-bearing short-term debt
　　Long-term debt
　　Capitalized lease obligations
　　Present value of noncapitalized leases

Equals:

　　Capital

Note: Exhibit based on information in G. Bennett Stewart III, *The Quest for Value* (New York: Harper Collins, 1991).

Exhibit 1 shows Stern Stewart's "top down" approach to estimating the firm's unlevered net operating profit after tax. As shown here, the analyst begins with sales (revenue), then subtracts the usual operating expenses such as cost of goods sold and selling, general, and administrative expenses. The LIFO reserve is added to the revenue figure, while accounting depreciation (in the Stern Stewart approach) is subtracted on the path to UNOPAT. Since the benefits of corporate debt financing (if any) are already reflected in the dollar cost of capital, $COC, the cash tax figure should be based on the marginal tax rate paid by the unlevered firm. A rigorous application of Stewart's approach to adjusting the firm's accounting operating profit to a cash operating profit figure for the EVA calculation is shown in an Association for Investment Management and Research (AIMR) publication by Pamela Peterson and David Peterson.[11]

As Stewart points out, the amount of capital employed within a firm can be estimated by making adjustments to the left hand or right hand side of the firm's balance sheet. As revealed in Exhibit 2, it is possible to estimate the firm's operating capital using the "asset approach" or the equivalent "sources of financing approach." The asset approach begins with the "net (short-term) operating assets." This figure represents current assets less *non*-interest bearing current liabilities (accounts/taxes payables, and accrued expenses for examples). To this amount, Stewart adds familiar items like the accumulated LIFO reserve, net plant and equipment, and goodwill-related items. The capitalized value of research and development and cumulative write-offs from special items are also figured into their asset-based view of capital.

In the equivalent "sources of financing" approach, the firm's economic capital estimate is obtained by adding "equity equivalents" to the firm's book value of common equity, along with debt and "debt equivalents." Exhibit 2 shows that in the Stern Stewart model, equity equivalents consist of preferred stock, minority interest, deferred income tax reserve, LIFO reserve, and accumulated goodwill amortization. Likewise, debt and debt equivalents consist of interest bearing short-term liabilities, long-term debt, as well as capitalized lease obligations. With the income statement (Exhibit 1) and balance sheet (Exhibit 2) converted to a cash operating basis, an analyst is able to *jointly* estimate the firm's unlevered net operating profit after tax and the economic capital employed within the firm. As mentioned before, the firm's after-tax return on capital is calculated by dividing UNOPAT by total capital.

Overview of Goldman Sachs' Approach Like Stern Stewart and others, Goldman Sachs has narrowed the field from 160 possible accounting adjustments down to a select number of accounting adjustments that can have a meaningful impact on the firm's assessed cash operating profit and its economic capital.[12] The key "equity equivalents" used by Goldman's U.S. Equity Research Group to measure the firm's economic capital (or equivalent financing thereof) are shown in the top portion of Exhibit 3. Based on the "sources of financing approach," they begin with stockholders equity on the firm's balance sheet and then "add back" (if any) the listed equity equivalents. On the income side, the increase in equity equivalents is added back to accounting net income as shown in the lower portion of Exhibit 3.

As shown in Exhibit 3, accounting-based items like deferred tax liabilities (and deferred assets resulting from *non*-recurring restructuring and environ-

---

[11] Using the 1993 Annual Report for Hershey Foods Corporation, Peterson and Peterson provide a step-by-step instruction on how to calculate the firm's cash operating profit, dollar cost of capital, and economic value added (EVA). This practical guide can be found in Pamela P. Peterson and David R. Peterson, *Company Performance and Measures of Value Added* (Charlottesville, VA: The Research Foundation of the Institute of Chartered Financial Analysts, 1996).

[12] See Einhorn, Napolitano, and Cohen, "EVA: A Primer."

mental cleanup costs), minority interests, and LIFO reserves have balance sheet and income statement consequences that can impact the correct estimation of the firm's after-tax return on capital — through their *joint* impact on UNOPAT and economic capital. Also, the taxes used in measuring a company's post-tax capital returns should be a reflection of the cash taxes actually paid by the *unlevered* firm — as the interest tax subsidy (if any) is already reflected in the cost of capital calculation for the levered firm. On the tax issue, Goldman Sachs uses the *statutory* corporate tax rate rather than the firm's effective tax rate.

Final Comments on UNOPAT Estimation in Practice Hence, there are many accounting adjustments that an analyst can make when attempting to measure a firm's after-tax return on capital, ROC (measured by the UNOPAT/TC ratio). These ROC challenges are independent of the empirical and academic issues that arise when attempting to calculate the firm's cost of capital, COC (to be discussed shortly). Because the economic profit message can get muted as the number of accounting adjustments grows, it is important for equity analysts to find a practical balance between the number of UNOPAT and capital adjustments while still protecting the integrity of the EVA model. Conformity in the number of accounting adjustments also makes economic profit comparisons across firms and sectors more reliable.

Exhibit 3: Equity Equivalents Approach Used by Goldman Sachs U.S. Research Group

Derivation of Total Adjusted Capital Employed

Common Equity
+ Equity Equivalents*
+ Preferred Stock
+ Minority Interest
+ Long-Term Debt
+ Short-Term Debt
+ Current Portion of Long-Term Debt
= Total Capital Employed

Derivation of NOPAT

Net Income Available to Common
+ Increase in Equity Equivalents
+ Preferred Dividend
+ Minority Interest Provision
+ After-Tax Interest Expense
− ESOP Accrual
= NOPAT

* Includes: Accumulated amortization of intangibles, deferred taxes, cumulative non-recurring charges, LIFO reserves, and ESOP accruals.

Source: Steven G. Einhorn, Gabrielle Napolitano, and Abby Joseph Cohen, "EVA: A Primer," *U.S. Research* (Goldman Sachs, September 10, 1997).

In general, important items like research and development expenditures should be capitalized on the balance sheet and amortized on the income statement over a long period of time — rather than "expensed" in the current year. Also, goodwill which arises from corporate acquisitions (namely, the acquisition "premium" paid by acquirers) should be treated as economic capital. An inspection of Exhibits 1, 2, and 3 reveals that the *major* adjustments to the accounting income statement and balance sheets made by U.S. Equity Research Group at Goldman Sachs as well as Stern Stewart & Co. are similar in scope and interpretation.

EVA Versus REVA

As a final layer of complexity, there is even a debate within the economic profit camp as to whether EVA should be estimated in the standard form employed by Stern Stewart *et al* or whether a refined version — called "Refined Economic Value Added" (REVA) — should be used in company-based research. As shown in this chapter, EVA is calculated by dividing UNOPAT by total economic capital employed within the firm. In this way, EVA measures the dollar "surplus" generated by the firm's (present and anticipated future) operating capital. Hence, in present value terms, it represents the value-added (or net present value) to the firm's physical (and human) capital. As such, REVA — which in effect measures the firm's unlevered net operating profit after tax (UNOPAT) over the market value of the firm — is not as firmly rooted in the NPV theory of the firm.[13]

Cost of Capital Estimation Challenges

Aside from any further accounting difficulties that may arise when calculating the firm's economic profit, there remains many challenging "cost of capital" issues that can impact the estimation of the EVA metric. These COC challenges have both theoretical and empirical foundations. In the former context, the standard approach — used by EVA players like Goldman Sachs and Stern Stewart — to calculate the cost of capital presumes that corporate debt financing is a "cheaper" source of financing in comparison with equity financing — thereby giving corporate managers an incentive to finance growth with debt versus equity.

Yet Merton Miller argues that even in a world of taxes with deductibility of debt interest expense, levered firms should be priced *as if* they were equivalent business-risk unlevered firms.[14] In his well-known "Debt and Taxes" model, the pre-tax rate of interest on taxable corporate bonds rises in the capital market to a level that offsets any perceived gains from corporate leverage at the firm level. As a result, Miller re-establishes the "capital structure irrelevance" predictions of the

---

[13] For an insightful discussion of the EVA *versus* REVA controversy, see the following two articles. The case for REVA is discussed by Jeffrey Bacidore, John Boquist, Todd Milbourn, and Anjan Thakor, "The Search for the Best Financial Performance Measure," *Financial Analysts Journal* (May/June 1997). The "back to basics" case for EVA is covered by Robert Ferguson and Dean Leistikow, "Search for the Best Financial Performance Measure: Basics are Better," *Financial Analysts Journal* (January/February 1998).

[14] See Merton H. Miller, "Debt and Taxes," *Journal of Finance* (May 1977).

riginal MM (Miller-Modigliani) framework. These powerful principles of corpo-
ation finance suggest corporate debt policy has *no* meaningful impact on the value
f the firm. In this view, the levered firm's weighted average cost of capital is the
ame as the capital cost estimate for the equivalent business-risk unlevered firm.

To illustrate the EVA-importance of Miller's arguments in a more direct
vay, consider the familiar expression of the relationship between the cost of capi-
al for levered and unlevered firms. In this context, the levered firm's after-tax
apital cost can be expressed in terms of (1) the after-tax cost of capital for the
quivalent business-risk unlevered firm (UCOC), and (2) the expected tax benefit
vailable to the company from the perceived debt-interest tax subsidy. In more
ormal terms, the levered firm's cost of capital (LCOC) can be represented as:

$$LCOC = UCOC \, [1 - t_e \times (D/C)]$$

vhere UCOC is the unlevered firm's cost of capital, t_e is the *effective* debt tax sub-
idy rate, and D/C is the firm's "optimal or target" debt-to-capital ratio.

In Miller's "Debt and Taxes" model, he argues that competition in the
narket for taxable and tax-exempt bonds dictates that the levered firm's cost of
apital (LCOC) will be the same as the capital cost for the equivalent business risk
nlevered firm, UCOC. This implies that the firm's weighted debt tax subsidy
erm, $t_e \times (D/C)$, in the cost of capital formulation must be *zero*. In effect, Miller's
ioneering work throughout the years reveals that corporate debt policy *per se* has
o impact whatsoever on the firm's after-tax cost of capital, and therefore, its over-
ll market capitalization. In this sense, only real corporate investment opportuni-
ies (positive NPV projects) can have a material impact on shareholder wealth.

Suffice it to say that the effective debt tax subsidy rate, t_e, that applies in the
eal world is considerably lower than the statutory corporate tax rate that managers
nd investors alike might use in the estimation of the firm's cost of capital. EVA esti-
nates that are calculated in this simple way would of course be biased upward. This
neasurement error would result from the inherent downward bias in the levered
irm's cost of capital due to the presumed debt-interest tax subsidy. Moreover, unless
his seemingly favorable subsidy to the levered firm's cost of capital is noticed by
nvestors, then the debt-induced EVA bias could lead to an overly optimistic assess-
nent of the market value of the levered firm and its outstanding shares.[15]

An especially problematic cost of capital issue arises for the equity ana-
yst in the context of estimating the required return on the firm's common stock.
n principle, using CAPM to estimate the firm's anticipated cost of equity seems
easonable enough because this *single factor* model is an integral component of
:stablished financial theory. However, in recent years CAPM has been challenged

---

[5] The equity analyst should also be aware that even the unlevered firm's cost of capital (UCOC) is
mpacted by economywide changes in interest rates and the market-based business risk premium. This
neans that a firm's required return on capital (therefore EVA) can change *independently* of company spe-
:ific happenings at the micro level. This macro economic concern is also voiced by Peterson and Peterson,
Company Performance and Measures of Value Added.

by many empirical studies that question the validity of the one-factor expected return-risk predictions of the model.

CAPM Alternatives There are well-known factor-based equity models that can be used in lieu of the single-factor CAPM. In this context, the analyst might consider the benefits of using a multi-factor approach to estimating the firm's expected return on common stock, and (therefore) the required return on invested capital. Fundamental factor models like BARRA have been used to build forecasts of equity returns based on beta, size, earnings momentum, and book-to-price ratios — among other "common factors" that influence security return. Macro factor models — such as Burmeister, Ibbotson, Roll, and Ross — have been used in practice to estimate the expected return on common stocks in the context of interest rate and economywide changes in corporate profits. At a later point, we'll describe an innovative approach to estimating the required return on equity capital developed by James Abate at BEA Associates.

CASH FLOW RETURN ON INVESTMENT

Although EVA is perhaps the most popular value-based metric, it is not the only one used in practice by corporate managers and investors. Another prominent measure that is also consistent with the principles of wealth maximization is *cash flow return on investment* (CFROI). This metric is used by two consulting advisory firms — Holt Value Associates, LP (dealing primarily with investment management firms) and Boston Consulting Group (on the corporate side). Although differences exist, Holt's CFROI measure is similar in concept to the well-known internal rate of return (IRR) method used in capital budgeting analysis.

In principle, CFROI can be viewed as the after-tax internal rate of return on the firm's existing assets. CFROI is that rate which sets the present value of the after-tax cash flows generated by the firm's existing assets equal to their investment cost. As a result, the firm's net present value is positive if CFROI exceeds the "hurdle rate" or cost of capital, while the firm's NPV is negative when the Holt estimated CFROI metric falls short of the required return on the firm's existing capital.

Since Holt's CFROI metric is based on both current *and* distant cash flows while Stern Stewart & Co.'s EVA measure appears — on the surface — to be a snapshot of the firm's current economic profit, it is tempting to argue that the former firm's measure is more closely aligned with promoting shareholder value added over the long term. Such a comparative interpretation is incorrect however when one realizes that economic profit (EVA) is the *annualized* equivalent of the firm's net present value (see below). Also, if for some reason the firm's managers compare CFROI to a hurdle rate that is inconsistent with the required return on the firm's capital, COC, then a wealth-destroying *agency* problem exists between the firm's managers and owners.

Wealth Equivalency of CFROI and EVA

Although Stern Stewart and Holt/BCG like to promote their respective metrics as the "best" among today's value-based measures, it is important to emphasize that EVA and CFROI are theoretically equivalent ways of looking at the firm's net present value (or shareholder value add). This wealth equivalency between the two value-based methodologies is based on the following considerations: on the Stern Stewart side of the wealth creator ledger, the firm's NPV can always be viewed as the present value of its anticipated economic profit stream. In this context, EVA is the *yearly* equivalent of the firm's net present value.

Additionally, on the Holt/BCG side of the wealth creator ledger, the firm's NPV is positive when CFROI or the internal rate of return exceeds the corporate-wide hurdle rate. But EVA, and therefore NPV, is positive *if and only if* the firm's residual or surplus return on capital (IRR *minus* COC) is greater than zero. In this context, it can be shown that the firm's net present value is equal to the present value of its anticipated future economic profit (EVA). In principle, it can be shown that the firm's cash flow return on investment (CFROI) is the internal rate of return (IRR) that drives the *sign* of the firm's EVA when measured relative to its cost of capital.[16]

CFROI: Real World Considerations

Pamela Peterson and David Peterson point out that the proprietary CFROI measure is very informative yet more complex than a typical IRR calculation.[17] The estimation difficulty arises because the inputs to the model are stated in *real* as opposed to nominal dollars.

Using the 1993 Annual Report for Hershey Foods Corporation, they provide an insightful discussion on how to calculate CFROI (as well as EVA) along with the important issues that arise when interpreting the results. After intensive examination of Hershey's financial statements, Peterson and Peterson discover the gross cash flow and investment items that are pertinent to the CFROI calculation. Their *nominal* findings from information gleaned from the Hershey Corporation financial reports at year-end 1993 are shown below:

Gross Cash Investment	=	$2,925.863 million
Gross Cash Flow (payment)	=	$427.156 million
Nondepreciating Asset (future value)	=	$522.968 million
Asset Life	=	18 years
IRR	=	13.31%

Based on the information provided in Hershey's 1993 Annual Report, they find that the internal rate of return on the firm's *existing* assets is 13.31%. Although many calculations were involved to arrive at this point, the estimated IRR percentage is *not* the firm's actual CFROI. As noted by Peterson and Peterson, there are

---

[16] For a demonstration of the link between NPV and EVA and between NPV and CFROI, see Fabozzi and Grant, *Equity Management.*

[17] See Peterson and Peterson, *Company Performance and Measures of Value Added.*

two practical differences between the standard IRR and CFROI calculations. First, the inputs to the CFROI model are stated in current monetary equivalents: past investments are "grossed up" to the current period by a historical inflation factor while gross cash flows are inflation-adjusted back to the present time period.

In light of the current dollar adjustments supplied by Holt Value Associates (to Peterson and Peterson), the CFROI measure for Hershey Foods Corporation drops from 13.31% to 10.25%. This percentage estimation difference is important. If the firm's "hurdle rate" were somewhere between the two figures, the unsuspecting (or less informed) analyst with a CFROI estimate of 13.31% might incorrectly gauge the firm as a "wealth creator" with positive NPV. Second, in the Holt/BCG approach, the firm's CFROI is actually stated in *real* terms as opposed to nominal terms. Hence, the real CFROI measure is impacted by the inflation assumption used by the analyst in the future cash flow and gross investment estimation processes (aside from the many nominal accounting adjustments that were already mentioned in calculating a firm's economic profit).

Peterson and Peterson also point out that CFROI measurement concerns arise because the estimated *real* return on the firm's existing assets is *not* compared to an inflation-adjusted cost of capital measure using the standard COC formulation. If correct, then the Holt/BCG approach to shareholder value added may give rise to an agency conflict between managers and owners, unless of course their estimated "hurdle rate" — perhaps in light of the many empirical challenges to CAPM — is somehow a more descriptive measure of the *equilibrium* required rate of return on the firm's economic capital. Given the proprietary nature of the Holt/BCG cost of capital benchmark, one is left wondering how the market would generally know this in setting the equilibrium real rate in the first instance.

THE BEA MODEL

Now let's look at an actual application of value-based metric analysis — the model used by the U.S. Active Equity Group at BEA Associates. This firm has found the economic profit framework particularly effective in its ability to describe both changes in corporate valuation and in their active attempt at capturing abnormal returns on securities of firms operating in different sectors of the economy.[18] The concept of economic profits utilized by BEA (like the commercial EVA® measure of corporate success) is defined as the after-tax operating cash flow return earned by a firm in *excess* of what its owners of equity and debt expect to earn on their invested capital. The firm's required rate of return (or weighted average cost of capital) is based on an assessment of market risk factors as well as company specific risk considerations.

---

[18] A complete discussion of BEA's economic profit approach to security analysis can be found in James A. Abate, "Select Economic Value Portfolios." The economic profit model discussed here is also consistent with the EVA-based company analysis approach recommended in Grant, *Foundations of Economic Value Added*.

Bottom-Up Approach

In BEA's "bottom-up" approach to security selection, the estimated residual profit measure is examined in terms of a firm's relationship with market or investor expectations of future returns. From this perspective, BEA's economic profit approach to equity management is an excellent way of gauging how effective the company's decision-making has been in allocating resources which will lead to shareholder wealth creation and changes in market value. The follow-on bridge is to identify not only good companies (corporate perspective) but the proper entry points so that those good companies are also good stocks (investment perspective).

The three key pricing elements used by BEA to assess the value of a firm's anticipated economic profits include: (1) capital growth rate, (2) after-tax operating return on invested capital, and (3) the required return on invested capital (weighted average cost of capital). BEA's desire is to isolate the market expectations for a company that are implied by its current market value.

Growth is crucial in BEA's bottom-up pricing assessment. This is where BEA analysts attempt to capture a reasonable and sustainable growth rate for a company in terms of revenues and profits. This is also where linking the balance sheet to the income statement is deemed important since the growth rate for revenues and profits is a function of investment, whether it is in new plant and equipment or intangible assets. BEA analysts also recognize that the after-tax operating return on invested capital is crucial when compared to the required return on invested capital. While this return spread is often referred to as the "residual return on capital" or the "surplus return on capital," BEA refers to the difference between the firm's after-tax operating return and the required (or expected) rate of return as the "excess return on invested capital."

In the BEA approach, the economic profit, capital growth, and valuation linkage is transparent: Those companies that generate positive excess returns on invested capital should continue to invest and grow their businesses, while firms having negative residual returns should not. In essence, the assessed spread between a company's operating return on capital and the required return on capital measures how much "economically profitable" reinvestment a firm can generate. Deprivation of growth in a high return on capital business is viewed as a signalling event that future revenue and economic growth rates may slow. From a corporate valuation perspective, any company that is deemed attractive from an economically profitable and judicious capital growth standpoint should trade at a premium when measured relative to replacement cost of assets. In this context, BEA recognizes that a company that generates an excess return on invested capital should trade at a premium to replacement value based upon market expectations of continued economically profitable reinvestment.

Economic profit analysis can be used to assess which companies are likely to generate positive abnormal returns. In the BEA model, this profit/valuation assessment involves the calculation and/or research assessment of:

1. the excess return on invested capital (positive or negative)
2. the growth rate of capital.
3. the ratio of market value to asset replacement cost.
4. the relationship between market implied growth rates and BEA's estimate through the use of an earnings discount model.

Excess Return on Invested Capital

The first step in BEA valuation analysis is to calculate the spread between the firm's operating return on capital and the required return on capital. The estimation of the excess return on invested capital is explained below.

Estimating the After-Tax Operating Return on Capital An essential component of economic profit analysis involves arriving at a measure of pre-interest, after-tax operating earnings generated by a firm, relative to the amount of capital which was required to generate such operating return. This well-known profitability ratio is simply the firm's after-tax operating return on capital.

To arrive at after-tax operating earnings, BEA deducts from revenues the cost of goods sold, selling and administrative expenses, marketing and promotional outlays, cash taxes on operating profits, and an amount to reflect required economic capital expenditures rather than "accounting" depreciation. This after-tax earnings calculation is used to approximate the firm's real operating cash flow.

In the BEA model, the amount of invested capital is determined without regard to capital structure and from a replacement cost basis. In this calculation, the estimated current replacement cost of assets is used rather than an accounting figure in an effort to eliminate accounting distortions that have little bearing to economic reality. (Examples include restructuring charges, accumulated depreciation, and reserves.)

Estimating the Required Return on Capital BEA uses a market-capitalization weighted average of the required return on equity and debt. Calculating some of the components in the required return on capital formula is a straightforward task. For example, the required return on debt can be determined mostly by the firm's credit rating. However, they also recognize that a significant, many times conflicting, amount of academic research has been focused on estimating the required return on equity.

To handle empirical regularities arising from systematic *non*-market phenomenon, BEA has constructed a proprietary scoring model akin to more fundamentally oriented measures like credit ratings which account for the shortcomings of an exclusively market based, backward looking measure of risk such as beta to estimate company specific required rates of return on equity capital. The focus is on assessing stability in future economic profit by not only using firm size, but also growth and variability of earnings, financial leverage, and other measures to adequately capture the impact of risk on required return. In effect, the higher the embedded fundamental risk for a company, the higher the required return or cost of capital.

Exhibit 4: Required Return versus Company Specific Risk Score

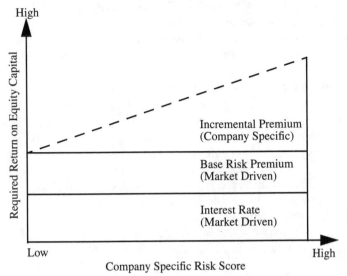

Source: James A. Abate, "Select Economic Value Portfolios," *U.S. Equity Product Overview* (BEA Associates, January 1998).

Along this line, BEA does a sizable amount of proprietary analytical research on determining the market driven base risk premium as well as the slope of the incremental premium, i.e., the difference between the least risky and most risky companies in the investable universe. Other things the same (market and *non*-market factors such as size), firms having demonstrated stability in their economic profit are assigned a low company-specific risk "score" in comparison with those firms with volatile economic profits. An illustration of BEA's "company specific" approach to estimating the required return on capital is shown in Exhibit 4.

Growth Rate of Capital

According to BEA, firms create economic profits by either investing in high return projects or by rationalizing underperforming assets in place. Invested capital management, otherwise referred to as capital budgeting analysis, is closely linked with changes in the level of economic profit — for it is corporate investments and/or divestitures that drive operating returns. Sources of funds (after-tax earnings, additional debt and equity financing, asset sales) when related to the ability to exceed the required rate of return on invested capital should be consistent with the use of funds (internal growth spending, corporate acquisitions, debt reduction, stock buybacks, and dividends).

The focus on value-creating firms by BEA is therefore twofold: (1) those companies that BEA analysts expect to experience an increase in market value when undertaking new projects, and (2) firms that BEA expects to increase in market value when reducing operations by divestiture or abandonment of projects in place. Exhibit 5 presents a display of excess returns measured relative to the capital growth rate for a sample group of companies. Note that the intercept on the horizontal axis is above zero. This is to reflect a nominal growth hurdle rate to identify real growth within a peer set.

Market Value-to-Asset Replacement Cost

BEA also looks at the market value-to-asset replacement cost ratio when assessing the investment merits of equity securities. As stated previously, it is not only important to identify good companies but also those that are good stock investments at today's price. Market value is defined as the current freely-tradable value of equity, debt, preferred stock, and minority interests. The value of cash and marketable securities is subtracted from market value and invested capital if it is viewed as *abnormal* relative to working capital requirements and linked to a specific timetable for distribution to shareholders.

A market value-to-asset replacement cost ratio in excess of *one* implies that existing and anticipated future capital investments have economic value added. Therefore, companies with ratios that exceed unity must achieve economic profit improvement at least at the growth rate which is implied within the current market value or a detrimental revaluation in the market value/asset replacement cost ratio will occur. On the positive side, those firms with excess returns on invested capital that consistently surprise positively will receive a favorable revaluation (higher ratio). A representative display of the excess return on invested capital versus the market value-to-asset replacement cost ratio is shown in Exhibit 6.

Exhibit 5: Excess Returns Relative to Capital Growth Rate

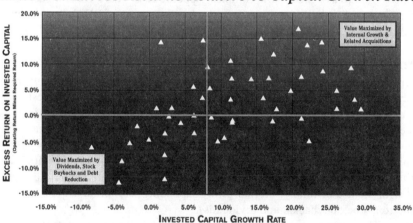

Source: James A. Abate, "Select Economic Value Portfolios," *U.S. Equity Product Overview* (BEA Associates, January 1998).

Exhibit 6: Risk-Adjusted Cash on Cash Valuation

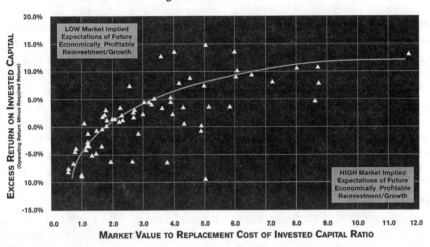

Analyzing Market Implied Growth Rates

In attempting to accurately value a company and thereby conclude whether or not a bottom-up market inefficiency exists, market implied growth rates should be compared to both past and forward looking estimates for operating performance. For specific securities BEA calculates market *implied* expectations of future economically profitable growth by using an earnings (after-tax operating cash flow) discount model, thought of sometimes as the discounted cash flow method. In this way, BEA examines the firm's market value as it relates earnings growth to its excess return on invested capital.

BEA employs the familiar Gordon-Shapiro dividend or earnings discount model. In this constant growth framework, the market value of the firm can be expressed as:

$$V = \text{Earnings}/(K - G)$$

where V is the firm's market capitalization (including debt and equity), K is the required return on capital, and G is the long-term sustainable earnings growth rate. Next, with knowledge of the firm's market value, after-tax operating earnings, and required return on capital, it is possible to estimate the market *implied* long-term growth rate, G, according to:

$$G = K - \text{Earnings}/V$$

That is, BEA backs into the market's *implied* expected growth rate for a company with knowledge of its after-tax operating earnings, market valuation of invested capital, and the required return on capital. The market's *implied* growth rate, G, for a company is then compared to a growth estimate — based upon

BEA's assessment of trends in capital growth as it relates to revenue and economic profit generation. If there is a *positive* spread between the BEA assessed growth rate and market-implied earnings growth, then there is a potential buy opportunity. In contrast, if BEA-assessed earnings growth falls short of market implied earnings growth rate then a potential sell opportunity exists. In this latter instance, upside surprise to the implied growth rate is not transparent. Therefore, economic profit growth appears to be expensively priced. In addition, a target price is calculated based upon BEA's growth expectations to determine the degree of opportunity, if any.

This is where BEA in its actively managed U.S. equity portfolios attempts to add value for clients from a *bottom up* perspective. Through use of proprietary models, BEA attempts to find those companies that are generating returns in excess of required return on invested capital. This tells BEA's analysts (1) which companies are gaining the most from their capital spending, and (2) those firms that are capable of using their cost of capital as a competitive advantage. BEA's detailed valuation analysis permits them to get a truer understanding of which, why, and to what extent, companies are selling for more than their asset replacement cost. In this way, BEA hopes to find the good, fast-growing companies with low disappointment risk and potential restructuring opportunities. That goal is especially important in an economic cycle where capital spending, mergers and acquisitions, and asset rationalizations are an integral part of corporate planning.

We have attempted to illustrate the significant *value drivers* in the BEA economic profit model. In actuality, an in-depth analysis of the relevant variables and their sub-components (e.g., operating return equals profit margin times asset utilization) is conducted through a variety of techniques. As part of the analysis, BEA uses (1) company-specific historical trend analysis, (2) multi-period benchmarking to peer firms, (3) compilation of qualitative information, including company visits and management meetings, and (4) determination of competitive advantage persistency in their bottom up approach to equity analysis. As a note, BEA's general feeling about competitive advantage is that it exists or doesn't and that arbitrary fade periods should be reflected in growth rates rather than introduce another level of long-term arbitrariness.

BEA's "Top Down" Approach

One of the distinguishing characteristics of BEA's U.S. portfolio management effort is its research focus on sector-specific economic profit influences. In their so-called *non-nucleus* or *peripheral sectors*, the principal driver of sector and individual stock selection process are macroeconomic profit trends that tend to affect most stocks in the sector in a somewhat equal manner. In other words, BEA's analyst will financially model the entire industry, first to assess opportunities before attempting to identify the best stocks. By nature, peripheral sectors tend to be commodity price and interest rate sensitive industries, generally those where no individual company's competitive advantage is dominant.

Exhibit 7: Financial Services (Banking)

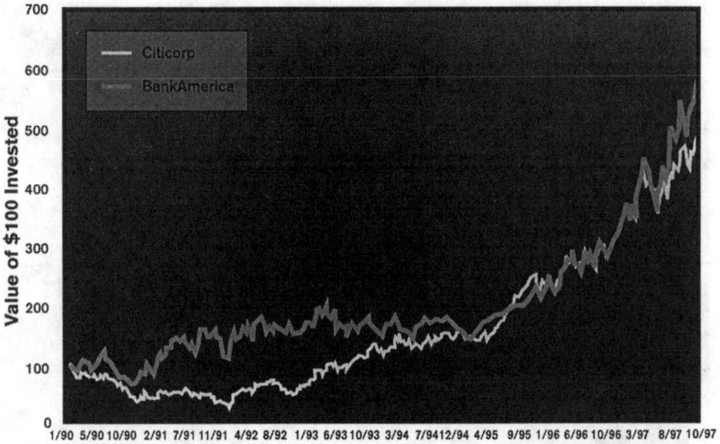

For instance, in sectors like oil (part of energy) and chemicals (part of basic materials), BEA finds that stocks are highly correlated with trailing periods capital spending and commodity prices. Thus, analysis of macro trends such as global capacity changes, GDP growth, utilization rates, and currency values adds more value to the portfolio decision than a purely bottom-up approach to security selection. In other words, the macro trend overwhelmingly influences the level of industry or sector-based economic profits (measured *net* of capital costs) and does so in a homogeneous way across the sector. The fundamental premise of economic profit is still intact — proper allocation of capital being essential to shareholders — but poor decisions by one or more companies can have great "headwind" effect on even the best companies within an industry, oil and mining being good examples.

Thus, the portfolio peripherals consist of a group of sectors where macro *themes* drive stock price to a great degree. For these industries, a *top-down* macroeconomic profit approach is first used in stock selection. Since these companies share many of the common influencing factors of operating and investment performance — such as commodity price or interest rate effects — stock price comovement is usually tight in the peripheral sectors. BEA's peripheral sectors include financial services, energy, utilities, basic materials and precious metals, transportation, and real estate trusts. To illustrate the peripheral comovement theme, Exhibits 7 and 8 show how $100 invested in two companies in the banking and utilities sectors, respectively, *jointly* moved in value over time.

In general, BEA's approach to sector analysis has three key elements. First, BEA feels that it is crucial to understand what point sectors are at in the economic or competitive development cycle, as is the case with utilities for example. Second, it is important to identify how the respective sectors stand to benefit or be hurt from current economic profit trends in the economy. Third, BEA deems it important to engage in a detailed analysis and modeling of particular macro variables for each of the peripheral sectors.

Exhibit 8: Utilities

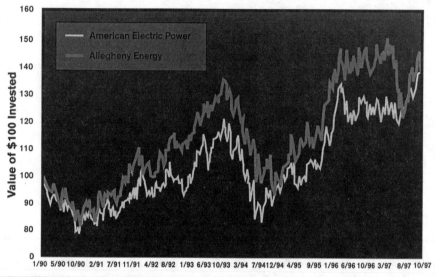

Sector Deviation from Benchmark

From BEA's view, sector emphasis or de-emphasis should *not* be made by a conventional value or growth style of investing. In fact, the style should be a derivative of the sector calls and the abundance of a sector's stockpicking opportunities — *not* the other way around. For example, if an investment manager is labeled as a traditional growth manager, then according to the S&P/BARRA Growth index, that manager is taking on significant benchmark risk unless he is consistent with a 20.1% or so current weight in health care stocks.

At the opposite end of the spectrum, the weight of health care in the S&P/BARRA Value index now stands at approximately 3.0%. In other words, the manager is almost forced to make an investment in a sector based solely on the style or investment label that is attributed to him which are driven by valuation measures like price to book, but not related to an appropriate fundamental measure such as return on equity. These sector deviations from benchmark issues can arise in many other industries as well.

Rather than focus on value or growth stocks *per se*, the primary task in determining sector emphasis results from an assessment of volatility and return comovement of stocks within various industry groups. In this way, BEA determines whether or not a "bottom up" economic profit framework for individual stock selection works best in comparison with a "top down" approach that allows the portfolio manager to emphasize a factor's homogeneous influence on stock prices within the sector. The result is what BEA calls a "true value" equity portfolio. Demonstrating successful application, the performance alpha generated in BEA's Select Economic Value Equity Portfolios has been positive thus far.

Summary of BEA Approach

Taken together, BEA uses microeconomic and macroeconomic profit analysis when selecting individual securities. Their "bottom up" approach to portfolio management works best in volatile (winners and losers) economic sectors such as health care and technology where significant return dispersion exists among securities due to distinct market share and competitive advantage differences which influence very different economic profit results even in a stable macroeconomic environment. In the "top down" portion of their active equity strategy, stocks in peripheral sectors are selected recognizing that they are significantly influenced by a common macroeconomic driver such as commodity price or interest rate happenings.

Chapter 10

Market-Neutral Portfolio Management

Michael P. McElroy, CFA
Senior Vice President
Independence Investment Associates, Inc.

INTRODUCTION

Market-neutral portfolios (also known as "long-short" portfolios) are portfolios that combine two (and sometimes three) separate components — a "long" portfolio, a "short" portfolio, and (in some cases) a futures overlay, which gives the strategy exposure to an underlying index. Market-neutral portfolios, while now commonly accepted by institutional investors, only date back to the late 1980s. Prior to this period, these strategies were known as "hedge funds," but stringent risk controls and disciplined stock selection processes have made these strategies more consistent and rewarding to institutional investors in recent years. Long-short portfolios, while "better" than long-only portfolios from a theoretical perspective, are not "better" than long-only portfolios, but just different. Along with the development and refinement of market-neutral portfolio management, though, has come a myriad of fanciful promises and misinformation, which we hope to debunk in this survey of the strategy.

This chapter will cover several topics. First, we will define what market neutral is, and how it differs from traditional "long-only" portfolio management. Second, we will discuss the skills that a manager must have in order to consider running a successful market-neutral strategy. Third, we will look at the benefits and risks of market-neutral investing from both the client and manager perspective, and finally we will discuss how we at Independence Investment Associates have taken a successful, long-term track record in long-only portfolio management and extended it to successful market-neutral portfolio management.

WHAT IS MARKET NEUTRAL?

Market-neutral portfolio management is not a new concept, but has only been receiving an audience from institutional investors over the past decade or so. His-

The author wishes to acknowledge the valuable input of David P. Canavan, CFA and Michael Even, CFA, and the assistance of Elizabeth A. Woodward and Emily E. Coupe.

torically, institutional equity managers had been limited to managing long-only portfolios. Active managers could put their investment insights into the portfolio in two ways — by overweighting the stocks they found attractive relative to the weight of these stocks in the benchmark portfolio, or by underweighting the stocks they did not find attractive. The difference between an asset's weight in the benchmark and in the portfolio is known as the asset's *active weight*. A positive active weight implies an overweight position in a stock, while a negative active weight means that the manager does not hold a benchmark weight of the stock. While long-only managers could make an almost unlimited active overweight on a given stock, without the ability to short-sell a stock in the portfolio any stock's active underweight was limited to the weight of the stock in the benchmark. This means that, in a long-only portfolio, a manager can only take a significant short position[1] in stocks that are the larger constituents of the benchmark. Market-neutral portfolio management relaxes this restriction, and allows active managers more freedom to efficiently take advantage of the information they identify, and maximum flexibility to produce excess returns.

Until recently, there were many regulatory (external) and operational (internal) constraints that investment managers faced in order to short securities. Today, more efficient financial markets and back-office operations staffs conversant in the issues associated with shorting securities allow the more sophisticated investment managers to successfully take advantage of both types of information — "good" information, used in the long portfolio, and "bad" information which is used to construct the short portfolio.

How Market Neutral Works — An Illustration

In order to make the above discussion a little more tangible, let's look at an example. An investment manager ranks stocks from most attractive (highest alpha) to least attractive (lowest alpha) using his/her own proprietary research information. This manager has been in business for many years, and has had a distinguished track record of success at discriminating between the top stocks and the bottom stocks. The measure we use to identify the manager's ability to discriminate between top and bottom stocks is a statistic called the *information coefficient*, or IC, which is the correlation between a manager's forecast of returns and the actual returns of the stocks in a subsequent period. Because the manager has a positive IC, the value from the discriminatory ability has yielded a long-term alpha (return in excess of the market return) of about 2.0% per year.

A client approaches the manager and asks whether the process can be applied to a market-neutral portfolio. Given the long-term success, the discipline, and the defined process, running a market-neutral strategy is not a stretch. In order to apply this stock picking process to a market-neutral portfolio, the manager now builds two portfolios — a "long" portfolio and a "short" portfolio. The "long" port-

---

[1] See the section on trading and back office requirements later in this chapter for a more detailed description of short selling stock.

folio is constructed using the manager's familiar process, and the "short" portfolio is almost a mirror image of the long portfolio, except it is made up of unattractive stocks that the manager short-sells (we will discuss the mechanics of the portfolio construction process in more detail later.) The long portfolio has a beta of 1.0, does not have any significant industry or style tilts, and is diversified. Because the manager has attained an annual alpha of 2% per year, he/she expects this portfolio to outperform the market by this margin. The manager also assumes the information in the ranked list is symmetric, meaning that a short portfolio built from the bottom of the ranked list should be expected to underperform the market by about 2.0% per year. This "short" portfolio will have a beta of −1.0, and will also be diversified and have no significant industry or style tilts. Note that the "market neutral" characteristic comes from the fact that equal-dollar amounts are held in a long portfolio with a beta of 1.0 and a short portfolio with a beta of −1.0. Therefore the portfolio's beta is zero $[(0.5) \times 1.0 + 0.5 \times (-1.0) = 0]$.

The manager then aggregates these holdings into the market-neutral portfolio, which consists of both long and short positions. How does this strategy make any money if it does not have any exposure to the market? From the skill the manager brings to the process with stock selection, that's how! Let's look at how this strategy performs in different market environments:

Case 1: Market up 10%

Long portfolio outperforms market by 2% → 12% gain in long portfolio
Short portfolio underperforms market by 2% → 8% gain to short portfolio
Total strategy outperforms by 4% → 12% − 8% = 4% alpha

Case 2: Market down 10%

Long portfolio outperforms market by 2% → 8% loss in long portfolio
Short portfolio underperforms market by 2% → 12% loss to short portfolio
Total strategy outperforms by 4% → (−8%) − (−12%) = 4% alpha

Case 3: Market unchanged

Long portfolio outperforms market by 2% → 2% gain in long portfolio
Short portfolio underperforms market by 2% → 2% loss to short portfolio
Total strategy outperforms by 4% → 2% − (−2%) = 4% alpha

The invariance to market conditions and the ability to add value in different environments is why the strategy is called market neutral. In fact, whenever the portfolio beta of the long portfolio is equal to the portfolio beta of the short portfolio, the portfolio is called a market-neutral portfolio, since the only source of volatility in the portfolio is uncorrelated with the market. Clearly, if the manager is wrong about which stocks outperform and which stocks underperform, this strategy can cause "double trouble." Yet, as we will show, the return-to-risk tradeoff of the market-neutral strategy is superior to the long-only case under any market conditions. Let's spend some time looking at the factors that differentiate a good market-neutral manager from an average or poor manager.

REQUIREMENTS FOR SUCCESSFUL MARKET-NEUTRAL MANAGEMENT

There are three necessary skills a manager must have to successfully manage a market neutral portfolio. First, the manager must be able to differentiate outperforming (positive alpha) stocks from underperforming (negative alpha) stocks. Second, because risk control is a key of successful market-neutral management, a manager must have skill at combining these return expectations with risk expectations in a disciplined manner. Third, implementation of the investment ideas from the first two steps is critical as compared with long-only management, as the manager must deal with short-selling restrictions and risk balancing between the long and short portfolios.

Stock Selection Skill

Stock selection is a critical skill for active management, but is "twice as important" when managing market-neutral portfolios, since either skill (or lack of it) will manifest itself in both the long and short parts of the market-neutral portfolio. As mentioned, stock selection skill can be expressed by a measure known as information coefficient (IC), which is the correlation between expectations of stock returns and the actual returns attained by the stocks over a measurement horizon. The IC can give a rough measure of predictive ability (if ranks of expected returns and ranks of realized returns are used) or an exact measure of return prediction (if expected returns are correlated against realized returns). Because market-neutral strategies (if implemented properly) are isolated from market effects, stock selection skill is the only skill that manifests itself in market neutral performance.

How are stock return predictions arrived at? Every manager has different ways of determining these expectations. A value manager might use techniques like low P/E, a dividend discount model framework or a combination of different techniques, the common thread among the techniques being a focus on price relative to some fundamental factor. A growth manager might determine relative stock attractiveness based on earnings or price momentum, estimate revision or some combination of these methods. The distinguishing characteristic of this style of management is looking for "growth" in some fundamental characteristic, while not being as concerned with the price paid for this growth potential. A third, more consistent style of predicting stock returns is to use a multi-factor valuation model that combines both value and growth models. The techniques these diversified managers use are similar to those of value and growth managers, but the difference is the combination of these techniques leads to less volatility and better predictive ability over the long-term than style-tilted managers attain. Multi-factor models can be constructed in different ways, from equal-weighted to quantitatively-combined using optimization techniques which differentially weight models based on their information coefficients and their correlation to other models.

Once the stock selection model is constructed, how can one be assured it has symmetric skill? That is, because a manager has been a successful long-only portfolio manager, does this provide any assurance that the process also provides skill at identifying stocks that underperform the market? This is a particularly important consideration from the investor's perspective, for as was mentioned above, market-neutral investment managers have only been seriously managing money using these techniques since the late 1980s, and many managers offering this management style have extended their long-only portfolio management process to a market-neutral process.[2] While there are not any hard and fast rules for assurance of symmetric skill, we recommend making sure at least three conditions are met to have confidence of a manager's extensibility to market-neutral investment. First, the manager's stock selection process should be derived from a defined philosophy that the manager believes in, which should be invariant. Second, the manager's stock selection process should be well defined, and use techniques which are logical, theoretically sound, and are applicable to all sectors of the market. Third, the manager should have a long track record of success, as statistical significance (confidence) grows with more observations.

The ability of a manager to discriminate between top-performing and bottom-performing stocks within each sector of the market cannot be stressed enough as a key skill for a successful market-neutral manager to have. A long-short strategy which uses unreliable stock return forecasts in portfolio construction can dramatically increase the chance of the portfolio generating large losses, rather than the more efficient gains that market-neutral managers have on average delivered. Yet, for the manager with good discriminatory ability and a high level of investment information compared to the consensus view, market-neutral management gives the manager additional flexibility to take advantage of the information, and this justifies pursing these returns via a long-short strategy.

Use of Risk Control

Effective use of risk modeling technology is another integral part of the market-neutral portfolio construction process. Both the opportunities for risk control, along with the complexities that go along with it, are amplified with market-neutral investing. How can this happen? If the manager's process tends to favor high-beta stocks, these stocks will be at the top of the manager's ranked list. Imagine the case where those high-beta stocks (stocks with betas greater than 1.0) are at the top of

---

[2] For a discussion of these ideas, see Daniel Cardell and Mitchell C. Krask, "Are Characteristics of Stocks that Underperform the Market the Same as Those That Outperform?" *The Journal of Investing* (Summer 1995), pp. 32-39.

the list, and low-beta stocks are at the bottom of the list. Without risk control, the market-neutral manager would buy a portfolio of the top stocks, which would have a portfolio beta of greater than one, and short a portfolio of the bottom stocks, with a portfolio beta of less than one. Combined, these two portfolios are certainly not market-neutral, as the aggregate portfolio has a beta different than zero (remember that market-neutral strategies have a beta of zero, which removes the market as the source of risk.) In fact, the strategy would have a net beta exposure that is double the net exposure the long-only strategy would have. While one could question the risk control being employed in the long-only strategy, this example should highlight the importance of risk control in market-neutral portfolio management.

Risk arises from many sources in a portfolio. In the previous example, having a portfolio beta for either the long or the short portfolio different than 1.0 gives the portfolio systematic risk different than the market. Yet even a portfolio having a beta of 1.0 (or −1.0 for a short portfolio) can still have some amount of extra-market risk. What is this type of risk? This risk — also known as common-factor risk — was quantified in the late 1970s from the fact that it is possible to put together a portfolio of stocks within one industry (such as banks) with a beta of 1.0, but clearly have a different risk than the market. Exhibit 1 gives an example of a portfolio that has a beta of 1.0, but clearly is not a portfolio that resembles the market. As can be seen, the bank positions in this hypothetical portfolio are larger for the lower-capitalization, lower-beta banks, and smaller for the higher-capitalization, higher-beta banks in order to get a portfolio beta of 1.0.

Exhibit 1: Sample Portfolio with Beta of 1.0

Name	Weight (%)	Beta	Name	Weight (%)	Beta
Suntrust Bks Inc	5.98	0.96	Northern Trust Corp	2.95	1.04
Wachovia Corp	5.73	0.93	Fleet Financial Group Inc	2.85	1.00
First Union Corp	5.34	0.94	Norwest Corp	2.78	1.10
National City Corp	5.33	0.93	Mercantile Bancorp	2.69	1.00
Republic NY Corp	5.32	0.94	Mellon Bank Corp	2.67	1.05
Corestates Finl Corp	5.2	0.97	Summit Bancorp	2.63	1.02
Wells Fargo & Co	4.94	0.99	PNC Financial Corp	2.57	1.03
US Bancorp Del	4.85	1.01	Synovus Financial Corp	2.29	1.02
Fifth Third Bancorp	4.02	0.99	BancOne Corp	2.16	1.08
Huntington Bancshares	3.76	0.94	Chase Manhattan Corp	1.98	1.10
Comerica	3.64	1.01	First Chicago Nbd Corp	1.96	1.06
Nationsbank Corp	3.53	1.04	State Street Corp	1.48	1.13
BB&T Corp	3.37	1.01	BankBoston Corp	1.09	1.09
Bank New York Inc	3.33	1.04	Citicorp	1.01	1.15
Keycorp New	3.22	1.00	BankAmerica Corp	0.88	1.17
			Bankers Trust NY Corp	0.43	1.09
Portfolio Beta:	1				
Portfolio Tracking Error*	9.37%		Factor Risk/Tracking Error	82%	

* Relative to S&P 500

Source: Independence Investment Associates, Inc.; Risk data from BARRA USE2 model, February 1998

This common-factor risk arises because market risk is not the only type of risk which individual stocks are exposed to. Industry risks, along with style risks (such as growth, high E/P, and other factors) help explain individual stock risks above and beyond market (beta) risk. While we stated earlier that a market-neutral portfolio has no exposure to the market (net portfolio beta of zero), we should extend our definition to state that an effectively run market-neutral strategy not only has a portfolio beta of zero, but also effectively neutralizes most of the common-factor risks. Not all of these common factor risks are necessarily bad, though. For instance, a manager whose stock ranking process focuses on stocks with low P/E (meaning having a high E/P, or common factor exposure) will want to have this risk in the portfolio, as the manager might have identified returns which come along with the risk. In some cases, though, managers have been successful because of their ability to "tilt" their portfolios toward beneficial common-factor risks, but these managers must watch out for any correlation of their common factors with systematic (market) factors, as a market-neutral strategy can tend to neutralize returns coming from market factors.

An important idea in modern portfolio theory is for a manager to maximize excess returns (alpha) relative to the excess risk (tracking error) that a manager is willing to accept in order to capture the excess returns. This ratio of return to risk is known as the *information ratio* (IR), and is the measure that investors should use to evaluate the success and consistency of a manager. We just discussed the different ways that managers attempt to identify excess returns, but how do managers control excess risk?

There are several methods managers use to control the excess risk, ranging from the simple to the more complex. At the simple end of the spectrum, a market-neutral manager might only ensure that both the long and short portfolios (either alone or combined) have a net beta of zero. As we discussed above, this is a necessary — but not sufficient — characteristic of a well-managed market-neutral portfolio, as the manager can have two separate portfolios that together have no market exposure, but alone are very biased either toward industries or styles.[3] A more sophisticated manager might do some industry and style matching between the benchmark (market) portfolio and the long and short portfolios, along with making sure that the net portfolio beta is equal to zero. These managers might use simple algorithms or more complex methods such as stratified sampling to match different characteristics of the market portfolio and the long and short portfolios relative to each other. One shortfall of these methods is that there are many different dimensions of risk the manager must match, and the problem becomes both confusing and overwhelming as the manager seeks to control multiple dimensions of risk simultaneously.

---

[3] Different practitioners have different opinions about the ability to separate the market-neutral portfolio into separate long and short portfolios, and the meanings of these separate portfolios. For a discussion of these ideas, see Bruce I. Jacobs and Kenneth N. Levy, "20 Myths about Long-Short," *Financial Analysts Journal* (September/October 1996), pp. 81-85.

At the most sophisticated end of the risk control spectrum is a method called portfolio optimization. Portfolio optimization is like stratified sampling "on caffeine." It takes the return expectations (alphas) for each stock and combines them in the most efficient manner with the risk characteristics that go along with the return. The advent of cheap computer power on investment manager's desks over the past decade has made this technology fast and easily available to managers. These programs don't run themselves, though. The portfolio manager must specify — in addition to the return expectations — a "risk aversion" parameter that defines the tolerance the manager, or client, has for risk with respect to attaining return. A high risk-aversion parameter means the portfolio is not tolerant of much risk, while a small number indicates the portfolio will seek high returns at the expense of risk. The "art" of portfolio optimization is to find the proper parameter that allows the manager to take best advantage of the return expectations with respect to their risk.

Trading and Back-Office Requirements

Market-neutral strategies require the management of two simultaneous portfolios. A firm's back office and trading operations are impacted by this requirement in different ways than they might be accustomed to in dealing with long-only portfolios. On the trading side, the trading desk must be able to deal with (at least) double the trading volume that a long-only portfolio would generate, and also manage the proper execution of the short sales. Because the rules for short-selling stocks requires that stocks can only be sold when on an uptick, cash management and compliance differ from the long-only trading scenario. Additionally, for clients that require equitization of the market-neutral portfolio, futures trading, hedging, and effective rolling of futures contracts to maintain constant market exposures as the underlying stock portfolios change value often add another complexity to the management of the portfolio.

Short-selling is worth discussing in more detail, as it is a process with five parties involved — the lender of the stock, the borrower (short-seller), a prime broker, the executing broker, and the buyer of the stock. The lender of the stock owns the stock, and is represented by a custodial bank that has permission to lend the stock. The borrower is the market-neutral manager that wants to sell the stock short, and the borrower works through a prime broker who is responsible for finding the lender and making sure that regulations are met while the stock is on loan. The executing broker serves the same role in the short selling as in a regular transaction — matching seller and buyer — with the additional responsibility of making sure the short sale only occurs on an "uptick." The buyer of the stock that the market-neutral manager has sold short is the same as any other buyer, and is not aware that he/she has had stock sold short to them.

For these five participants, the short sale has four parts: initiation, transaction, settlement, and maintenance. The initiation of the short sale has the borrower contact the prime broker, who determines whether a lender can be found and whether the borrower can meet all regulatory requirements, such as maintaining adequate collateral on account. In a market-neutral portfolio, the long portfolio serves as collateral for the short portfolio. Once the prime broker gives its approval, the borrower can contact any executing broker to execute the short sale. The broker must be informed it is a short sale so that it can make sure the uptick rule is enforced. The uptick rule can be circumvented by use of broker's "principal packages" or options, though each of these options are either costly or limited by fairly illiquid markets and limited profit potential.

Once the short sale is done, settlement entails the prime broker transferring the stock from the lender to the buyer, and the dollar amount the buyer pays is transferred to a margin account that the lender controls. This cash serves as additional protection (in addition to the stocks held in the long portfolio as collateral) by giving the lender "ready cash" to buy back the short position at any time. This margin account is kept invested in interest-bearing securities, and the lender returns some percentage of this interest to the borrower as a rebate rate, the amount of which depends on how easy the stock is to borrow, and how much "clout" the borrower has in the market. As market-neutral strategies have become more accepted and managed in larger size, managers are receiving larger portions of the rebate for their use.

At the operations end of the process, the back office must also handle twice the amount of transactions as for a long-only portfolio, and must also be able to report on and reconcile the long positions with the short positions (and futures, if they are part of the portfolio strategy.) One major responsibility of the operations area is to handle the daily maintenance ("mark-to-market") required for a market-neutral portfolio. On a daily basis, while the short position is open, cash is moved to or from the lender's margin account to keep the account at exactly the right level needed to buy back the stock. If the price of the shorted stock goes up, money is transferred to the margin account, and if the price goes down, money is transferred from the lender's margin account to the borrower's account.

Because the market-neutral portfolio return is the manager's value-added combined with the rebate rate (approximately the Treasury bill return), an operations area that cannot handle the additional mechanics required can be a liability for the market-neutral manager. The ability to monitor the return and risk profiles of the aggregate portfolio and efficiently manage the margin accounts is critical to successful market-neutral management.

BENEFITS OF MARKET-NEUTRAL PORTFOLIOS

There are three clear benefits to choosing market-neutral management over traditional long-only management — the ability of a manager to use the full range of stock selection skill, the ability to increase risk control, and the ability to make the skill "portable." We have already discussed the ability of a manager to take full advantage of his/her stock selection skill above, so let's talk about the risk control and portability advantages.

Risk control is enhanced in a market-neutral portfolio by allowing the manager to simultaneously manage both a long and a short portfolio. While these portfolios can be run either aggressively or well-diversified, depending on client risk tolerance, the dynamics of the two portfolios relative to each other allow the manager to tightly control risk exposures much more precisely than with a long-only portfolio. For example, a manager's stock selection process may have a bias toward utility stocks, and getting this information into the portfolio will likely lead to the portfolio beta being less than 1.0, which will lead to a market exposure bet. Additionally, even if the manager only wants to get the specific stocks into the portfolio, he or she can still be forced into making a beta bet. A market neutral framework allows the manager to buy the utility stocks the process finds attractive, and short the utility stocks the process finds unattractive. When the holdings are combined, the beta bet is neutralized, and the concentration in the portfolio is toward the best utilities and away from the worst.

Tracking error — also known as residual risk — is also reduced relative to the long-only portfolio with respect to the return level. If a manager's process for identifying attractive and unattractive stocks generates independent investment ideas, the risk of the combined long-short portfolio (assuming dollar equivalency between both portfolios) increases not by a factor of two but by a factor of less than two due to the non-linear relationships when combining risk.[4] When the alphas used in the long portfolio and short portfolio are uncorrelated, the efficiency of the portfolio rises since excess returns are additive (doubled) while residual risk is only increased by 1.4 times, leading to an information ratio (return/risk) 43% higher than for the long-only portfolio. While this analysis does not take into account any additional transactions costs that arise with a market-neutral portfolio, it still shows that market neutral is an efficient way to take advantage of superior investment information.

Market-neutral portfolio management also allows a manager to make his/her value-added "portable," which is becoming a much more desirable characteristic for sophisticated institutional investors.[5] Fund policy and asset allocation decisions can be made independently of the decision to use a market-neutral manager, since the long-short spread can be combined with different asset classes. In fact, for institutional investors whose charters allow them or their managers to short-sell securities, long-short managers can simplify the plan's structure because it allows separation of security selection from asset allocation.

By eliminating market exposure, volatility is neutralized in a long-short portfolio. Any volatility in a properly managed market-neutral strategy comes

---

[4] For a discussion of this relationship, see Richard O. Michaud, "Are Long-Short Equity Strategies Superior?" *Financial Analysts Journal* (November-December 1993), p. 44-49.

[5] For discussion of this idea, see Marvin L. Damsma and Gregory T. Williamson, "Managing Risk in the Aggregate Portfolio: The Rewards of Portable Alpha," Chapter 1 in *Alpha: The Positive Side of Risk* (Washington Depot, CT: Investors Press, 1996) and William C. Fletcher, "Value Investing in a Style-Neutral World," in *Value and Growth Styles in Equity Investing* (Charlottesville, VA: Association of Investment Management and Research, 1995), pp. 14-20.

only from the variability in the manager's alpha, and not from market sources. Though derived from long and short positions to the equity markets, this alpha is not bound to any particular market, so the strategy can be "attached" to different market returns — fixed income, domestic or international equities or other asset classes can be overlayed on top of the manager's value added. In addition, certain types of managers stand to gain from using a market-neutral implementation, particularly managers who are index-constrained due to illiquidity away from the top few large index stocks. This situation can arise with a small-capitalization manager, who could potentially use market neutral to increase risk.

As mentioned above, the "pure" return of a market-neutral strategy is the manager's value-added from both the long and short portfolios, combined with the rebate rate the manager receives from the lender. This return is known as a "pure alpha," as it is gained without any exposure to sources of risk. Many institutional investors, however, have actuarial assumptions that require them to have exposure to stocks and/or bonds in order to earn a required return for meeting liabilities. These investors will often instruct a market-neutral manager to "equitize" a strategy to get the market exposure cheaply and to add the alpha via the market-neutral strategy.

To gain exposure to a market, futures contracts for the market the client wants to gain exposure to can be used. In cases where the asset the client desires exposure to does not have either traded or liquid futures available, swaps and/or forwards can be used, though not at as low a cost as futures. Futures allow the investor to gain market exposure with only a single security and at low cost. For example, an investor can get $10 million of broad stock market exposure with only 35 S&P500 futures contracts, which requires a cash outlay of $367,500.[6] This is ideal, as the low cost to gain exposure allows almost every dollar to be deployed in the market-neutral strategy. Because futures investing requires almost no cash compared to investing in the underlying market, futures are priced to return the market return less the risk-free rate. The sources of return to a market-neutral strategy are summarized in Exhibit 2.

As can be seen, the source of return on the long portfolio (having a beta of one) is the market return plus the manager's value-added. For the short portfolio, the manager will lose the market return (with the beta of -1.0, since it is owed to the lender of the stocks) but will gain from the manager's value-added on the short side derived from the shorted stocks underperforming the benchmark. The manager will make the alpha on the long side, the alpha on the short side, and the risk-free rate (from the rebate on the short selling). The manager may then "swap" the risk-free rate for futures in order to gain market exposure.

In summary, the main attraction of long-short strategies is the potential for them to deliver high absolute returns that are not correlated with the market, and are obtained with a lower volatility than in a long-only portfolio.

---

[6] These numbers are based on a notional S&P500 contract value of $250 times the index value, and a variation margin of $10,500 per contract as of this writing. These numbers will change with market level and margin requirements changing.

Exhibit 2: Return Sources to Market-Neutral Strategy

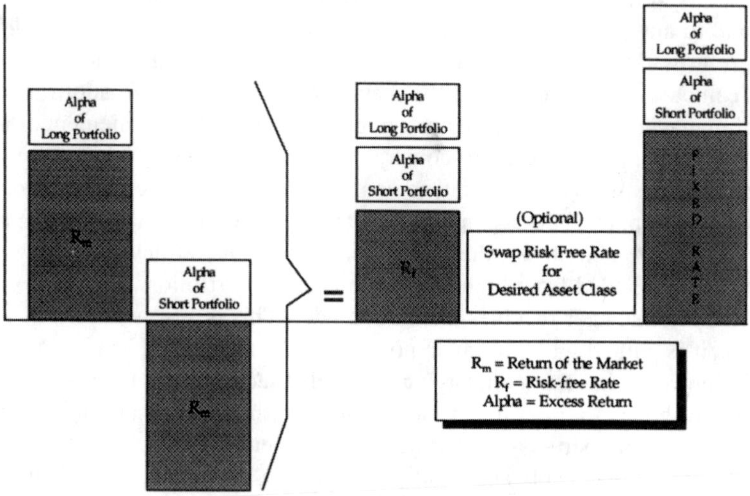

Alpha of Long Portfolio

Alpha of Long Portfolio

Alpha of Long Portfolio

Alpha of Short Portfolio

R_m

Alpha of Short Portfolio

Alpha of Short Portfolio

(Optional)

Swap Risk Free Rate for Desired Asset Class

FIXED RATE

R_f

Alpha of Short Portfolio

=

R_m

R_m = Return of the Market
R_f = Risk-free Rate
Alpha = Excess Return

Source: Independence Investment Associates, Inc.

MARKET NEUTRAL IN PRACTICE

Until now we have discussed the conceptual issues with market-neutral management. We will now go through the process a manager might use to create and maintain a market-neutral portfolio. In particular, we shall discuss how market-neutral portfolios are constructed in our investment firm.

Step 1: Forecast Stock Alphas

Forecasting a stock's extra-market return (alpha) is both an art and a science. In addition to forecasting stock performance on a relative basis, the use of portfolio optimization requires that we properly scale the return estimate so that it can be properly combined with the risk estimate that it is being compared to.

To determine the relative positions of stock performance, we use a multifactor model to identify stocks that will outperform and underperform the market return on an annual basis. The model is based on the philosophy we adhere to, which is that any stock that combines cheapness and improving fundamentals is attractive. For the past 15 years, we have implemented a consistent process that uses different valuation techniques (such as dividend discount models, P/E models, estimate momentum, and diffusion models) to rank stocks based on the different criteria. To build a composite valuation model from the individual constituent models, we combine the models based on their ability to forecast returns (the information coefficient of each model) and their correlation to each other. It is often easier to think of our composite valuation model as a diversified portfolio — of models.

The goal in constructing this portfolio is to find the best models that give the highest forecast return while yielding the lowest volatility of forecasting ability.[7]

The composite model tells us the position of each stock within our universe of 540 stocks, but does not tell us how to convert these positional scores to expected returns. We use a technique to convert our scores to alphas known as the alpha scaling "rule of thumb."[8] This technique takes the scores, and multiplies them by our accuracy (the information coefficient for our universe of stocks) and each stock's residual volatility. The logic behind this transformation is simple — our score gives us a ranking for each stock, the IC tells us the correlation between our rankings and actual returns, and the volatility tells us how to differentiate between stocks with similar scores. If our accuracy (IC) is high, we want to take the most advantage of our ranking system; however, a good manager's IC is in the range of 0.03-0.10, so this factor serves as a "haircut" factor which tells us how much confidence to put in our score. Likewise, for stocks with similar scores, we need to ensure that the optimizer will trade stocks off equally with different volatilities.

Proper scaling of alphas is vital in order to eliminate an effect known as "alpha eating" which happens when alphas are scaled improperly. Without proper scaling, an optimizer — which trades off return for risk — will be biased toward low-volatility securities if the alphas do not reflect the potential variability of returns that stocks can have relative to their risks. This phenomenon was noted by Michaud recently when he noted that the portfolio optimization process typically creates a downward-biased estimate of a portfolio's true risk characteristics, and subsequently these portfolios are significantly more volatile than assumed.[9] One other thing to note about alpha scaling is that the scaling methodology employed should be consistent with the realization that a long-short strategy that uses an unreliable forecast can dramatically increase the probability of large losses. By using the IC to scale our scores, we directly tie our predictive accuracy to the range of expected returns.

Step 2: Construct Market-Neutral Portfolio

The next step is to take these return forecasts we have developed and combine them into a market-neutral portfolio. There are a few schools of thought on how to construct the market-neutral portfolio — some managers advocate stratified sampling, while others champion the simultaneous optimization of both the long and short portfolios. Even though a market neutral portfolio does not have any final exposure to a market, it is necessary for the market-neutral manager to build the portfolio relative to some index. We use sequential portfolio optimization to construct the market-neutral portfolio.

---

[7] In fact, the mathematics for model combination is very similar to that of portfolio combination. For more discussion on how to do this in practice, see Richard C. Grinold and Ronald N. Kahn, *Active Portfolio Management* (Chicago, IL: Probus Publishing, 1995).

[8] See Grinold and Kahn, *Active Portfolio Management*, for more details on this technique.

[9] See Michaud, "Are Long-Short Equity Strategies Superior?" for more discussion on this point.

Exhibit 3: Iterative Portfolio Construction Process

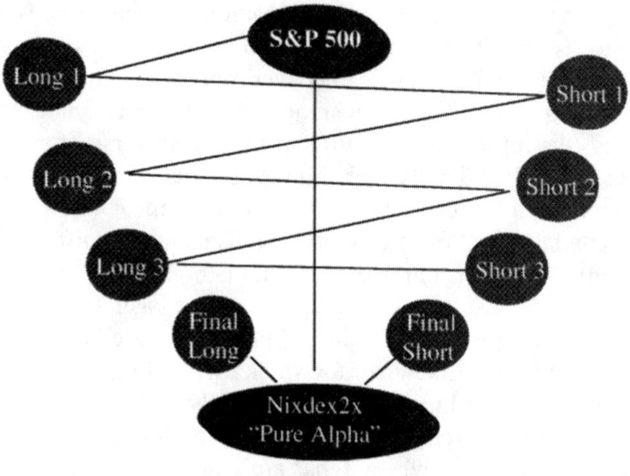

Source: Independence Investment Associates, Inc.

Because most managers' alpha generation process has some bias in it, we feel the best way to build the market-neutral portfolio is to sequentially construct it. Exhibit 3 shows how this is accomplished. In the first iteration, a "long" portfolio is built relative to a broad-market index, such as the S&P500 or the Russell 1000 Index. The index chosen should be representative of the stocks that the alpha generation process is forecasting returns for — it would not make any sense for us to choose a small-capitalization index as the reference, as we do not have stocks with similar characteristics in our investment universe. The first iteration constructs the long portfolio relative to the chosen index, with the selection universe being our entire investment universe that we calculate expected returns for. Some of the portfolio and risk characteristics of this first long portfolio are shown in Exhibit 4, while the short portfolio is shown in Exhibit 5.

As can be seen in Exhibit 4, the long portfolio is run with tight risk control, demonstrated by the 1.81% tracking error. The initial portfolio has 167 names in it, which we do not start paring down — based on minimum position size — until we get to the final long and short portfolios. Notice also that the beta of this portfolio is 1.00, as will be required for the short portfolio as well in order to run a true market-neutral portfolio. Exhibit 5 shows similar characteristics for the short portfolio created during the first iteration.

The long portfolio from the first iteration is then used as the benchmark for the construction of the short portfolio, rather than building the short portfolio with reference to the S&P500 Index. This is done in order to neutralize any biases that might have entered the long portfolio due to alpha scaling tilts. As in the case of the long portfolio, the entire ranked list is used to select the stocks for the short portfolio — with the one modification that we apply an alpha "multiplier" of –1.0 to the list in order to make the bottom stocks the most "attractive" for the short portfolio construction. Once this short portfolio is has been constructed, the iterative process continues as in Exhibit 2; however, in subsequent iterations we do not select from the entire ranked list of securities, but only from the existing securities selected from the previous portfolio of the same type. For instance, once the "Long 1" and "Short 1" portfolios are built, portfolio "Long 2" is built selecting securities only that are in "Long 1," rather than the entire ranked list. The same is true for the short portfolios as well.

Exhibit 4: Portfolio Characteristics of First Long Portfolio

Number of Assets	167
Tracking Error	1.81%
Risk Aversion Parameter	30
Portfolio Beta	1.00
Portfolio Alpha	1.92%
Specific Risk/Residual Risk	78.6%

Common Factor Exposures	Net Active Exposure
Variability In Markets	0.00
Success	0.06
Size	-0.12
Trading Activity	0.03
Growth	0.04
Earnings/Price	0.10
Book/Price	0.02
Earnings Variation	0.01
Financial Leverage	-0.14
Foreign Income	-0.18
Labor Intensity	0.11
Yield	-0.03

Largest Industry Overweights	% Difference from Benchmark
Services	3.64%
Other Insurance	2.56%
Banks	1.33%

Largest Industry Underweights	% Difference from Benchmark
Telephone	-3.51%
Beverages	-1.67%
International Oil	-1.59%

Source: Independence Investment Associates; BARRA US E2 risk analytics

Exhibit 5: Portfolio Characteristics of First Short Portfolio

Number of Assets	208
Tracking Error	1.45
Risk Aversion Parameter	30
Portfolio Beta	1.00
Portfolio Alpha	1.65
Specific Risk/Residual Risk	85.2%

Common Factor Exposures	Net Exposure Relative to Benchmark
Variability In Markets	-0.01
Success	-0.02
Size	-0.14
Trading Activity	0.01
Growth	0.02
Earnings/Price	-0.01
Book/Price	0.06
Earnings Variation	0.00
Financial Leverage	-0.08
Foreign Income	0.00
Labor Intensity	0.01
Yield	-0.01

Largest Industry Overweights	% Difference from Benchmark
Chemicals	1.65%
Thrift Institutions	1.45%
Retail (Food)	0.70%

Largest Industry Underweights	% Difference from Benchmark
Tobacco	-1.17%
Services	-0.97%
Agriculture, Food	-0.90%

Source: Independence Investment Associates; BARRA US E2 risk analytics

A second difference is that as each successive iteration is completed, the risk aversion parameter (or risk multiplier, as it is sometimes called) is increased in order to "force" both the long and short portfolio to "look like" each other. Raising the multiplier increasingly squeezes out differences between portfolios. In a long-only portfolio construction, the higher the risk multiplier, the more the portfolio looks like the benchmark (since if a manager is very averse to risk, he/she wants the portfolio to have minimal active weights, which leads to minimal risk.) The risk multiplier has the same effect in the long-short framework — a high risk multiplier leads to active "bets" (such as style or industry) being squeezed out, so as to leave a portfolio which gets its value-added from the specific stocks either outperforming or underperforming the market.

While this is not a "simultaneous" optimization, since the portfolios are constructed separately, the portfolios are closely linked to each other, and each individual portfolio would not be held in the absence of the other. Some practitioners do not follow this recipe, but rather build both the long and short relative to the same index, rather than to each other. This certainly leads to a different outcome, since each of these portfolios would be held in the absence of the other, do not reflect any leveraging of the information the manager has, and could have embedded biases that we discussed earlier which the true market-neutral manager should seek to eliminate. The portfolio characteristics of the final market-neutral portfolio are shown in Exhibit 6.

The beta of the combined portfolio in Exhibit 6 is zero — since each constituent portfolio had a beta of 1.0, buying and selling similar portfolios yields no net market exposure. Also notice the alpha of the portfolio, which is an expected 4.02%. This is about double the level of the long-only portfolio, because the returns are additive between portfolios. Also notice that the tracking error is only 3%, whereas the individual tracking errors for the long and short portfolios were about 2% each. How does this happen? Remember that the risks (standard deviations) are not additive, but the variances are additive. Each constituent portfolio had an approximate tracking error of 2%, or 4 units of variance. Combination of these two portfolios (assuming no correlation between the two portfolios) would lead to a tracking error of $\sqrt{4+4}$ or 2.82%.

Exhibit 6: Portfolio Characteristics of Final Market Neutral Portfolio

Number of Assets	316
Tracking Error	3.04
Risk Aversion Parameter	50
Portfolio Beta	0
Portfolio Alpha	4.02
Specific Risk/Residual Risk	90.1%

Common Factor Exposures	Net Active Exposure
Variability In Markets	0.12
Success	0.09
Size	-0.30
Trading Activity	0.03
Growth	0.13
Earnings/Price	0.10
Book/Price	0.03
Earnings Variation	0.13
Financial Leverage	-0.17
Foreign Income	-0.37
Labor Intensity	0.14
Yield	-0.09

Largest Industry Overweights	% Difference from Benchmark
Services	5.77%
Business Machines	2.07%
Insurance (Other)	1.86%

Largest Industry Underweights	% Difference from Benchmark
Telephone, Telegraph	-2.58%
Producer Goods	-2.46%
Thrift Institutions	-2.04%

Source: Independence Investment Associates; BARRA US E2 risk analytics

The tracking error of 3.04% implies that there is some correlation between the long and short components. The final two things to note about the combined portfolio is that factor exposure differences between the two portfolios are small, which leads to a ratio of specific risk to residual risk of over 90%. This shows the result of "distilling" the market-neutral portfolio down to an almost "pure" alpha, which has minimal style and industry exposure. The result of all these iterations is that the ratio of expected return to expected risk is approximately 4%/3%, or 1.33 — this is much higher than most managers can attain with long-only management, and a ratio of 0.5 is considered very good for a manager.

Why do we choose an iterative optimization process, rather than the simultaneous optimization process? As we mentioned, many processes to identify superior stocks have some bias in them. Some biases are good (such as looking for value or growth), while other biases might not be good or intended. For instance, a manager might have a beta bias in the process (high beta stocks attractive, low beta stocks unattractive) or an industry bias (oil stocks attractive, airline stocks unattractive). Simultaneous optimization that does not control risk at each step of the process risks creating a problem portfolio that we had discussed above for a manager that might have a "beta-bias" in the ranked list. Using the iterative approach, though, will not allow for a beta bet to get into the portfolio.

In Exhibits 4 and 6, it can be seen that there are some biases in the portfolio — tilts toward the earnings/price, growth, and other factors. While the goal is to be market-neutral and factor-neutral in a long-short portfolio, remember that our alpha creation process is designed to capture both cheapness and improving fundamentals, and so these characteristics are manifest by positive exposures to these two factors. We have shown over time that there has been positive alpha associated with ranking stocks based on the criteria of cheapness and improving fundamentals, so we have been comfortable with positive exposures to these characteristics.

Step 3: Trading the Market-Neutral Portfolio

Once the orders for the 316 stocks have been created, the next step is to trade the orders with the broker. As was mentioned above, the first step is to contact a prime broker who will tell us a list of securities that are either difficult to or impossible to "borrow" for different reasons. If it turns out that none of the stocks are problematic, the next step is to find the lowest-cost execution broker to trade the orders.

Typically, because risk control is paramount with the start-up of a market-neutral portfolio, it is important to have all the orders executed as a package. For this reason, principal package trading is often employed on start-up to make sure that every order gets executed during the day, and we know just what execution prices we will get. The process to have principal package trading done is to give the different candidate executing brokers a broad profile of the risk "characteristics" of the portfolio — some of the basic statistics might be the number of stocks in the long and short portfolios, the tracking errors of each portfolio relative to an index, the industry/sector breakdown or other descriptive statistics which the brokers require. The broker then comes back with a "bid" for how much they will execute the package for — this is either quoted in cents per share, or in basis points of portfolio value, depending on the broker's convention. This bid, if accepted, gives us the confidence to know that there will be no "left-over" at the end of the day, so that the risk characteristics will be in line with what we expected when we put the orders together. With the growth and acceptance of package trading and market-neutral management, principal packages are now very routine ways to get orders executed quickly and efficiently.

Step 4: Maintenance of the Portfolio

Many of the ideas behind maintenance of the portfolio have already been touched upon. Successful maintenance of the portfolio requires that the risk statistics can be accurately measured on a timely basis (so as to know when to rebalance the portfolio), and that from the operations end margin requirements are met. The margin requirements are handled by close coordination of the prime broker with our operations staff to ensure that money is available if cash is required, and that money is put into an interest-bearing account if margin frees up.

Trading of the market-neutral portfolio after inception is handled like any other trading on a trading desk, with two exceptions. First, since the portfolio is a "package" which must remain both risk-balanced and cash-balanced, coordination on the trading desk is required when trading in market neutral-portfolio names, particularly when the same assets perhaps are being bought or sold for long-only accounts at the same time. Second, coordination of order transition is important — for instance, the valuation parameters of a stock currently held short in the portfolio can change, and the manager might want to have the stock in the "long" portfolio. To accomplish this, the shorted stock must first be "covered" (or returned to the lender) before any new purchases are made for the stock. This coordination requires good accounting and execution systems to be done properly and efficiently.

CONCLUSION

This chapter has given a brief overview of what market-neutral portfolio management is, and how it can benefit pension plans and other institutional investors. Though brief, the chapter has touched on what has motivated the growth of this style of management, the key characteristics that one should look for in a market-neutral manager, and the benefits that can come from it. The section on how a market-neutral portfolio is run in practice hopefully showed how one manager has used a successful process and its familiarity with risk control techniques to efficiently combine information into a market-neutral portfolio.

Market-neutral portfolios are an exciting extension of long-only portfolio management. For a manager who has a very well defined stock ranking process and is proficient in the combination of these expectations with the risks that accompany them, the management of market-neutral portfolios allows the manager to extend the use of information he/she has. We expect to see the continued growth of this type of portfolio management as the institutional plan sponsor community recognizes the increased efficiency and portability benefits that a plan gains from using the style of management as part of their overall structure.

Chapter 11

Enhanced Indexing

Michael L. Steinberg
Associate
Smith Breeden Associates, Inc.

Gerald J. Madigan
Principal
Smith Breeden Associates, Inc.

INTRODUCTION

Tales of passive asset investment strategies are not likely to be the subject of cocktail party banter. On the contrary, many more entertaining stories will encompass how John or Jane Investor sleuthed the market once again by picking XYZ stock. It is, however, a uniquely human behavior pattern that enables these same investors to omit mention of any market *underperformance* they may have experienced (due to "selective asymmetrical returns memory" or "realized loss amnesia"). The important question here is whether John and Jane are boasting of overall market outperformance from year to year (assuming they weren't so obnoxious as not to receive a return invitation to each year's cocktail party). In other words, was their ingenious investment strategy consistent over time? Those partygoers who stood quietly in the corner smiling and shaking their heads during this conversation would probably say "no" and would likely be advocates of passive investment styles, or indexing.

Given the realization that indexing lacks the flair worthy of party chatter, investment professionals now offer an alternative for both passive and active investors alike: *enhanced indexing.* The lure of enhanced indexing lies in the possibility of combining the diversification and reliability advantages of passive index management with investment returns exceeding the relevant index. This chapter is comprised of four sections. The first section discusses the growing trend toward passive investing and the role of enhanced indexing in the evolving investment marketplace. The second section introduces three distinct contemporary approaches to enhanced index investment management. The third section discusses the factors that determine the success or failure of the "enhanced cash" management approach. The final section describes the implementation of this "enhanced cash" approach by Smith Breeden Associates as it relates to S&P 500 Index "enhanced index" accounts.

Exhibit 1: Growth of Institutional Indexed Assets (1973-1997)
(U.S. Tax-Exempt Holdings)

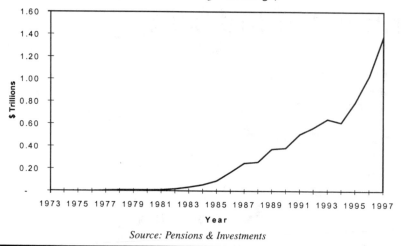

Source: Pensions & Investments

THE GROWING ROLE OF
PASSIVE INVESTMENT APPROACHES

While enhanced indexing involves both active and passive management techniques, it has principally evolved from the practice and growing recent popularity of indexing. In the scope of investment management history, indexing is a relatively recent phenomenon. In late 1997, *Pensions & Investments* magazine reported that the holdings of U.S. tax-exempt institutions in indexed assets rose to approximately $1.4 trillion from less than $100 billion only 12 years earlier (see Exhibit 1). The use of indexing within the mutual fund sector has also grown rapidly (see Exhibit 2). While $1.5 trillion was held in U.S. diversified actively-managed equity mutual funds, $136 billion was in diversified domestic equity index funds as of year-end 1997. Enhanced indexing is younger still, with significant investment only in this decade.

Many factors have contributed to the growth of indexing. Chief among them has been the increased awareness of the importance of asset allocation decision to ultimate performance and the spotty record of active managers in specific investment categories. The emergence of standardized quantitative measures of risk and return and wide market acceptance of the importance of diversification flowed directly from the introduction of Modern Portfolio Theory (MPT) in 1970. More recently, a study by Brinson, Singer, and Beebower investigated the performance of 82 large U.S. pension funds for the period of 1977 to 1987.[1] This study revealed that 91.5% of the total variation in these funds' performance could be

---

[1] Gary P. Brinson, Brian D. Singer, and Gilbert L. Beebower, "Determinants of Portfolio Performance II: An Update," *Financial Analysts Journal* (May/June 1991).

attributed to asset allocation policies while security selection and market timing only accounted for the small remainder of variation. As investors have become more accepting of the role of investment policy on one's returns, they have focused more on the selection of asset classes. Since indexing provides very precise and consistent definitions of the risk and return parameters of an asset class, the use of indexing to more closely mirror the investor's selected asset classes has grown.

The increased popularity of indexed funds can also be attributed to increased investor scrutiny of the value of active management in highly competitive market sectors. As demonstrated in Exhibit 3, active managers of domestic equity securities have not been able to consistently outperform the S&P 500 Index. Furthermore, the higher level of trading activity involved in actively managed funds passes along a higher cost structure to investors. These factors, in addition to growing investor patience in long-term strategies coupled with the ease associated with monitoring passive investments, have all played a part in the growth of indexed funds.

Exhibit 2: Mutual Fund Assets of U.S. Diversified Equity Funds ($ billions)

Year	Amount in U.S. Diversified Actively-Managed Equity Mutual Funds	Amount in U.S. Diversified Equity Index Mutual Funds	Amount in U.S. Diversified Enhanced Index Equity Mutual Funds
1997	1,462.4	135.7	14.1
1996	1,067.4	80.0	8.0
1995	786.4	46.6	5.9
1994	522.1	26.0	3.2
1993	460.6	22.3	2.5
1992	338.7	15.0	1.6
1991	257.9	9.4	0.9
1990	170.7	4.6	0.5
1989	177.8	3.6	0.5
1988	137.4	2.3	0.2

Source: Morningstar, Inc.

Exhibit 3: Percent of U.S. Diversified Actively-Managed Equity Funds Outperforming the S&P 500 Index*

Year	Percentage
1997	10
1996	25
1995	17
1994	24
1993	65
1992	59
1991	62
1990	38
1989	22
1988	46

*Excludes index and enhanced index equity funds. Net-of-fees, before taxes.
Source: Morningstar, Inc.

Exhibit 2 also illustrates the growth demonstrated in enhanced index equity funds. At the end of 1997 $14 billion was held in U.S. diversified enhanced index equity funds. The growth of these funds can be seen as resulting from both increasing investor interest in passive management styles and a desire to achieve returns in excess of the average for the selected asset class.

Modern Portfolio Theory and Active and Passive Management

As stated previously, the practice of enhanced indexing involves the uses of both active and passive management styles. To better understand how these methods differ, a review of the Capital Asset Pricing Model (CAPM)[2] is useful.

In equilibrium, or under the conditions of efficient markets, the CAPM defines a security's expected rate of return as:

$$E(Return_i) = r_f + \beta_i[E(R_{market}) - r_f] \qquad (1)$$

where

r_f = the risk-free rate of return.

β_i = the *market risk*, or the covariance of security *i*'s return with respect to the return of the market.

R_{market} = a random variable representing the return of the market.

This theory posits that the expected return of a security should equal the risk-free rate plus a risk premium that is commensurate with its market risk, or β.

While the benefits of diversification are accepted under both management styles, it is the belief in efficient markets that separates the two. In active portfolio management, the presumption of efficient markets must be relaxed. When applied in terms of the CAPM, this rationale implies that securities may demonstrate returns that are not equal to their return in equilibrium. This difference between a security's expected return and its return in equilibrium is known as alpha (α). Equation (1) can now be amended to include alpha and can be written as:

$$E(Return_i) = \alpha_i + r_f + \beta_i[E(R_{market}) - r_f] \qquad (2)$$

In a strictly efficient market, a security's alpha will be equal to zero and its return will be dictated solely by its response to changes in the overall market. In the context of a portfolio of securities, the formula's variables can be extended to demonstrate that:

---

[2] William F. Sharpe, "Capital Asset Prices: A Theory of Market Equilibrium under Conditions of Risk," *The Journal of Finance* (September 1964), pp. 425-442; John Lintner, "The Valuation of Risk Assets and the Selection of Risky Investments in Stock Portfolios and Capital Budgets," *Review of Economics and Statistics* (February 1965), pp. 13-37; and, Jan Mossin, "Equilibrium in a Capital Asset Market," *Econometrica* (October 1966), pp. 768-783.

$$\alpha_{Port} = \Sigma w_i \alpha_i$$
$$\beta_{Port} = \Sigma w_i \beta_i$$

where

    α_{Port} = the weighted average alpha of a portfolio.
    β_{Port} = the weighted average beta of a portfolio.

Given that active managers believe that inefficiencies exist, they will attempt to identify, through various valuation approaches, securities which may have either positive or negative alphas. Active managers will then buy securities deemed to have positive alphas and/or sell securities deemed to have negative alphas.

    Passive managers, or "indexers," generally respect the efficiency of the markets, and the concept of zero alphas. A prototypical index fund will simply hold all of the securities included in the index at the index weighting. If that approach is impractical for some reason, a very close proxy is created by replacing securities such that, in the aggregate, the portfolio replicates the risk characteristics, or beta, of a designated benchmark.

CONTEMPORARY APPROACHES TO ENHANCED INDEXING

Armed with a theoretical understanding of both active and passive management dogmas, one can conceptualize the approach of enhanced equity indexing. In the context of the risk and return framework, an enhanced equity index fund targets the risk attributes, or beta of a selected equity index, while attempting to generate returns in excess of that index. Thus, again it can be said that an enhanced indexing strategy will involve elements of both indexing and active management. These approaches seek to placate the growing number of indexers while also satiating the more aggressive appetites of active investors. While there are numerous strategies that may be attempted to achieve this, there are four approaches which dominate the practice today. The essence of the differences among these approaches is the source of the alpha generation. In each, the manager chooses a part of the portfolio in which he/she has expertise to provide better than index results on a consistent basis. Clearly, the key question for the investor is "what is the source of the alpha?" The first approach, "underlying security/sector selection," springs from the practice of varying holdings only slightly from the index weights. The other three, "index arbitrage," "active synthetic contracts management," and "enhanced cash management" derive from continuous or intermittent replication of the index through use of synthetic contracts.

Underlying Security/Sector Selection

The security/sector selection methods of enhanced equity indexing provide an extension of active equity management. The goal of the security selection method is to utilize stock valuation measures to identify both undervalued and overvalued securities within the benchmark's index. From these findings, a portfolio that is beta (risk) neutral to the index is created by establishing overweighted positions in the undervalued securities. Similarly, under sector selection, the goal is to identify sectors of the benchmark's index that are either over or undervalued. Again, a beta neutral portfolio is constructed, this time by overweighting the sectors of the index deemed undervalued.

As mentioned above, both methods utilize the disciplines of active equity management. Thus, the gains from these techniques are subject to *the ability of the manager to identify any positive or negative alphas in the stocks and/or sectors of the underlying index.* For this reason, this method of enhanced indexing may not appeal to strict passive investors who believe in the efficiency of the equity markets. Another drawback associated with this style is that frequent security/sector rotation will produce higher transaction costs than those incurred by a passively managed fund. Additionally, by overweighting certain stocks/sectors within an index while underweighting others, these funds may contain more *security-specific risk.* That is to say, it is the risk that would otherwise be "diversified-away" by holding all the stocks within the index. Finally, the likelihood of *tracking error*[3] may prove to be more significant for this strategy than for some of the alternatives. This measure relates to the differences in returns demonstrated by a fund versus its benchmark. For these reasons, many investors have concluded that security/sector approach essentially represents a diluted version of traditional active management and often does not achieve the goals of a passive mandate.

Approaches Utilizing Synthetic Replication of an Index

These enhanced indexing approaches begin with synthetic construction of a targeted index using futures, options, and/or swaps. The leveraged nature of these tools allows for the investment of most of the account assets in money market instruments. The synthetic contracts are typically priced such that holding the contracts with a notional value equal to account total assets, plus money market securities with a face amount equal to account total assets, will consistently produce a return equivalent to a like account with all account assets invested in the securities underlying the target index. This relationship for an S&P 500 Index account is depicted below (see Exhibit 4).

---

[3] Mark W. Riepe and Matthew D. Werner, "Are Enhanced Index Mutual Funds Worthy of Their Name?" Ibbotson Associates, 1998. In the paper, tracking error is defined as follows:

$$\text{Tracking Error} = \sqrt{\frac{\Sigma(E_t - \bar{E})^2}{T-1}}$$

$E_t = Rfund_t - Rbenchmark_t$

$\bar{E} = (1/T)\Sigma E_t$

where
$Rfund_t$ = the return of a fund over period t.
$Rbenchmark_t$ = the total return of the benchmark for period t.
T = the total number of periods.

Exhibit 4: Synthetic S&P 500 Index

Money Market Return	+	S&P 500 Overlay Using Synthetic Contracts	=	Return on S&P 500 Index Including Dividends

This relationship is most easily visualized by creating an account that uses a single swap contract to obtain the derived S&P 500 Index exposure. If the account assets total $100 million, a swap with a $100 million notional amount would be created. For a specified period of time, the account would agree to pay a money market interest rate (approximately LIBOR) based on the notional amount and the counterparty would agree to pay the S&P 500 Index total return to the account based on the notional amount. The account then would invest the account assets in money market securities with a combined yield approximately equal to the rate it must pay the counterparty. Thus, the money market investment and swap obligation interest nets out to approximately zero for the account and it receives the S&P 500 Index total return from the counterparty. In the end, the account's net return is the S&P 500 Index total return.

    Receive S&P 500 Index Total Return Based on $100MM Notional Amount
  − Pay Money Market Return Based on $100MM Notional Amount
  + Earn Money Market Return on $100MM Cash Invested
  = S&P Index Total Return on $100MM

At first blush, it may seem unusual to expect a counterparty to be willing to trade a stock market return for a money market return. However, if you envision the position of a sophisticated, well-capitalized counterparty, it becomes clear why this type of contract is available at such a price. Some institutional investors are able to purchase the underlying stocks and obtain financing at a rate less than money market rates. Then by executing a contract such as the one described above, the net result would be a locked-in spread between their financing rate and comparable short-term rates. These counterparties keep the pricing of swaps, futures, and options in line on a continuous basis.

The following example demonstrates how S&P 500 Index futures can be used to replicate a portfolio of stocks in proportion to the S&P 500 Index. A manager wishes to replicate a $100 million stock portfolio that has a beta of 1.0 with respect to the S&P 500 Index with S&P 500 Index futures. The current spot value of the index is 950.00 and each point of the S&P 500 Index is worth $250.

The number of contracts required for replication will be (assuming any variation on futures will be realized at expiration):

Contracts = (Portfolio Assets × β)/
(Spot Value of Index × Value of one point of the Index)
= ($100,000,000 × 1.0)/(950 × 250)
= 421

The relative ease with which a stock portfolio can be constructed by using futures or other synthetic securities plus cash-like investments provides for the following three different enhanced index strategies using synthetic replication.

Index Arbitrage

The index arbitrage approach entails constant monitoring of the relationship between the pricing of futures (plus money market securities) versus pricing of the underlying securities and purchasing the cheaper alternative in place of the richer alternative. To understand this technique, one must first understand the pricing of a futures contract. By definition, the fair or theoretical price of an index future is:

$$F_{theoretical} = S \times (1 + (r - d) \times t/360) \tag{3}$$

where

S = the spot value of the index.
r = the annualized risk-free rate.
d = the annualized dividend yield of the index.
t = the days to expiration of the contract.

The price of the futures contract should trade very near its fair value. If these values deviate too much, arbitrage will drive the futures contract's value back to its fair value. For example, if the actual market value of the futures (F_{market}) is trading above its fair value, or $F_{market} > F_{theoretical}$ (after considering transaction costs), an arbitrageur will buy the stocks of the underlying index and sell a notionally equivalent amount of futures. Conversely, if the contract is trading below its fair value, or $F_{market} < F_{theoretical}$, an arbitrageur will short the stocks of the underlying index and buy a notionally equivalent amount of futures. Given these forces, an enhanced portfolio manager using the index arbitrage technique will *attempt to generate alpha by being long the underlying stocks of the index when the futures are trading rich.* Antithetically, if the market value of the futures is trading cheap, the manager will *attempt to generate alpha by holding futures.*

Early in the life of S&P 500 Index futures market, well-executed index arbitrage programs produced significant profits by exploiting the frequent and significant inefficiencies in the pricing of futures versus the cash market. These opportunities, however, have become scarcer as the market has matured and the pricing of futures contracts has become more efficient. Now, any mispricings are quickly corrected through the rapid actions of a large number of sophisticated arbitrageurs. In addition, the market circuit breakers and other trading restrictions aimed at limiting "program trading" that have been implemented in recent years have reduced further the reliability and attractiveness of this activity.

Active Synthetic Contract Management

A second enhanced indexing approach, which relies on synthetic replication of the index can be described as active synthetic contract management. Managers subscribing to this approach invest a small amount of the portfolio in synthetic contracts designed to provide exposure equal to the account capital level and invest the remainder in cash-like instruments which produce a return similar to the short-term funding cost, as described above. Where these managers *attempt to generate alpha is in the active management of the futures, options, and swap contracts.* The goal of active management here is to take advantage of perceived inefficiencies in and among those markets. In other words, the money market portion of the portfolio is managed to obtain a money market return just as though pure index replication was the goal. While the beta of the portfolio will be maintained at 1.0 versus the index, the makeup of the synthetic contracts providing the beta are actively managed to attempt to produce excess returns. Thus, the success of this approach is dependent on the number and degree of mispricings (inefficiencies) in the markets for the synthetics and the skill of the manager in recognizing and taking advantage of them.

Enhanced Cash Management

The third and final approach utilizing synthetic replication of the index is the enhanced cash approach. Under this approach, synthetic contracts are used to obtain the market index exposure just as for a pure index replication. However, instead of investing the account cash in money market instruments earning a short-term rate of return, the cash is invested in an actively managed portfolio of securities designed to reliably outperform money market returns without adding significant risk. Thus, the manager *attempts to generate alpha by outperforming in the money market portion of the account.*

One unusual characteristic of this approach is that its success is not dependent on the existence of inefficiencies in the markets for the securities underlying the index or in the futures and option markets related to the index. The alpha generated by outperforming in the cash portion of the account is portable among markets, as long as synthetic contracts are available to effectively create the desired index exposure at fair prices. The cash portion of the enhanced cash strategy portfolio could be invested in any type of securities as long as the risk level can be controlled to limit the tracking error between the portfolio returns and money market returns to an acceptable level.

THE ENHANCED CASH MANAGEMENT APPROACH

As briefly described above, the enhanced cash management approach represents one of several ways in which enhanced indexing can be accomplished. The use of synthetic replication allows for portability of alpha from less efficient markets into markets demonstrating greater efficiency. The following discussion explores the applicability of the strategy and the key factors, which determine the success or failure of the approach. The evaluation of the following factors stand out as the most important in gauging the relative success and applicability of the activity: the suitability of the benchmark index and the inefficiency of the securities within the market utilized to outperform money market instruments and the ability of the individual manager to take advantage of these mispricings to generate an excess return.

Evaluation of the Suitability of the Benchmark Index

In determining a benchmark for an enhanced index strategy, several items should be considered. Of these considerations, the ability to create a reliable synthetic replication of the index, or *overlay*, should be paramount. The reliability here will be determined by the ability of the overlay account to consistently demonstrate minimal tracking error with respect to the benchmark. This tracking error can be greatly mitigated by selecting a benchmark with highly liquid tools for replication that predominantly demonstrate arbitrage-free pricing. These instruments often include futures, swaps, and options. While the availability of all three instruments as vehicles for replication is preferable, an index that at the very least has comparable futures contracts that exhibit fair prices is preferred. Futures are preferable due to the default risk contained in swaps and the "richness" or "cheapness" that options may exhibit. Thus satisfying the conditions of efficient, safe, and fairly priced derivative availability with respect to a selected benchmark will generally lead to a greater predictability of overlay returns.

Another factor to consider when selecting an index would be the historical performance of active managers versus the index. The inability of active managers to consistently outperform a specific benchmark generally indicates their participation in an efficient market. This may provide an opportunity for a more favorable result using an enhanced indexing approach due to the portability of alpha (from a less efficient market) that a synthetic replication plus bonds approach may provide.

The cost structures of actively managed equity funds also warrants consideration. Compared to certain benchmarks, active equity managers may incur significantly higher costs associated with their strategies. These costs may include more frequent turnover of their portfolio, larger bid-ask spreads that may be present in less liquid markets, and higher management fees. Therefore, employing an enhanced index strategy where cost savings may be realized may also present a more attractive alternative to active equity management.

Evaluation of the Alpha Generation Activity

The second major part of the enhanced cash approach to enhanced indexing involves the generation of alpha. In contrast to determining the ideal market benchmark, one where mispricings and repeatable profit opportunities are limited (more efficient), the ideal market for generating alpha should present significant and repeatable opportunities for an effective manager to outperform the market return (less efficient). This opportunity to outperform is provided by the combination of an existence of significant numbers of volatile mispricings and the ability of a limited number of participants to consistently take advantage of those opportunities. The long-term feasibility of this repeatable outperformance is further dependent upon the selected market demonstrating both liquidity and long-term promise for this strategy. In other words an inefficient market, demonstrating liquidity, in which certain participants have an advantage in evaluation and trading will provide the most favorable conditions for this strategy.

Since the benchmark for the cash enhancement (alpha generation) portion of the activity is a money market-like return, the risk characteristics of the securities utilized must, either naturally or through hedging, resemble those of a short-term money market investment. An additional consideration is the correlation of the securities utilized in alpha generation with the securities in the benchmark index. Inclusion of securities in the alpha generation portion of the account which are correlated with the benchmark index in a meaningful way will increase the beta of the portfolio relative to the benchmark index. An example of a portfolio with such a potential correlation problem would be a portfolio benchmarked to the S&P 500 Index which is fully replicated synthetically but also holds low grade U.S. corporate bonds which display significant correlation with the U.S. stocks.

Finally, even if a market is chosen which provides opportunities for reliable generation of excess returns, the particular manager executing the strategy must possess skill in identifying mispricings. Furthermore, consistent demonstration of this skill is essential for the long-term success of this strategy.

Additional Considerations

The level of turnover resulting from the use of synthetic replication in addition to an active approach in the management of the cash portion under the enhanced cash management strategy may produce taxable capital gains. Due to this, these accounts are often more appropriate for either nontaxable or tax-deferred funds.

CREATING AN S&P 500 ENHANCED INDEX FUND

The Standard & Poor's Composite Stock Price Index (S&P 500) is composed of 500 common U.S. exchange-traded stocks. The index represents a diverse industry base and is priced on a market-value-weighted average. Several tools exist that allow for the leveraged replication of this index. These tools include futures, swaps, and options. The highly liquid nature of these instruments coupled with their propensity to be fairly priced with respect to the S&P 500 Index and the sketchy record of active managers attempting to outperform this index makes it an attractive benchmark for an enhanced index approach.

Smith Breeden Associates' S&P 500 Index Overlay Construction

The following will demonstrate how, with the use of synthetic instruments, an S&P 500 overlay account can be constructed. Furthermore, the use of a low risk portfolio of hedged mortgage-backed securities (MBS) as the cash enhancement segment generates the alpha under this approach.

Futures

In the example presented earlier in this chapter, the replication of a $100 million stock portfolio with S&P 500 Index futures was illustrated as:

Contracts = (Portfolio Assets × β)/
(Spot Value of Index × Value of one point of the Index)

The leveraged nature of this approach to replication requires that a little over 5% of the fund's assets be posted for margin. This allows for investment of almost 95% of the fund's assets in securities replacing the money market portion of the portfolio. It can therefore be said that two segments exist within this structure: (1) an account representing almost 95% of the assets and (2) an S&P 500 overlay account with the remaining assets held in margin (money market securities). If the larger account is not actively invested, one can assume that it will earn a short-term rate of return. Therefore, assuming a short-term rate of return on this segment plus the return of the overlay account, the replication of the S&P 500 Index is thus shown by Exhibit 4.

As illustrated in the exhibit, the proper construction of the overlay account is a key element in achieving returns similar to the index. By revisiting the earlier example, it can be shown how this approach can be fine-tuned to create a more efficient futures overlay account. In determining the number of contracts held in the overlay account in the example, it was assumed that the variation in the price of the futures would be realized only at expiration. In reality this is not the case, as prices change daily and these daily gains and losses accrue interest. The interest-earning feature of these accounts is important in that must be considered when calculating the number of S&P 500 Index contracts needed. More specifically, the number of contracts required can be reduced to account for the interest earned by the margin account. Furthermore, by reviewing the theoretical value formula for the S&P 500 Index futures contract in equation (3), it can be seen that another component of the overlay account remains. The theoretical value of the futures contract depends upon the relevant risk-free rate assumed from the date of investment until contract expiration. The contract's fair value will increase when rates rise and decrease when rates fall. This sensitivity to changes in interest rates can be hedged, however, and the majority of its interest rate risk can be removed. Given the assumption that the relevant rate will be the risk-free rate to the time to expiration of the futures contract, short-term money market rate futures can be used to hedge this interest rate risk.

Equity Swaps

In addition to the use of S&P 500 Index futures for composing the overlay account, S&P 500 Index equity swaps may also be used. Equity swaps are over-the-counter (OTC), or non-exchange traded contracts designed to closely track the return of the S&P 500 Index. A manager wishing to replicate a portfolio would enter into an equity swap with a counterparty. This counterparty will usually be a commercial bank or an investment bank. The counterparty will agree to pay the dividends and capital gains of the S&P 500 Index as determined by the contract's notional amount in exchange for a floating rate of interest (typically LIBOR) on the notional amount. Thus the return on the swap should be the gain or loss on the notional amount plus dividends on the stocks of the S&P 500 Index less the interest paid on the notional amount. The use of equity swaps will be linked to both the "fairness" of the swap's price and creditworthiness of the counterparty.

The price of a swap for the investor receiving any capital gains and dividends will generally be quoted as a spread to LIBOR. As with futures, the fair value of a swap should reflect an arbitrage-free level. In this case, that level would be the cost of hedging a similar arrangement using the cash market and forward contracts as shown in equation (4).

$$P_{forward} = P_{spot} \times (1 + repo) \tag{4}$$

where

$P_{forward}$ = the price of a forward contract on the index.
P_{spot} = the spot value of the index.
$repo$ = repo rate, or interest rate on such short-term cash transactions

A swap contract will be fairly priced when the spread to LIBOR (or LIBOR minus the swap spread) is equal to the repurchase agreement (repo) rate. As mentioned previously, the attractiveness of these agreements will also be related to the financial soundness of the counterparty. This is due to the default risk they contain. The creditworthiness will directly affect the level of the swap spread as counterparties demonstrating strong credit ratings will command a lower spread and vice-versa.

Options

The use of both exchange-traded and OTC options also represent vehicles for index replication. As with swaps and futures, the "fairness" in their prices will also determine the prudence of their use. A detailed discussion of the use of these instruments is beyond the scope of this chapter. It should be noted however, that use of these instruments will be most beneficial when used to complement either a futures or swap position. The implied volatility of the underlying index value that is inherent in the prices of these options often dictates their use. For example a manager may buy or sell these depending on their "richness" or "cheapness." This decision will be based on a comparison of the options' implied volatility versus their historical norms.

The Enhanced Cash Management Segment: A Look at Mortgage-Backed Securities

As discussed earlier, the ability of a manager to generate an excess return in the enhanced cash segment will primarily determine the success of this approach to enhanced indexing. Various fixed income market sectors contain features which may generate inefficiencies. These inefficiencies are more likely to exist in markets containing bonds with uncertain cash flows. In these markets, managers possessing superior skills at valuing these securities may be able to generate consistent excess returns (alpha). Understanding the rationale behind the use of certain fixed income markets for alpha generation, Exhibit 4 can now be revised as in Exhibit 5.

As shown in Exhibit 5, rather than simply holding the non-overlay assets in a fund earning short-term interest, these assets will now be actively invested in fixed income assets. The goal here is to achieve a higher return on these assets than the return they would have earned had they simply been held in an account earning a short-term rate of interest and after taking operating expenses into account without introducing meaningful tracking error.

Long-Term Feasibility and Liquidity — The Use of Mortgage-Backed Securities

As mentioned previously, for the strategy to be viable for a long period of time, the assets must be invested in a continuously liquid market. Exhibit 6 provides the sizes of some of the largest areas of the fixed income markets in the United States.

Mortgage debt represents a sizable component of total credit market debt. Within this sector, the amount of the mortgage debt that has been securitized, or pledged as collateral for securities, is substantial. These securities, representing pools backed by the cash flows of underlying individual mortgages, make up the mortgage-backed securities (MBS) market. The recent size of this market is in excess of $2 trillion (Exhibit 7). The size, liquidity, and growth in the MBS sector indicate that these securities possess characteristics desirable for use in the alpha-generation portion of an enhanced index strategy

Exhibit 5: Enhanced S&P 500 Index

Short Duration Fixed Income Portfolio Designed to Generate Excess Returns ("Alpha") over the Money Market Return	+	S&P 500 Overlay Using Synthetic Contracts	=	S&P 500 Index Including Dividends + Alpha

Exhibit 6: Total Credit Market Debt, Domestic and Foreign, Owed by Financial and Nonfinancial Sectors
($ billions, end of period)

	1997*	1996	1995	1994	1993
U.S. Treasuries	6,467	6,390	6,014	5,665	5,217
Municipal Securities	1,316	1,295	1,294	1,342	1,378
Corporate and Foreign Bonds	3,158	3,066	2,793	2,481	2,328
Mortgages	5,162	5,022	4,692	4,463	4,261

* End of Second Quarter 1997.

Source: Federal Reserve Bulletin

Exhibit 7: Outstanding Principal Balance of MBS (End of Period)

	1997*	1996	1995	1994	1993
Mortgage-Backed Securities ($bb)	2,134	2,056	1,861	1,726	1,570
As a Percent of Mortgage Debt (%)	41.3	40.9	39.7	38.7	36.8

* End of Second Quarter 1997.

Source: Federal Reserve Bulletin

Another favorable aspect of MBS relates to the minimal credit risk associated with most of these bonds. The majority of mortgage securities are backed by the United States government or United States governmental agencies (GNMA, FNMA, and FHLMC) and carry AAA ratings.

It should be noted that while a market's size and overall credit rating does contribute to its liquidity, this measure is easily determined by examining the market prices of these securities, or more specifically their bid-ask spread. A wide spread between where a security can be bought (ask) and sold (bid) indicates unfavorable liquidity properties. The excellent liquidity of the most common MBS, known as *passthrough securities*, is indicated by the narrow spreads (generally in the order of $1/32$ to $4/32$ of 1%) that they display. By investing in these securities which possess minimal bid-ask spreads, liquidity risk can be greatly reduced.

Alpha in the MBS Market

MBS, as well as some corporate and agency securities, contain embedded options, generally call features. Mortgages allow borrowers to prepay at any time. Corporate and agency bonds often contain options which permit the bonds' issuers to retire the outstanding debt and reissue it when interest rates are more favorable (lower). The presence of these options tags these securities with what is known as *call risk*. Call risk creates several complexities for investors. One complexity lies in the unpredictable nature of the embedded option and the resulting difficulty in determining the cash flows of the bond. Additionally, an investor may experience *reinvestment risk* when a security is called. This is the risk that the proceeds returned to an investor after a bond is called may have to be invested at lower rates of interest. A final and nontrivial trait of bonds with embedded call options is known as *negative convexity*. This characteristic limits the upside price potential of a bond given the threat of its being called if interest rates fall. These bonds thus demonstrate asymmetrical price movements in response to interest rate movements in that their price will decline more for a given rate increase than their price will rise for an equal decrease in rates.

Given the risks that exist in bonds with embedded calls, these securities generally display higher yields than Treasuries of comparable maturity. These higher yields are commonly quoted as spreads over the term structure of interest rates, or as a *spread-to-the-curve* (Treasury yield curve). This spread equates to the incremental yield that would be earned over the Treasury curve assuming the bonds are held to maturity and market conditions do not change. Realizing that call risk exists in these bonds, and therefore the fragility of the assumption that they are held to maturity, a spread adjusted for the call risk of a bond proves to be a more appropriate measure. The measure used to reflect the call risk is known as the *option-adjusted spread* (OAS). The calculation of the OAS incorporates volatility in the term structure of interest rates, that is — changing market conditions. This methodology allows the investor to consider probable future paths of interest rates and the examination of a bond's cash flows in each possible scenario. The OAS is the spread over Treasuries that equates the average present value of the cash flows from each of these paths to a bond's price.

Since the OAS attempts to value the incremental risk-adjusted yield that can be earned over the least risky securities (in this case Treasury securities), its size and range of values varies across different fixed income asset classes. The size and variance of spreads are ultimately related to the predictability of their cash flows. A direct relationship will exist between this predictability and the agreement among market participants regarding the assumptions underlying the calculation of the OAS. Said another way, bonds displaying a greater predictability of cash flows will have a more simple and standard set of assumptions for determining their OAS.

Generally, the more elementary these assumptions, the lower and more stable the OAS. For example, most non-mortgage, corporate, and agency securities possess fairly uniform price characteristics. With the exception of the inherent credit risk in corporates, the price sensitivity of these classes to interest rates is usually the major determinant of the exercise of the embedded option. As a result, the size and variance of related risk-adjusted yields will be modest. With MBS, a broader diversity of structures exists. Moreover, by their construction (i.e., various collateralized mortgage obligations), some of these structures may contribute more uncertainty to the evaluation of their cash flows. Finally, factors other than interest rates will determine whether the mortgages underlying an MBS will be prepaid. These factors are primarily related to individual decisions contributing to the sale of a property. Thus, the broader range of structures and the additional contingencies related to the exercise of the MBS's option require a more extensive and complex set of assumptions when calculating the OASs of these securities. This complexity contributes to difficulty in modeling the OAS of an MBS and directly results in both a larger and more variant risk-adjusted result and more opportunity for investors. A hypothetical representation of these spreads can be seen in Exhibit 8 where the points represent hypothetical individual securities.

The resulting higher mean and wider variance of OASs in MBS provides for the possibility that a greater average spread can be earned over Treasuries versus other markets. The key in realizing these spreads will be related to a manager's skill in accurately assessing the risk/return characteristics of individual securities. To further understand this, a more detailed look at the MBS investment process is helpful (see Exhibit 9).

Exhibit 8: Comparative Risk-Adjusted Yields on Low Credit Risk Securities

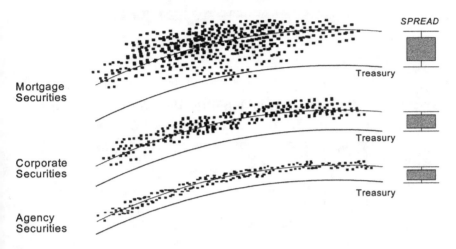

Exhibit 9: The MBS Investment Process

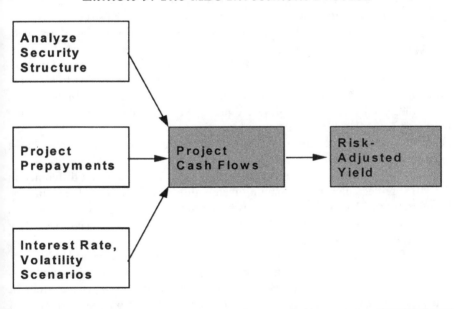

Exhibit 10: Lifetime Prepayment Estimates of Various Wall Street Firms (CPRs)

Coupon	7 Dealer Avg.	Firm A	Firm B	Firm C
8.0	15.8%	15.4%	17.8%	6.4%
8.5	20.5%	22.1%	29.4%	6.6%
9.0	19.7%	31.3%	17.5%	7.6%

Source: Bloomberg Information Services, July 1997

Exhibit 11: Comparison of Various Wall Street Firms' OAS on 30-Year Fixed Rate MBS

Coupon	Firm 1	Firm 2	Firm 3	Firm 4	Min	Max	Range
6%	19	28	34	24	19	34	15
7%	24	25	47	33	24	47	23
8%	32	27	60	39	27	60	33
9%	1	-15	67	33	-15	67	82
10%	98	N/A	33	52	33	98	65

Source: Published Mortgage Market Research, June 1997

Exhibit 9 illustrates the importance of the underlying assumptions used in modeling the projected cash flow of a MBS and determining its risk-adjusted spread. As stated earlier, these assumptions relate to the bond's structure, the volatility of the term structure of interest rates, and its call rules. Any disparity among the underlying assumptions used by different managers will result in a difference in the perceived fair values for these securities. These differences in valuation create inefficiencies and opportunities to earn excess returns. Differences in the assumptions will occur more often with respect to the call rules. In the case of MBS, these call rules are the projected prepayments on these bonds' underlying mortgage loans. Looking at a comparison of prepayment forecasts used by various Wall Street firms, demonstrates the significant variance of assumptions among market participants (see Exhibit 10).

This variance in prepayment assumptions translates into a difference in the MBS' projected cash flows and ultimately different OAS fair value estimates. Examination of Exhibit 11 illustrates how broad the range of results are with respect to different securities' risk-adjusted yields given the variance of modeling assumptions that exists.

Exhibit 11 provides convincing evidence that a divergence of beliefs exist as to actual fair values within the MBS arena even among sophisticated market participants. These differences, arising from the disparate assumptions of MBS market participants regarding prepayment expectations, are evidence of inefficiencies in the MBS market. A skilled manager should then be able to earn an excess return in the large, highly liquid but complex MBS market. A manager who also possesses the skill of measuring risk and hedging risk will further enhance these returns.

Success in Finding Alpha

While it has been shown that alpha can exist in the MBS market, consistently realizing this alpha will be critical to the success of the enhanced cash approach. Given the complexity of the assumptions involved in predicting the projected cash flows of a MBS, a manager demonstrating consistent proficiency in modeling these will hold a competitive advantage in locating alpha within this market. This proficiency will result from a diligence in detailed research used in generating the underlying assumptions used in modeling MBS. This will be further augmented by continually developing one's MBS model to reflect both additional contingencies within the assumptions as well as state-of-the-art developments in the area of financial engineering. Although no model will ever be able to perfectly predict homeowners' prepayment behavior, those coming the closest will be more successful in consistently earning excess returns.

CONCLUSION

The diversification and reliability advantages of passive management along with the possibility of earning returns greater than a desired index have all contributed the to development of enhanced indexing. In the risk and return context, enhanced indexing targets the risk attributes of a selected index while attempting to generate returns in excess of that index. Numerous strategies can be utilized to attempt this. One specific strategy involves an enhanced cash management approach. As with other enhanced indexing approaches the key to its long-term success is contingent upon a number of factors. One factor lies in the benchmark selected and the means employed in replicating the benchmark. Furthermore, the sources for generating excess returns and the manager's skill in identifying these will determine the feasibility of the enhanced indexing strategy used.

Chapter 12

Dynamic Style Allocation

Bruce D. Westervelt, CFA
Executive Director, CIO
First Madison Advisors

INTRODUCTION

The concept that equity styles are the key to realized risk and return for a diversified equity portfolio has recently received a great deal of attention. The purpose of this chapter is to summarize the evidence on equity style management and show how it is applied to First Madison Advisors' investment approach called Dynamic Style Allocation.

MAKING THE CASE FOR EQUITY STYLE MANAGEMENT

The work by Nobel Laureate William F. Sharpe on style analysis and his contention that 98% of a multi-manager pension fund's performance can be explained by style, has created considerable interest in the topic.[1] Sharpe has indicated in correspondence that, "For a single equity mutual fund the typical number is more like 85% to 90% (out of sample)." This, of course, is why investment management consultants have been placing equity managers in style boxes (i.e., large cap value, small cap growth) for evaluation purposes for quite a while. However, the idea of controlling exposure to equity styles as an active process for adding excess return has only been prevalent a short while. Those who are comfortable with the notion that asset class allocation is key to overall portfolio returns, should recognize the value of equity style allocation within the equity asset class.

Are Equity Styles As Important As Traditional Asset Classes?
Sharpe refers to equity styles as asset classes when doing style analysis. He indicated that, "The asset class returns should either have low correlation with one another or, in cases where correlations are high, different standard deviations,"[2] (see Exhibit 1). This suggests that equity style should be of equal importance in

---

[1] William F. Sharpe, "Setting the Record Straight on Style Analysis," *Dow-Jones Fee Advisor* (November/December 1995), pp.50-56.
[2] William F. Sharpe, "Asset Allocation: Management Style and Performance Measurement," *The Journal of Portfolio Management* (Winter 1992), pp. 7-19.

explaining returns as traditional asset classes. Exhibit 2 shows the magnitude of difference and potential opportunity for adding excess return by shifting classes.[3] The study was segmented into two parts, the first being an assessment of the potential value added through traditional asset allocation using four asset classes (long bond, intermediate bond, S&P 500, and cash). The second part assessed the opportunity to add value by shifting between four equity styles (large cap growth, large cap value, small cap growth, and small cap value).

Exhibit 1: Equity Style Standard Deviations
January 1980 to December 1997 — Based on Monthly Returns

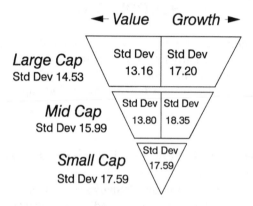

◄ Value   Growth ►

Large Cap
Std Dev 14.53

| Std Dev 13.16 | Std Dev 17.20 |

Mid Cap
Std Dev 15.99

| Std Dev 13.80 | Std Dev 18.35 |

Small Cap
Std Dev 17.59

| Std Dev 17.59 |

Conclusion: The standard deviations are quite different, particularly by Growth versus Value and by Size.
Source: First Madison Advisors

Exhibit 2: The Importance of Equity Style Allocation
For the 18 Years 12/31/79 through 12/31/97

By taking only the best quarter for one of the asset classes each quarter in asset allocation and equity style allocation respectively and linking them together, the "potential" to add extra return through shifting is revealed.

Asset Allocation:		*Equity Style Allocation:*	
Long Bond	Intermediate Bond	Large Value	Large Growth
Cash	S&P 500	Small Value	Small Growth

* Note: Small includes Mid Cap and Small Cap

Best of Asset Allocation	32.32%	Best of STYLE Allocation	31.88%
vs Traditional 60/35/5 Mix	14.73%	vs Wilshire 5000	16.43%
Maximum Potential from Shifts	17.59%	Maximum Potential from Shifts	16.79%

Conclusion: Style Allocation rivals Asset Allocation in potential.

---

[3] Bruce D. Westervelt, "The Importance of Equity Style," First Madison Advisors, January 1998 (additional information may be requested: firstmad@ix.netcom.com).

Exhibit 3: Yearly Differences Between Styles

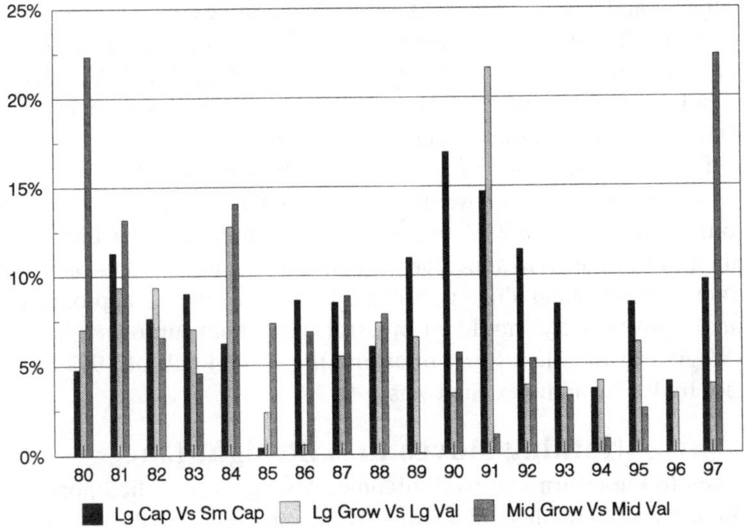

Source: First Madison Advisors

The study found that over the 18-year period covered, the return on a portfolio of 60% stocks, 35% bonds, and 5% cash was 14.73%. It went on to show that if, at the beginning of each quarter, the assets of the portfolio were 100% allocated to the asset class that performed best during the quarter (assuming no transaction costs or market impact), the annualized rate of return exploded to 32.32%. The difference, 17.59%, represented the potential value added by asset class allocation and helped explain investors' interest in asset allocation. Similarly, the study showed that perfect quarterly allocation of an equity portfolio's assets to the best performing equity style generated an annualized rate of return of 31.88%. The Wilshire 5000's performance over the same period was 16.43% The difference, 16.79%, represented the potential value added by equity style allocation within the equity asset class. This suggests that large differences between the annual returns of the styles existed, as Exhibit 3 demonstrates. It also suggests that the value added through equity style allocation rivaled that of traditional asset class allocation.

HOW TO CAPTURE THESE STYLE DIFFERENTIALS

To capture style, broadly diversified portfolios are used to capture the differences in returns caused by common characteristics of the market segments. Examples of fundamental characteristics include earnings yield and book-to-price. Broadly diversified portfolios are often associated with indexing, suggesting the possibility of using index funds to capture style differences. However, large or institutional investors may not accept the high turnover of style index funds. Examples of style indexes include the BARRA/S&P Growth and Value indexes. The indexes are constructed by splitting the S&P 500 into high price-to-book stocks (i.e., growth stocks) and low price-to-book stocks (i.e., value stocks). The overall S&P 500 Growth and Value portfolios are rebalanced every six months in this fashion. The resulting turnover in the portfolio as calculated by BARRA's Performance Analysis software was about 23% annually. Other style indexes generate as much as 20%-40% turnover and the expenses become prohibitive.

If one maintained a 60% growth and 40% value weighting (a 10% under-weight to value and a 10% overweight to growth), with no active shifting the portfolio would still suffer the 23% turnover. By comparison, over First Madison's five years as an active style allocator the entire active process has only generated 22% turnover, using stand alone portfolios versus the indexed approach requiring 40% plus turnover. Why should an investor care about turnover? According to Wayne Wagner of the Plexus group, during the second half of 1997 the cost for each share traded by an index fund was 1.40%.[4]

Nothing Moves In A Straight Line

Style is key to the return and risk outcome. A single diversified portfolio is the most efficient way to implement the tilts. However, modeling the shifting between the five or six styles is challenging. What looks like a relatively simple process of running a multiple linear regression to derive sensitivities to economic and fundamental factors, turns out to be not so simple. In a recent article, Daniel Coggin shows that equity style indexes do not exhibit mean reversion.[5] When a statistical test on the two differential return indexes — value versus growth (CRSP Deciles 1-2 split on growth) and small versus large (CRSP Deciles 3-9 versus Deciles 1-2) — was performed, it was found that the relative style performance relationship is non-linear. This means that the use of a linear mean reverting methodology probably would not lead to a process that can successfully add value over time. By accommodating nonlinearities in the mean and variance, these data characteristics can be overcome. In addition, Coggin stated "It is at least possible to predict stock index returns (or index differentials) by *conditioning* such predictions on some *outside* information, such as the business cycle and interest rates."

A DIFFERENT MODEL

A case against the efficient-markets constant-returns model was put forth in the mid-1970s by Nobel Laureate Robert Merton.[6] An intertemporal model for the

---

[4] Wayne Wagner, "Those Hidden, Sometimes Hefty Transaction Costs Can Be a Drag," *The New York Times* (March 8, 1998).

[5] T. Daniel Coggin, "Long-Term Memory in Equity Style Indexes," *The Journal of Portfolio Management* (Winter 1998), pp. 37-46.

[6] Robert C. Merton, "An Intertemporal Capital Asset Pricing Model," *Econometrica* (September 1973), pp. 867-887.

capital market is deduced from portfolio selection behavior by an arbitrary number of investors who act so as to maximize the expected utility of lifetime consumption. In addition these investors "are affected by the possibility of uncertain changes in future investment opportunities." They may collectively shift their preference from investment to spending or within the equity portfolio from "high risk" small cap growth to "lower risk" large cap value. This would be a function of what changes were occurring in the collective expectation for the future, rationally shifting their demand for assets classes and styles through time. Merton indicates that preferences and future opportunity sets are state-dependent. Research attempting to identify these state variables would eventually follow.

State Variables To Explain Return

The idea that economic variables play a significant role in influencing equity valuations was highlighted by the empirical research of Nai-Fu Chen, Richard Roll, and Stephen Ross.[7] They hypothesized that "From the perspective of efficient-market theory and rational expectations intertemporal asset-pricing theory, asset prices should depend on their exposures to state variables that describe the economy." Noting that, "By the diversification argument that is implicit in capital market theory, only general economic state variables will influence the pricing of large stock market aggregates." It is interesting that in this attempt to estimate APT state variables, they limit their discussion to *large stock market aggregates or equity styles*. They concluded that several economic variables such as "industrial production, twists in the yield curve, unanticipated inflation, ... were found to be significant in explaining expected stock returns."

Two Types of Information

The nature of the information affecting the equity market may have a varying impact on the pricing of assets. The efficient markets hypothesis (EMH) indicates that changes in asset prices should follow a random walk.[8] This would be true for the impact of one type of information, daily news that was not broadly known prior to its release (EMH semistrong form). A second type would not act in this fashion — information on the state variables coming through time and often having a trending characteristic. As changes in the economy unfold, asset prices reacting to state-variables in varying degrees may not follow the random walk.

Recent Research

In a recent article, Fama and French argue that "previous work shows that the average returns on common stock are related to firm characteristics like size,

[7] Nai-Fu Chen, Richard Roll, and Stephen A. Ross, "Economic Forces and the Stock Market," *Journal of Business* (1986), pp. 383-403.

[8] Paul A. Samuelson, "Proof That Properly Anticipated Prices Fluctuate Randomly," *Industrial Management Review* (Spring 1965), pp. 41-50 and Eugene F. Fama, "Efficient Capital Markets: A Review of Theory and Empirical Work," *The Journal of Finance* (May 1970), pp. 383-417.

earnings/price, cash flow/price, book to market equity, past sales growth and short term past return. We find that, except for the continuation of short-term returns, the anomalies largely disappear in a three-factor model. Our results are consistent with rational Intertemporal CAPM or APT asset pricing."[9] The Fama-French three-factor model is a three-factor multiple regression model. The three factors are beta (β), company size (small minus big premium [SMB]), and a financial distress factor represented by the company's book-to-market ratio (high minus low premium, [HML]). If the return of the market minus the risk-free rate, SMB, and HML are the expected premiums, the time-series regression equation can be written as follows:

$$R_i - R_f = b_i(R_M - R_f) + s_i SMB + h_i HML + e_t$$

where R_i is the return of the portfolio, R_f is the risk-free rate, R_M is the return of the market, and the factor sensitivities or loadings, b_i, s_i, and h_i, are all slopes in the time series regression, and e_t is a random error term.

French and Fama have now created a multi-factor model to which individual equity security's loadings can be estimated to explain their returns. Being a version of traditional finance equilibrium model, French and Fama would suggest that factor loadings are proxies for risk and are priced in equilibrium.

A DIFFERENT PERSPECTIVE

Recently Kent Daniel and Sheridan Titman found that:

> Most of the comovement of high book-to market [HML] stocks is not due to distressed stocks being exposed to a unique "distress" factor, but rather, because stocks with similar factor sensitivities tend to become distressed at the same time. Second, our evidence suggests that it is characteristics rather than factor loadings that determine expected returns. We show that factor loadings do not explain the high returns associated with small and high book-to-market stocks beyond the extent to which they act as proxies for these characteristics. Further, our results show that, with equities, the market beta has no explanatory power for returns even after controlling for size [SMB] and book-to-market ratios [HML].[10]

---

[9] Eugene F. Fama and Kenneth R. French, "Multifactor Explanations of Asset Pricing Anomalies," *The Journal of Finance* (March 1996), pp. 55-84.

[10] Kent Daniel and Sheridan Titman, "Evidence on the Characteristics of Cross Sectional Variation is Stock Returns," *The Journal of Finance* (March 1997), pp. 1-33.

This is consistent with the findings of Chen, Roll, and Ross in that stocks with similar state-variable sensitivities tend to act in the same fashion at the same time.

If two types of information are working on stock prices — daily news and macro economic data — then the randomness of the returns of individual securities remains. However, when market segments are represented by large numbers of securities, which cancels out the random behavior of individual securities, the returns associated with those segments are captured. The segments themselves are not factors. They simply have a large enough population to capture common characteristics. The economic "state variables" will still impact the aggregate styles and have their own separate effect through time.

Composite Assets

Style is key to the return and risk outcome. A single diversified portfolio is the most efficient way to implement style tilts. Styles represent the characteristics of a segment of the market. These market segments can be viewed as composite assets. When bundled together, they look like a single stock. The segment will have an aggregate price/earnings ratio, growth rate, price to book, etc. Not surprisingly, Fama and French observed that "But for small stocks, the recession of 1981 and 1982 turns into a prolonged earnings depression; on average, small stocks do not participate in the boom of the middle and late 1980s."[11] These composites have all the valuation characteristics that individual equities have.

Do Fundamentals Impact Style Performance?

In a recent research report published by *The Bank Credit Analyst* (BCA), the importance of earnings for these composites was driven home.[12] BCA segmented the U.S. equity market as follows:

$20 billion and over	: Super-caps
$1 billion - $20 billion	: Large-caps
$250 million - $1 billion	: Small-caps
less than $250 million	: Micro-caps

BCA found that: "EBIT margins for the super-caps have more than doubled, skyrocketing from a trough of 7% in 1993 to 15% in the first quarter of 1997." An analyst's job is to figure the present value of an asset based on future earnings power. The rising trend in margins has benefited the largest capitalization companies. BCA found,

In the micro-cap sector, earnings growth has remained below sales growth and thus margins have contracted to an astonish-

---

[11] Eugene F. Fama and Kenneth R. French, "Size and Book-to-Market Factors in Earnings and Returns," *The Journal of Finance* (March 1995), pp. 131-155.
[12] BCA Publications, "Dissecting the Two-Tier Equity Market: Large Caps Versus Small Caps," *The Bank Credit Analyst* (September 1977).

ingly-low 3.5%, half their level of the late 1980s. Small-caps earnings growth is about flat over the last ten years at about 7.5% and both mid and small have been experiencing a declining annual sales growth from about 24% in late 1993 to 12% in 1997. In the Super-caps and Large-caps the sales growth has remained about flat over the same time frame.

Consequently, Small-caps have underperformed Super+Large-caps since January 1, 1993 by roughly 3.61% annually over the time period analyzed. (See Exhibit 4.)

Valuation: In Style Management Everything Is Relative

By comparing the composites relative exposure(s) to fundamental factors such as earnings/price, book/price, growth, etc. a process can be built that reflects when there is a high probability of valuation realignment. By using a relative approach to valuation rather than a discount approach, the difficulties in estimating discounting factors are avoided. This indicates that the market *segments* do not trade at some precise equilibrium point but around a dynamic valuation which is subject to the effect of changes in state-variables and investor preferences. This allows for the large annual differences that can be seen in Exhibit 3.

Exhibit 4: Relative Performance of Small Cap versus Large Cap
1993-1997

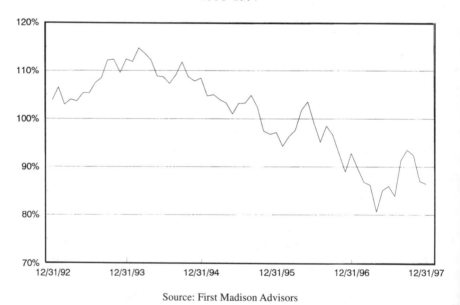

Source: First Madison Advisors

A NON-EQUILIBRIUM APPROACH

Although the market is efficient in that known information is rapidly incorporated into stock prices, the efficient market hypothesis is not embraced by First Madison's methodology. The EMH as put forward by Paul Samuelson and Eugene Fama, assumes *general equilibrium* (a perfect balance between investor decisions and the evolution of the economy) and *market efficiency*. This means that securities are always fairly priced and that investors have equal access to information, have homogeneous rational expectations (arrive at the same conclusions), share the same collective utility function (desire for risk and return), and have the same aggregate time horizon. However, the market can also be viewed as a "rational market" that allows for variation through time of expected (and realized) return in the market segments. At any single point in time securities appear to be priced relatively efficiently. It is only when expectations change through time that the persistence in returns for market segments (versus the broad market) occurs, resulting in non-random walk behavior.

Adaptive Modeling and Non-Linearities

If the mean and variance of the data are not linear as mentioned earlier, an adaptive modeling approach must be developed for dealing with the non-stationary relationships of both the data and the style relationships. To accommodate the non-linearity of the data a number of methodologies have become popular. Autoregressive conditional heteroskedasticity (ARCH) and generalized ARCH (GARCH) models parsimoniously model volatility of financial time series. By allowing conditional variance to affect the expected returns, ARCH and GARCH allow just enough non-linearity into an otherwise linear model to avoid overfitting and a nice gain in explaining differentials. The models allow a parsimonious use of factors, resulting in a better performance in out-of-sample tests.

Another type of model is the loglinear probability model. In generalized form, using only one logistic function which operates on a linear combination of factors, a model can be created that performs well out of sample and also allows for non-linearities in a disciplined way, by keeping the number of parameters down. This is in contrast with neural networks, which effectively end up using many logistic functions aggregated together, the feature contributing to overfitting.

First Madison uses the BARRA factor model to derive exposures for the styles, test state-variable sensitivities, and perform optimizations. In a recent study, Daniel and Titman note in their closing remarks:

> Our research suggests that after controlling for *stock characteristics*, factor sensitivities provide no information about a stock's expected rate of return. This suggests that investors can build superior portfolios with mean-variance optimizers that use characteristics to generate the expected return inputs along with covariance estimates either calculated with historical data or

provided by a vendor such as BARRA. Such a strategy would
have done exceptionally well in the past.[13]

THE DYNAMIC STYLE ALLOCATION PROCESS

First Madison Advisors' investment approach, called Dynamic Style Allocation
(DSA), actively shifts between five distinct and broadly diversified equity styles:
large cap growth, large cap value, mid cap growth, mid cap value, and small cap.
The process is implemented as a single portfolio comprised of an average of 500
U.S. equities, which are constituents of the 3,500 U.S. equity universe with a market capitalization greater $125 million. DSA uses quantitative techniques to
assimilate data from fundamental, macro-economic, and trend factors for determining the relative weight or representation of each equity style in the portfolio.
DSA adds value by actively overweighting equity styles which are showing positive relative performance, and by using passive portfolio construction and trading
techniques to minimize cost and diversify investment risk.

Although there has been interest in equity style management for quite a
while, recently Coggin and Fabozzi coedited the first book on the topic.[14] In that
book Richard Roll warns of possible non-stationarity in the style relationships
and indicates that an intertemporal model that captures non-stationary effects,
may produce better investment performance.[15] In a subsequent book, Focardi and
Jonas,[16] cover a broad range of issues that arise when equilibrium, linear, and sta-
tionarity assumptions are relaxed. Commenting on non-linear adaptive methods in
his book, Blake LeBaron, a leading authority in this area, notes that "adaptive
methods can show a significant advantage over the human observer in areas such
as finding patterns in multivariate series."

Defining the Styles

The first step in the development of a style process is defining what constitutes a
"style." The most convenient way to research styles by size is to use the historic
data on U.S. traded equity securities available from The University of Chicago
School of Business — Center for Research in Security Prices (CRSP). This database segments the market into capitalization deciles, which allows for the fact that
the dollar definition for size changes through time. The advantage here is that
returns for different market cap segments of the market can be produced all the

[13] Kent Daniel and Sheridan Titman, "Characteristics or Covariances?" *Journal of Portfolio Management*
(Summer 1998).

[14] T. Daniel Coggin and Frank J. Fabozzi, *The Handbook of Equity Style Management* (New Hope, PA:
Frank J. Fabozzi Associates, First Edition 1995, Second Edition 1997)

[15] Richard Roll, "Style Return Differential," Chapter 5 in *The Handbook of Equity Style Management.*

[16] Sergio Focardi and Caroline Jonas, *Modeling the Market: New Theories and Techniques* (New Hope, PA:
Frank J. Fabozzi Associates, 1997)

way back to December 31, 1925. Because much of the broadly used economic data are not available until 1945 or later, the post World War II period is a good starting point for several reasons. First, the pre-1945 small cap sectors were made up of companies that had fallen on hard times earnings-wise and the stock price reflected this (known as a "fallen angel"). Second, trading in the smaller cap segments had a couple of enormous relative performance fluctuations versus the broad market in the earlier periods (1932-1937 and 1942-1946), most likely due to the lack of liquidity in combination with economic, political, and world events.

By adopting the CRSP decile convention, Deciles 1-2 represent Large Cap, 3-5 represent Mid Cap, and 6-9 represent Small Cap. The 10th decile contains micro-cap companies that are so small and illiquid that if an active process moves in and out of this area, the extra returns that would be required to offset the implementation costs are prohibitive. Currently the investable universe starts with companies that have a total market capitalization of $125 million or greater.

Growth and value are broken out only in the large cap and mid cap segments of the market. Small cap is, once again, a segment where one should limit turnover. Because of the high correlation of mid cap growth to small cap growth (0.97) and mid cap value to small cap value (0.95), the process can pick up return benefits of the small cap growth and value by using the more liquid mid cap growth and value segments of the market.

Using this methodology, First Madison does *not* attempt to overlay a process that has a unique design (the segment deciles) onto a platform of commercial indexes. The need for a custom portfolio becomes clear as one examines the characteristics of the vendor indexes. The major vendors offer size and style indexes that have a definition quite different than that above, an obvious problem if one's modeling is built around a differently defined grouping of stocks. Vendors' style definitions are subject to change over time and a few represent active processes of their own. Additionally, these indexes typically have annual turnover in the range of 20% to 40%. If one attempts to overlay an active strategy on top of a platform with that much turnover, excess return can evaporate quickly by implementation costs such as market impact, commissions, and opportunity costs. When the constituent lists are revised for such indexes, a huge amount of concurrent trading among indexers occurs as stocks deleted from the list are sold down while additions are bid up. Often this process results in large unnecessary expenses to the index portfolio, where the manager's goal is simply to minimize tracking error to its respective index.

Quantitative Techniques

Financial data are notorious for being hard to predict, and this fact has gradually led to rejection of traditional linear dynamic models. Most often in the short run the data are non-stationary, and new robust techniques are required to deal with these features. The goal is to come up with a model which, while rich and flexible enough to explain historical data, doesn't fall into the trap of overfitting. This trap is especially treacherous when dealing with low frequency data where the number of sample data points is small. Hence, identifying good parsimonious specifications takes on great importance.

First Madison uses a class of the ARCH/GARCH family of models to account for dynamical changes not only in conditional mean but also in conditional variance of future returns. This strategy allows us to develop a better sense of the risk involved in taking a particular position. By using multivariate versions of the above models, First Madison identifies an optimal mix of asset styles, while keeping the estimation error small. These models are estimated by using nonlinear maximum likelihood techniques, which tend to reduce aggregate error.

The DSA model is comprised of a combination of sub-models that allow for non-linearity in fundamental factors and economic variables, and the interrelationships between the styles. These sub-models have different orientations in what they are attempting to predict. One grouping is focused on predicting short-term changes in style relationships, while another grouping is focused on longer-term relationships. The interplay between the two creates synergies resulting in superior results otherwise not available from either on a stand alone basis.

Sources of Data

Fundamental data such as earnings/price, book/price, growth, and yield can render a great deal of information about the relative valuation of the styles. As noted earlier, when small cap stocks' earnings growth has failed to keep up with the growth of larger capitalization segments, small cap relative performance has suffered. The same is true for growth and value. When large stocks become too overvalued versus small stocks, the performance of large stocks suffers on a relative basis to small stocks. The process incorporates the "active exposures to the fundamental factors," on the basis of these relationships: mid versus large, small versus large, large growth versus large value, and mid growth versus mid value. When the fundamental valuations are stretched, and economic or trend inputs indicate the probability of deteriorating relative performance, a shift away from overweighting that particular style will occur.

The literature on economic data is so vast in security valuation that it is beyond the scope of this chapter. However, the fact that security pricing is linked to the economic environment is generally accepted. A few of the most broadly used economic factors are: industrial production, capacity utilization, employment, GDP, U.S. dollar, term spread, and default premium. For example, when the default premium (the difference in returns between corporate bonds and long-term government bonds) is falling, small cap stocks tend to benefit because they are viewed as having higher risk. When the premium required to compensate investors is decreased, the present value of that segment increases.

Trend is a part of the style process as well. In addition to trends in relative performance between styles, trends in the fundamental factors and economic variables are also integrated into the style process. There may be a direct linkage between the default premium and size, or a linkage between the default premiums trend and size, or both. The transformations that may be applied to the data may take on an unlimited number of forms. Some may attempt to mimic the way time series data are acted upon by the market, while other variations may capture a surprise versus expectations. Even though there may be multiple ways to incorporate the same variable or relationship, each component contributes to the overall process.

Testing the Model

As variables are added to the submodels, through the estimation procedure itself, descriptive statistics about that variable and the effectiveness of the submodel itself are developed. When the models are combined in the composite model, traditional descriptive statistics are inadequate to provide a measure of efficacy. Because of the interactive effects between the various models, the results are actually a joint test of simultaneous models. In addition, because the short term model predictions of valuation are near term in nature while the long-term model derives probabilities of a conditional state (i.e., growth versus value), traditional tests — such as mean absolute deviation (MAD), root mean square error (RMSE), mean absolute percentage error (MAPE), R-Squared, or percentage of turning points forecasted — are not as telling as the actual live performance of the process itself.

Results

Dynamic Style Allocation reached a 5-year track record on March 31, 1998. The results were +1.52% annually versus the Wilshire 5000, "a broad market index" (see Exhibit 5). DSA had a correlation to the Wilshire 5000 of 0.98, which indicates that it is an appropriate benchmark. Because the realized risk was lower than that of the benchmark, the annual risk-adjusted return was +2.26%. In addition, DSA had an information ratio of 0.74 and a t-statistic of 1.64, indicating that the performance was due to skill. Finally, according to BARRA's Performance Analysis software, the average tracking error was 1.83%. While a highly diversified process will rarely hit a home run, consistent singles and doubles will often win the game.

CONCLUSION

Equity style exposure is rapidly becoming recognized as the most important driver of realized returns for diversified equity portfolios. When implemented as a stand alone equity portfolio, there is the opportunity to add excess return while experiencing lower residual risk, and lower volatility than the market. When included with an existing traditional multiple manager structure, the shifts in exposure toward styles either fill in for a potential lack of exposure to that style or increase aggregate exposure to the style amplifying the alpha (excess return). This return is difficult to capture with traditional linear methodologies and requires an adaptive approach to modeling. As the market becomes increasingly efficient at the individual stock level, the opportunity to add value through style allocation will be of increasing importance.

Exhibit 5: DSA versus Wilshire 5000 (Benchmark) April 1, 1993 (Inception) to March 31, 1998

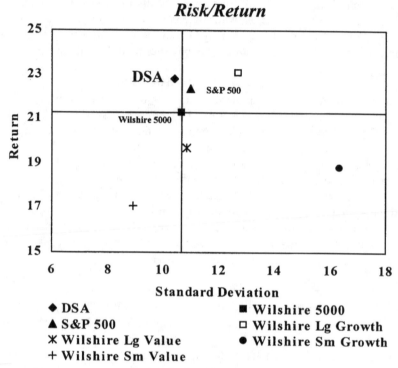

Risk/Return

DSA ◆
▲ S&P 500
Wilshire 5000

- ◆ DSA
- ▲ S&P 500
- ✳ Wilshire Lg Value
- ✚ Wilshire Sm Value
- ■ Wilshire 5000
- □ Wilshire Lg Growth
- ● Wilshire Sm Growth

Summary Statistics

Annual Excess over Wilshire 5000	+ 1.52%
Risk Adjusted Excess Return	+ 2.26%
Average Tracking Error	1.83
Beta	0.96
Information Ratio	0.74
t-statistic	1.64
Correlation to Wilshire 5000	0.98
Annual Portfolio Turnover	22%
Average # of Stocks in Portfolio	500

Chapter 13

Exploiting Global Equity Pricing Anomalies

Gary L. Bergstrom, Ph.D.
President
Acadian Asset Management

Richard O. Michaud, Ph.D.
Senior Vice President
Acadian Asset Management

Brian K. Wolahan, CFA
Senior Vice President
Acadian Asset Management

INTRODUCTION

Many numerical measures of a firm's "value" are used in investment analysis. These include financial ratios such as past or expected earnings-to-price. Additional commonly utilized measures of value include dividend yield, book-to-price, cash earnings-to-price, normalized earnings-to-price, and dividend discount model (DDM) alpha.[1]

Over the past 20 years, considerable empirical evidence suggesting the existence of statistically significant relationships between a number of such value-oriented measures of companies and *ex-post* returns has been uncovered.[2] Similar long-term evidence indicates that equities for smaller-capitalization companies have experienced returns in excess of the general market.[3] While most of the original studies focused on U.S. equities, many have subsequently been extended to non-U.S. markets, with similar relationships reported.[4] Based in part

---

[1] DDM alpha is a variation of the internal rate of return measure from the standard dividend discount model used by many organizations. See Richard O. Michaud and Paul Davis, "Valuation Model Bias and the Scale Structure of Dividend Discount Returns," *Journal of Finance* (March 1982). Normalized earnings-to-price is the inverse of current price-to-book ratio divided by the time-weighted average return on equity.

[2] See, for example, Eugene Fama and Kenneth French, "The Cross-Section of Expected Returns," *Journal of Finance* (June 1992).

[3] *Stocks, Bonds, Bills, and Inflation Yearbook*, annual (Chicago: Ibbotson Associates, 1996).

[4] See, for example, Gabriel Hawawini and Donald Keim, "On the Cross-Sectional Behavior of Common Stock Returns: A Review of the Evidence Around the World," in William Ziemba and Donald Keim (eds.), *Security Market Imperfections in Worldwide Equity Markets* (Cambridge: Cambridge University Press, forthcoming 1998).

on this evidence, more active investment managers appear to be attempting to exploit such perceived marketplace pricing anomalies in their stock-selection strategies.

One reason that many asset managers use multiple measures of stock value is that any return relationships can vary significantly over time. For global investors, multiple value measures are even more critical, since their effectiveness also often varies market-by-market. The question of which measures to use in a given market and time period is then likely to be a key investment decision.

EMPIRICAL EVIDENCE

To help identify which, if any, factors have been useful for global equity investing, Exhibits 1 through 4 show the relationship between seven value- and size-based factors with subsequent local equity returns. The analysis estimates the correlation between year-end measures for each of the seven factors and the next 12-month return on a year-by-year basis. This analysis was performed for each calendar year from 1975 through 1997 for four major non-U.S. markets: France, Germany, Japan, and the United Kingdom. The years on the exhibits refer to the return period, with the factors measured as of the end of December of the preceding year.

The company samples used are based largely on stocks included in the Morgan Stanley Capital International (MSCI) universe for each country. There is no look-ahead bias in the data since the information was taken from published sources available as of the date indicated. The ratios are presented such that a positive correlation indicates a positive return to value or small capitalization. For example, earnings-to-price is used rather than the more frequently quoted price-to-earnings ratio, since the former will correlate positively with future returns if there are positive returns to value-based investing. Other than that, the data has generally not been normalized or adjusted prior to the correlation estimation process.[5] The return numbers also have not been adjusted for either systematic or unsystematic risk. Finally, the correlations have been estimated on an equal-weighted basis. In addition to the year-by-year correlations, summary statistics are shown for the time periods 1975-1985, 1986-1997, and 1975-1997.

Exhibit 1 indicates that single-factor, value-based strategies have had limited effectiveness in France over the full 23 years. For the sub-period of 1975-1985, some factors did have a positive correlation with returns and this correlation was statistically significant. However, over the subsequent 12 years, none of these factors had significantly positive returns. Overall, book-to-price, dividend yield, DDM alpha, and normalized earnings-to-price had significant positive returns for the full period.

---

[5] The exception is "Small-Cap," which is the log of the inverse of U.S. dollar market capitalization [small cap = log (1/cap size in $million)]. A positive coefficient indicates a positive return to smaller-capitalization stocks.

Exhibit 1: Factor Correlations for France (1975-1997)

Year	Earnings-to-Price	Book-to-Price	Dividend Yield	DDM Alpha	Normalized Earnings-to-Price	Cash Earnings-to-Price	Small-Cap
1975	0.30	0.15	0.07	0.34	0.12	0.34	0.09
1976	0.19	0.24	0.10	0.23	0.23	0.09	−0.03
1977	0.20	−0.18	0.27	−0.05	−0.18	0.18	0.05
1978	0.13	−0.13	0.17	0.08	−0.14	0.09	0.21
1979	0.14	0.32	0.22	0.31	0.32	0.32	−0.04
1980	0.28	0.04	0.20	0.03	0.04	0.10	0.04
1981	0.17	0.33	0.03	0.27	0.32	0.24	0.06
1982	−0.08	−0.03	0.03	−0.02	−0.03	−0.08	0.10
1983	0.12	−0.07	0.01	−0.11	−0.07	−0.12	−0.15
1984	0.21	0.14	0.15	0.11	0.14	0.18	0.09
1985	−0.13	−0.07	0.11	0.02	−0.07	−0.25	0.06
1986	−0.20	−0.27	−0.04	−0.16	−0.27	−0.30	−0.28
1987	−0.13	0.07	0.01	0.04	0.07	−0.06	0.01
1988	−0.07	0.73	−0.20	0.53	0.73	0.04	0.39
1989	−0.04	0.08	−0.05	0.02	0.08	0.06	0.15
1990	−0.16	0.06	0.16	−0.09	0.07	−0.05	−0.05
1991	−0.02	0.23	−0.11	0.23	0.22	0.10	−0.03
1992	−0.05	0.01	−0.04	−0.02	0.02	−0.04	0.04
1993	0.05	0.29	0.15	0.26	0.29	0.18	0.28
1994	−0.08	0.15	−0.18	0.18	0.14	0.00	0.11
1995	0.08	−0.18	0.09	−0.10	−0.18	−0.09	−0.25
1996	−0.02	−0.17	−0.12	−0.01	−0.05	−0.28	0.18
1997	−0.03	0.27	0.07	0.21	0.27	0.28	−0.11
Summary Statistics:							
1975-1985							
Average Correlation	0.14	0.07	0.12	0.11	0.06	0.10	0.04
Standard Deviation	0.13	0.18	0.09	0.15	0.18	0.18	0.09
T-Statistic	3.45	1.24	4.77	2.36	1.16	1.78	1.56
1986-1997							
Average Correlation	−0.06	0.11	−0.02	0.09	0.12	−0.01	0.04
Standard Deviation	0.08	0.27	0.12	0.20	0.26	0.17	0.20
T-Statistic	−2.35	1.38	−0.63	1.61	1.57	−0.26	0.63
1975-1997							
Average Correlation	0.04	0.09	0.05	0.10	0.09	0.04	0.04
Standard Deviation	0.15	0.22	0.13	0.17	0.22	0.18	0.15
T-Statistic	1.24	1.86	1.82	2.76	1.98	1.08	1.24

Value and small-capitalization investing also had limited effectiveness in Germany over 1975-1997 (see Exhibit 2). Earnings-to-price, DDM alpha, and cash earnings-to-price showed significant positive returns for this period. Small-capitalization investing had negative returns, though these results were not statistically significant. This is consistent with the capital structure of this market during this period.

Exhibit 2: Factor Correlations for Germany (1975-1997)

Year	Earnings-to-Price	Book-to-Price	Dividend Yield	DDM Alpha	Normalized Earnings-to-Price	Cash Earnings-to-Price	Small-Cap
1975	0.13	0.40	0.05	0.04	0.40	0.28	−0.30
1976	0.33	0.24	0.24	0.26	0.21	0.36	−0.21
1977	0.26	0.06	0.16	0.23	0.04	0.14	0.33
1978	0.07	0.03	−0.16	0.06	0.02	−0.14	0.32
1979	0.28	−0.26	0.28	0.09	−0.29	−0.02	−0.16
1980	0.22	−0.45	−0.14	−0.05	−0.45	−0.24	0.06
1981	0.26	−0.17	−0.02	0.11	−0.19	0.01	−0.06
1982	0.29	−0.03	0.13	0.07	−0.04	0.08	0.11
1983	−0.12	0.22	−0.26	0.06	0.24	0.43	−0.02
1984	0.04	0.09	−0.19	−0.07	0.11	0.05	−0.22
1985	−0.26	−0.10	−0.18	0.02	−0.09	−0.31	−0.30
1986	0.13	−0.10	0.06	0.13	−0.10	−0.05	0.14
1987	0.33	0.26	0.44	−0.04	0.27	0.35	0.03
1988	0.23	0.41	0.01	0.39	0.39	0.22	0.34
1989	−0.20	0.03	−0.27	0.06	0.02	0.09	0.19
1990	0.00	−0.22	0.08	0.03	−0.24	−0.12	0.20
1991	0.36	0.41	0.36	0.28	0.39	0.39	−0.28
1992	−0.09	−0.15	0.04	0.01	−0.17	−0.12	−0.29
1993	0.35	0.47	0.39	0.57	0.45	0.50	0.05
1994	0.17	0.17	−0.09	0.15	0.16	0.02	−0.03
1995	0.06	−0.15	0.12	−0.08	−0.14	0.04	−0.37
1996	0.27	−0.07	0.15	0.05	−0.07	0.15	−0.33
1997	−0.08	0.06	−0.07	−0.11	−0.10	0.16	−0.20
Summary Statistics:							
1975-1985							
Average Correlation	0.14	0.00	−0.01	0.07	0.00	0.06	−0.04
Standard Deviation	0.19	0.24	0.19	0.10	0.25	0.24	0.23
T-Statistic	2.40	0.03	−0.13	2.46	−0.05	0.82	−0.60
1986-1997							
Average Correlation	0.13	0.09	0.10	0.12	0.07	0.14	−0.05
Standard Deviation	0.19	0.25	0.21	0.20	0.25	0.20	0.24
T-Statistic	2.32	1.32	1.69	2.06	1.00	2.36	−0.66
1975-1997							
Average Correlation	0.13	0.05	0.05	0.10	0.04	0.10	−0.04
Standard Deviation	0.19	0.24	0.20	0.16	0.24	0.22	0.23
T-Statistic	3.41	0.99	1.17	2.95	0.70	2.19	−0.91

Exhibit 3 shows that all of the value factors had significant positive returns in Japan for the full 23-year period, as well as for most sub-periods. Returns to small-capitalization stocks were positive, but not significant.

Exhibit 3: Factor Correlations for Japan (1975-1997)

Year	Earnings-to-Price	Book-to-Price	Dividend Yield	DDM Alpha	Normalized Earnings-to-Price	Cash Earnings-to-Price	Small-Cap
1975	0.19	0.14	-0.09	0.24	0.19	-0.03	0.22
1976	-0.01	0.03	-0.18	0.00	-0.05	-0.11	0.11
1977	0.08	0.46	0.47	-0.06	0.01	0.27	0.19
1978	-0.02	0.26	-0.09	0.09	0.10	0.12	0.32
1979	0.03	0.12	0.06	0.02	0.08	0.13	-0.08
1980	0.16	0.06	0.11	0.14	0.09	0.16	-0.02
1981	0.19	0.25	0.20	0.11	0.17	0.21	-0.33
1982	0.25	0.08	-0.16	0.31	0.26	0.03	-0.07
1983	0.11	0.01	-0.09	0.24	0.23	-0.05	0.16
1984	0.00	0.02	0.00	-0.09	-0.06	0.02	-0.10
1985	0.06	0.25	0.22	0.01	0.08	0.12	0.08
1986	-0.02	-0.07	0.03	-0.14	-0.15	-0.02	-0.13
1987	0.12	0.26	0.22	0.13	0.20	0.13	0.19
1988	0.06	0.12	0.21	-0.06	0.07	0.09	0.07
1989	0.03	0.13	-0.02	0.00	0.05	-0.03	0.52
1990	0.15	0.16	0.00	0.17	0.16	0.11	0.11
1991	-0.01	0.07	0.02	0.05	0.04	0.03	0.11
1992	-0.01	0.04	0.20	0.02	0.02	0.03	0.03
1993	0.11	0.27	0.20	0.23	0.27	0.23	-0.18
1994	-0.17	0.25	-0.01	0.05	0.14	-0.07	0.33
1995	0.21	0.07	0.11	0.18	0.19	0.13	-0.12
1996	0.16	0.05	0.10	0.11	0.05	0.13	-0.09
1997	0.08	-0.27	-0.04	0.03	-0.10	0.01	-0.38
Summary Statistics:							
1975-1985							
Average Correlation	0.10	0.15	0.04	0.09	0.10	0.08	0.04
Standard Deviation	0.09	0.14	0.20	0.13	0.11	0.12	0.18
T-Statistic	3.43	3.65	0.66	2.35	3.11	2.24	0.78
1986-1997							
Average Correlation	0.06	0.09	0.09	0.06	0.08	0.06	0.04
Standard Deviation	0.10	0.15	0.10	0.11	0.12	0.09	0.24
T-Statistic	1.99	2.05	3.00	2.09	2.20	2.57	0.54
1975-1997							
Average Correlation	0.08	0.12	0.06	0.08	0.09	0.07	0.04
Standard Deviation	0.10	0.15	0.15	0.12	0.11	0.10	0.21
T-Statistic	3.76	3.94	2.00	3.20	3.74	3.42	0.92

As in Japan, the U.K. experienced positive and statistically significant returns to all value factors for the entire 23-year period (see Exhibit 4). For most value-factors, this was also true for the sub-periods of 1975-1985 and 1986-1997. Returns to small-capitalization resulted in negligible value-added in the second sub-period, but was more effective during the 1975-1985 period.

Exhibit 4: Factor Correlations for the United Kingdom (1975-1997)

Year	Earnings-to-Price	Book-to-Price	Dividend Yield	DDM Alpha	Normalized Earnings-to-Price	Cash Earnings-to-Price	Small-Cap
1975	0.25	0.03	0.07	0.34	0.01	0.33	0.30
1976	−0.03	−0.06	−0.02	0.17	−0.07	0.20	−0.11
1977	0.12	0.17	0.02	0.11	0.16	0.18	0.32
1978	0.19	0.11	0.02	0.19	0.10	0.29	0.05
1979	0.02	−0.01	−0.17	−0.02	−0.01	0.21	−0.09
1980	−0.11	−0.12	−0.24	−0.18	−0.12	−0.01	−0.12
1981	0.21	0.19	0.09	0.21	0.18	0.26	0.18
1982	0.11	−0.04	−0.04	0.06	−0.05	0.05	0.01
1983	0.23	0.15	0.28	0.21	0.14	0.33	0.25
1984	0.23	0.10	0.25	0.13	0.09	0.21	0.18
1985	0.13	0.04	0.33	0.10	0.03	0.19	0.01
1986	0.15	0.08	0.15	0.12	0.07	0.21	−0.04
1987	0.11	0.37	0.27	0.30	0.36	0.37	0.25
1988	0.08	0.35	0.23	0.11	0.36	0.25	0.07
1989	0.09	−0.02	0.12	0.09	−0.02	0.21	−0.24
1990	0.15	0.05	0.02	0.05	0.04	0.11	−0.14
1991	0.20	0.01	0.07	0.03	−0.01	0.29	0.00
1992	−0.02	0.02	−0.22	0.04	0.02	0.01	0.05
1993	−0.06	0.66	0.26	0.42	0.66	0.11	0.42
1994	0.19	0.14	0.03	0.15	0.14	0.12	0.06
1995	0.03	−0.05	0.00	0.02	−0.05	0.08	−0.12
1996	−0.03	0.04	−0.04	−0.15	−0.16	0.11	−0.17
1997	0.21	0.09	0.19	0.04	0.01	0.01	−0.15
Summary Statistics:							
1975-1985							
Average Correlation	0.12	0.05	0.05	0.12	0.04	0.20	0.09
Standard Deviation	0.12	0.10	0.18	0.14	0.10	0.11	0.16
T-Statistic	3.44	1.66	0.98	2.92	1.39	6.36	1.79
1986-1997							
Average Correlation	0.09	0.14	0.09	0.10	0.12	0.16	0.00
Standard Deviation	0.09	0.21	0.14	0.14	0.23	0.11	0.19
T-Statistic	3.38	2.39	2.17	2.42	1.77	4.91	−0.01
1975-1997							
Average Correlation	0.11	0.10	0.07	0.11	0.08	0.18	0.04
Standard Deviation	0.11	0.17	0.16	0.14	0.18	0.11	0.18
T-Statistic	4.87	2.82	2.18	3.83	2.17	7.90	1.13

More generally, the evidence indicates that in markets with strongly positive returns to value factors, these returns remained relatively stable between the periods of 1975-1986 and 1986-1997. This was the case in Japan and in the U.K. This suggests that the returns to value measures have been relatively consistent over longer-term periods (greater than 10 years) in these countries. This also suggests that in these two markets returns to value factors had not been arbitraged away during this period.

However, the relationship of returns to value factors has clearly not been consistent on a year-by-year basis. Even a long-term, significantly positive predictive factor, such as book-to-price in Japan, experienced several consecutive years (1982-1984, 1995-1997) of trivial or negative value-added. Such lagging or mediocre performance could have serious business consequences in the practical world of institutional investment management, with its emphasis on consistent value-added. In the case of the earnings-to-price ratio in the U.K., only two of the past six years have provided appreciable value-added. Similar situations pertain to other factors in other markets.

In addition to varying in magnitude year-by-year, the returns to different value factors have varied significantly within the same market during the same time period. For example, in 1994 for Japan, book-to-price and normalized earnings-to-price had positive correlations with returns. However, earnings-to-price, dividend yield, and cash earnings-to-price were all negative in that year.

Across markets, the predictive power of identical factors has differed significantly within the same period. In 1992, Japan had strong positive returns to dividend yield. In the U.K. for this same period, returns to this factor were negative. Similar results for this factor were also experienced in 1980.

The universe of companies being considered also impacts the findings. Exhibit 5 shows the results for Japan of expanding the companies in the sample beyond the MSCI universe. Beginning in 1992, the number of Japanese companies available in the test sample was expanded from approximately 480 to well over 1,000. Most of the additional companies were smaller in size than those in the MSCI-only sample. This expanded universe exhibited somewhat different return characteristics to value-factors. There are differences in individual years, such as for the return to earnings-to-price in 1995. Most notable was the reduction in correlations for the expanded universe associated with earnings-to-price and DDM alpha for the full period. This indicates that care must be taken when extrapolating the results of this type of analysis to different investment universes, even within the same market.

PRACTICAL IMPLEMENTATION ISSUES

The practical investment challenge is how to use factors to forecast active returns and add value. The challenge stems primarily from the fact that no single factor has been, or is likely to be, beneficial in all time periods. In addition, factors have varied measurably in their predictive power across markets and time periods. Adding value becomes even more challenging when trading costs, which include broker commissions, stamp taxes, market impact, and opportunity costs,[6] are considered. These can have a significant impact on performance when implementing any active equity management strategy.

---

[6] Opportunity costs are the costs, or lost opportunities, associated with the performance of equity orders that do not get executed. For further information on trading costs, see Wayne Wagner (ed.), *The Complete Guide to Securities Transactions* (New York, NY: John Wiley and Sons, 1989).

Exhibit 5: Factor Correlations for Expanded Universe of Companies in Japan (1992-1997)

Year	Earnings-to-Price	Book-to-Price	Dividend Yield	DDM Alpha	Normalized Earnings-to-Price	Cash Earnings-to-Price	Small-Cap
1992	0.14	0.15	0.15	0.16	0.17	0.17	-0.01
1993	0.02	0.22	0.11	0.07	0.08	0.10	-0.06
1994	-0.05	0.24	0.02	-0.06	0.06	0.10	0.27
1995	-0.02	0.01	0.02	0.02	0.03	0.04	-0.05
1996	0.05	0.09	0.08	0.05	0.05	0.02	-0.01
1997	0.04	-0.10	0.02	0.03	-0.04	0.05	-0.36
Summary Statistics: 1992-1997							
Average Correlation	0.03	0.10	0.07	0.05	0.06	0.08	-0.04
Standard Deviation	0.07	0.13	0.06	0.07	0.07	0.05	0.20
T-Statistic	1.13	1.92	2.96	1.54	2.10	3.49	-0.45
Results From Exhibit 3 For MSCI Companies							
1992	-0.01	0.04	0.20	0.02	0.02	0.03	0.03
1993	0.11	0.27	0.20	0.23	0.27	0.23	-0.18
1994	-0.17	0.25	-0.01	0.05	0.14	-0.07	0.33
1995	0.21	0.07	0.11	0.18	0.19	0.13	-0.12
1996	0.16	0.05	0.10	0.11	0.05	0.13	-0.09
1997	0.08	-0.27	-0.04	0.03	-0.10	0.01	-0.38
1992-1997							
Average Correlation	0.06	0.07	0.09	0.10	0.09	0.08	-0.07
Standard Deviation	0.14	0.19	0.10	0.09	0.13	0.11	0.24
T-Statistic	1.14	0.86	2.30	2.91	1.73	1.76	-0.72

A more sophisticated strategy is required to overcome the shortcomings exhibited by single-factor investment approaches. Such strategies could include a focus on shorter-term analyses, such as semi-annual or even monthly returns-to-factors. Further, multiple valuation frameworks utilizing more than one factor have been shown to enhance the forecasting power of models when the underlying predictive factors have relatively low correlations with each other.[7] Finally, recent work has indicated that value is a multi-dimensional concept. The evidence presented here demonstrates that no one measure of value has been effective across all markets. Instead, a multi-factor framework which utilizes classes of value measures, developed on a country-by-country basis, may provide a sounder framework for more significant and consistent value-added.[8]

[7] Richard O. Michaud, "Demystifying Multiple Valuation Models," *Financial Analysts Journal* (January-February 1990).

[8] Richard O. Michaud, "Is Value Multidimensional? Implications for Style Management and Global Stock Selection," *The Journal of Investing* (Spring 1998).

One critical issue is whether the observed relationships between these factors and returns are likely to persist. If such factors are proxies for unmeasured or time-varying systematic risk, then they are likely to be persistent but may not be economically meaningful for active management. If instead, the relationships are true market inefficiencies, their investment value may be significant, but they may not persist. Another important issue is the risk associated with style-based investing. If a portfolio deviates substantially from its benchmark on a style characteristic, such as value or capitalization, it may carry significant benchmark-relative and absolute risk.[9] The central question becomes whether an investor is rewarded with sufficient excess returns for assuming additional risk. This issue should be carefully considered in seeking to exploit these types of anomalies in a global equity management program.

---

[9] For more information on risk-adjusted style investing, see Richard Roll, "Style Return Differentials: Illusions, Risk Premiums, or Investment Opportunities" in T. Daniel Coggin and Frank J. Fabozzi (eds.), The Handbook of Equity Style Management (New Hope, PA: Frank Fabozzi Associates, 1995) and Richard O. Michaud, "Investment Styles, Market Anomalies, and Global Stock Selection," (Charlottesville, VA: The Research Foundation of the Institute of Chartered Financial Analysts, forthcoming in 1998).

Index

229

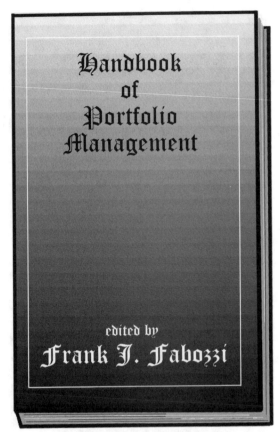

HANDBOOK OF PORTFOLIO MANAGEMENT

Frank J. Fabozzi, Editor

1998 Hardcover $89

HANDBOOK OF EQUITY STYLE MANAGEMENT:
SECOND EDITION

T. Daniel Coggin, Frank J. Fabozzi, and Robert D. Arnott, Editors
1997 Hardcover $65

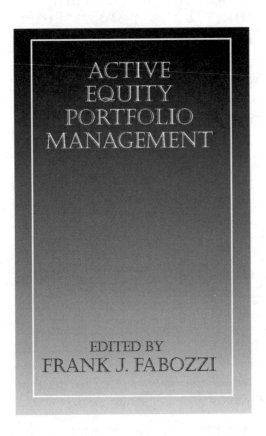

ACTIVE EQUITY PORTFOLIO MANAGEMENT
Frank J. Fabozzi, Editor
1998 Hardcover $70

Books available from
Frank J. Fabozzi Associates

Fixed Income Securities, Analysis, and Portfolio Management

Book	Price	QTY	Sub Total
Bond Portfolio Management	$65.00		
Fixed Income Securities	$65.00		
Managing Fixed Income Portfolios	$75.00		
Valuation of Fixed Income Securities and Derivatives 3rd. Ed.	$60.00		
Selected Topics in Bond Portfolio Management	$45.00		
Advanced Fixed Income Analytics	$65.00		
Treasury Securities and Derivatives	$53.00		
Managing MBS Portfolios	$60.00		
Corporate Bonds: Structures & Analysis	$65.00		
Collateralized Mortgage Obligations: Structures and Analysis	$50.00		
The Handbook of Corporate Debt Instruments	$87.00		
Handbook of Structured Finance Products	$95.00		
Asset-Backed Securities	$75.00		
The Handbook of Commercial Mortgage-Backed Securities – 2nd Ed.	$95.00		
Trends In Commercial Mortgage-Backed Securities	$85.00		
Handbook of Nonagency Mortgage-Backed Securities	$95.00		
Basics of Mortgage-Backed Securities	$42.00		
Advances in the Valuation & Mgmt. of Mortgage-Backed Securities	$65.00		
Valuation of Interest-Sensitive Financial Instruments	$55.00		
Perspectives on International Fixed Income Investing	$60.00		
Handbook of Emerging Fixed Income and Currency Markets	$75.00		
The Handbook of Stable Value Investments	$95.00		
Inflation Protection Bonds	$42.00		
Bank Loans: Secondary Market and Portfolio Management	$69.00		

Equity and Fixed Income

Book	Price	QTY	Sub Total
Handbook of Portfolio Management	$89.00		
Analysis of Financial Statements	$55.00		
Introduction to Quantitative Methods For Investment Managers	$58.00		

Risk Management and Derivatives

Book	Price	QTY	Sub Total
Measuring and Controlling Interest Rate Risk	$55.00		
Dictionary of Financial Risk Management	$45.00		
Risk Management: Framework, Methods, and Practice	$90.00		
Perspectives on Interest Rate Risk Management for Money Managers and Traders	$60.00		
Essays In Derivatives	$42.00		

Equity Portfolio Management

Book	Price	QTY	Sub Total
Active Equity Portfolio Management	$70.00		
Applied Equity Valuation	$65.00		
Handbook of Equity Style Management – Second Edition	$65.00		
Foundations of Economic Value-Added	$49.00		
Selected Topics in Equity Portfolio Management	$45.00		
Professional Perspectives on Indexing	$75.00		
Equity Management	TBA		
Investing By the Numbers	$58.00		

Other investment topics

Book	Price	QTY	Sub Total
Modeling the Market: New Theories and Techniques	$55.00		
Securities Lending and Repurchase Agreements	$85.00		
Pension Fund Investment Management – Second Edition	$95.00		
Credit Union Investment Management	$55.00		
Investment Management for Insurers	$125.00		
Perspectives on Investment Management of Public Pension Funds	$65.00		
The Use of Derivatives in Tax Planning	$150.00		
Issuer Perspectives on Securitization	$60.00		

Other Books Distributed By Frank J. Fabozzi Associates

Book	Price	QTY	Sub Total
The Handbook of Fixed Income Securities – 5th Ed. (Irwin, 1997)	$95.00		
Fixed Income Mathematics 3rd. Ed.(Irwin, 1996)	$60.00		
The Handbook of Mortgage-Backed Securities 4th Ed.(Irwin, 1996)	$85.00		
Advanced Fixed Income Portfolio Management (Probus, 1994)	$65.00		
Active Total Return Mgmt. of Fixed Income Portfolios (Irwin, 1995)	$65.00		
Handbook of Fixed Income Options – Revised Ed. (Probus, 1995)	$65.00		
Handbook of Asset/Liability Management – Revised Ed. (Irwin, 1996)	$75.00		

Totals:

Shipping Charge*:
(Domestic orders, $4 for the first book, $1 each additional)

Total:

To order: please check the books you would like to order, fill out the form below, and send along with check to Frank J. Fabozzi Associates, 858 Tower View Circle, New Hope, PA 18938.

Name:

Company:

Address:

City:

State:

Zip:

Phone:

FAX:

Email:

FORTHCOMING BOOKS:

ANALYSIS OF FINANCIAL STATEMENTS
Pamela Peterson and Frank J. Fabozzi
1998 Handbook $55

Tentative Table of Contents: 1 Sources of Financial Information; 2 Financial Statements; 3 The Quality of Financial Information; 4 Financial Ratios; 5. Earnings Per Share and Related Measures; 6 Tax Issues; 7 Cash Flow Analysis; 8 Value-Based Metrics; 9 Credit Analysis

DERIVATIVES AND EQUITY PORTFOLIO MANAGEMENT
Bruce M. Collins and Frank J. Fabozzi
1998 Hardcover Price $65

Tentative TOC: 1 Introduction; 2 The Derivatives Process for Equity Investors; 3. Listed Equity Derivative Contracts; 4. Using Listed Options in Equity Portfolio Management; 5. Pricing Stock Index Futures; 6. Arbitrage Trades with Stock Index Futures; 7. Basis Trading with Stock Index Futures; 8. Risk Management with Stock Index Futures; 9. Asset Allocation with Stock Index Futures; 10. Overview of OTC Equity Derivatives; 11.Applications of Equity Derivatives to Portfolio Management; 12. Pricing Issues with OTC Options; Appendix: The Influence of Taxation on Equity Investment Decisions

EQUITY MANAGEMENT
Frank J. Fabozzi and James L. Grant
1998 Hardcover $TBA

Tentative Table of Contents: 1. Introduction; 2. Modern Portfolio Theory; 3. Blueprint for Passive-Active Investing; 4. Equity Management Styles; 5. Traditional Fundamental Analysis; 6. Security Analysis using Value-Based Metrics; 7. Discounted Cash Flow Equity Valuation Models; 8. Factor-Based Equity Models; 9. Profiles in Equity Management; 10. Equity Trading Costs and Technology; 11. Measuring Equity Performance